LIGHTS!
CAMERA!
SUB ACTION!

Mike Seares

Jeremy,

Many thanks for all your help.

Best wishes,

Mike

ISBN: 978-0-9957339-3-0 (Paperback)

Edited by: Richard Sheehan - www.richardmsheehan.co.uk
Cover design by: Jeremy Hopes - www.publishing.graphics

Cover photos ©: Front: Mike Seares. Spine: Phil Barthropp.
Rear: Mike Seares, except left. 2nd and 4th down: John Cocking

For more great titles and to keep up to date with upcoming projects,
go to:
www.mikesearesbooks.com

CONTENTS

Foreword 7

Preface 9

Photographs 11

Introduction 13

1) Paddling Pools 15

2) Big Break 27

3) Stranded in Paradise 36

4) Tooty Fruity 65

5) Terrors of the Deep 92

6) Best of the Best 126

7) Going with the Flow 141

8) Legwork 161

9) Helicopters and Hedonism 183

10) Skulls and Danes 200

11) Battle Ensign 231

12) In the Loop 274

13) Ad Break 314

14) Digital Diving 324

15) Whale War III 354

16) On Reserve 383

APPENDIX 387

Photographs link 400

Foreword

I first met Mike on a confidential diving project in the Baltic Sea in 1992. He was the safety diver for a dive team I had contracted to investigate a recent wreck that had sunk in deep water under mysterious circumstances. What struck me about him during that operation was his cool professionalism. He was completely unfazed not only by the demanding and risky diving conditions but also the potential for serious political/military complications.

Since then our paths have crossed on countless occasions, mainly associated with Pinewood Studios and the Society for Underwater Technology.

I suppose the main feeling I have towards his career is pure envy, tempered with a grudging level of admiration and, I have to admit, 'respect' as well.

Being in a group of divers swapping stories is a situation I generally avoid if it includes Mike. After him relating any one of his seemingly endless adventurous escapades there is that inevitable embarrassing silence when everybody flounders hopelessly in a vain attempt to 'follow that if you can!'

Having read the manuscript of *LIGHTS! CAMERA! SUB ACTION!* cover to cover, I now feel quite justified in my opinion of Mike's career. He really has had some amazing adventures and achievements. But his success is clearly the direct result of his almost superhuman enthusiasm, dedication and commitment. Add to this his proven wide range of professional skills and you have a recipe for five-star accomplishments.

The literary world is in for a treat now that Mike is turning his attention to writing. He has a natural style. He writes as if it were the camera talking. The reader is instantly immersed (excuse the pun) in a vivid three-dimensional setting, a sort of word-induced virtual reality.

LIGHTS! CAMERA! SUB ACTION! also reveals the secrets and special effects of the hidden world behind the camera, both above and below the water. It's a bit like a magician revealing how the tricks are done. By the time you've turned the last page you'll be able to walk around a film set and chat like a pro!

And what is more, you will almost certainly end up looking at Mike Seares the way I do, through a cocktail of envy, admiration and respect.

And that's a wrap.

Dr John Bevan BSc MSc PhD FSUT FAE FRSA
Managing Director of Submex Ltd
Chairman of the SUT Diving and Manned Submersibles
Committee
Chairman of the Historical Diving Society
Past Technical Manager of Comex Diving Ltd (UK)
World depth record holder, 1,535 feet (1970)

June 2018

Preface

LIGHTS! CAMERA! SUB ACTION! has been a work in progress for a number of years.

It came about from a desire to tell the story of working in an industry where remarkable things can happen all in a day's work.

The aim of the book is to give the reader a sense of what goes on in creating underwater material for film, TV and other media projects, and to share some of the incredible adventures that can happen along the way.

To go underwater is an amazing experience. Film and television is an amazing industry. When you put the two together, the results can be extraordinary.

The industry itself covers such a broad spectrum of work that no two jobs are ever alike.

There is the high-powered world of feature films, with glamorous locations, expensive hotels and all the trimmings - and there is the run-and-gun excitement of following a developing news story or documenting an underwater expedition.

There are the crazy ideas thrown up by commercials and pop promos, which often boggle the mind and require creative thinking to make happen - and there is the careful planning and preparation necessary when designing and producing a documentary to inform and entertain.

Where required, care has been taken to explain in simple terms any technical aspects of the diving and filmmaking process, so that the reader will have an understanding as to the background of the actions being described.

But above all, it is hoped the book will provide an entertaining tale of adventure and discovery in an often misunderstood industry.

Thanks must go to all the colleagues who are mentioned throughout the text. Film and TV work is, above all else, a collaborative effort - and when that collaboration comes together, the results can be truly spectacular.

Mike Seares
August 2018

Photographs

Please go to the Photographs Link page at the end of the
book to find a link to over 300 photographs that
illustrate the contents of
LIGHTS! CAMERA! SUB ACTION!

Introduction

'Action!' yelled Steven Spielberg.

A second later, all hell broke loose.

The four feet of water I was standing in turned into a frothing maelstrom as two wave machines thumped their large wedge-shaped blocks up and down.

At the same time two massive aero engines spun up to speed with a frenzied whine that sent a hurricane of wind across the outdoor tank on the backlot at Elstree Studios ten miles north of London.

A couple of seconds later a massive sheet of flame from five flamethrowers shot across the jet-black sky only feet above, forming a curtain of fire that warmed my freezing face.

Suddenly, one of the world's greatest stuntmen, Vic Armstrong, was airborne overhead, landing in the water ten feet away.

He had barely hit the surface before two dustbin-sized containers, filled with gas, ignited at the sides of the tank, blasting debris high into the sky to crash down around the figure that was now in the water.

As the figure turned around, I found myself staring at Indiana Jones struggling to stay afloat in a storm-tossed ocean.

It was all I could do to help steady the bulky camera housing the cameraman was trying to line up on the action as the waves repeatedly knocked us against the concrete wall at our backs.

Five seconds later and...

'Cut!' blasted out over a loud hailer.

The wind, rain and fire were turned off.

The world returned to normal.

I relaxed, and as the adrenaline subsided, I could feel the cold of the near freezing water making its unwelcome presence felt through my suit. My teeth started to chatter. I'd barely got my breath back when a shout came from above.

'Right, let's go again!'

The broadest of grins spread across my face, and for the briefest of moments time seemed to stand still, as I wondered just how the heck the twists and turns of my life had led up to this point, rubbing shoulders with the best of the best and having the adventure of a lifetime.

And then all hell broke loose...

...again.

1

Paddling Pools

All around it was blue, a hazy, indistinct tone that seemed to carry on forever.

Above, there was a shimmering, but it was some way away and almost indistinguishable from the void that encircled me. Below was the murky dark of a bottomless pit. I should have been scared, but somehow I felt warm, comfortable, secure.

A shadow fleeted to my right, fading into the gloom. It reappeared, this time to my left. My curiosity was aroused. I moved forward, but how was I moving? Glancing down, I saw that my legs were performing the smooth up and down motion of an experienced scuba diver.

I kept on advancing.

Suddenly, the shadow materialised ahead, growing in intensity. The haphazard form became hardened, the outline clearer. The haze morphed itself into a head, with small, beady eyes, and behind it, the sleek body sprouted fins and a tail. As it approached, I watched, transfixed by the shape weaving its way through the water towards me, but still I felt warm and safe.

The great white shark was closer now, the pointed snout no longer a beautiful example of nature's ever diverse design. A gaping mouth, lined with rows of serrated triangular teeth, replaced the streamlined form.

I didn't feel safe any more.

I tried to move back, away from this approaching horror, but I was unable to do so. Some power held me captive, forcing me to stay and witness my impending doom. At the final moment, my jaw fell open in blind terror, pathetically mimicking that of the shark.

Then it was upon me. Man's worst nightmare was eating me alive!

As the precision killing machine closed its jaws, I sat bolt upright.

All around it was blue. I could feel the sweat running down my back, making my skin damp and clammy, but there was no shark. I glanced down at my legs. They were gone. I gasped, throwing my hands to where my knees should have been. I felt the soft contours of the blue downy sleeping bag that covered my lower body. I breathed a sigh of relief.

The phenomenon that was *Jaws* had done its worst. It had only been seven hours since I'd left the cinema in a state of nerve-shredded exhilaration.

I managed a strangled laugh and fell back on the thin Karrimat that lined the floor of the tent, the blue interior, now diffuse with light from the approaching dawn.

Everything was all right.

I started to slowly drift off, remembering pitching the

tent on a sloping green field near the small, picturesque town of Charlestown in Cornwall.

Charlestown? What the hell was I doing there?

I sat bolt upright again, this time checking my watch. In four hours on the 23rd of July 1976, aged fifteen, I was going to jump into the sea for my first ever scuba dive.

The sweat returned.

The 23rd of July 1976 was a landmark date in the course of my life. Everything I would do from that moment on, every decision made, every penny saved, would be devoted to the lure of the underwater world.

It was almost inevitable that I should have arrived at this juncture. A series of events over the years had grouped themselves together in my mind and come up with one word - UNDERWATER - and there was no going back.

My earliest memorable encounter with the liquid medium, which covers two-thirds of the Earth's surface, was in an austere Victorian swimming pool in Stockport, Cheshire. I had found myself there for swimming lessons at the tender age of four and right from the start I felt at home in the water. This would become a weekly occurrence and one I would look forward to with relish. After all, it was fun and the grown-ups thought it was good for me, so it was a win-win situation all round.

Not long after the regimental regime of Mrs Fox's swimming classes started, I had a goal - a ten-shilling note my great uncle had promised me for when I completed a length.

After much anguish on behalf of the long-suffering Mrs Fox, and following many covert dashes from the

17

protective custody of the shallow end, I finally made it – my first length, and the closest I would ever come to the world of professional sport.

Further, less mercenary interest in water came through the wonder of television. It was only black and white, but the images from *The Undersea World of Jacques Cousteau* that shone from the small square box in the corner of the living room were to have a profound effect on my life, as indeed they would on many others.

It was the blend of excitement, adventure and technology that did it, and while the same could be said of the astronauts who blasted into space and would eventually land on the Moon, that was something that, however appealing, always seemed totally unattainable – out of this world if you will. Diving, on the other hand, was something within reach, and I knew that one day I would join the privileged few who plunged beneath the waves to explore the oceans of the planet.

My first real brush with divers up close came when I was fourteen. We always seemed to make epic journeys as a family and this one involved a caravanning trek across Europe, ending up in the mountainous vistas of Corsica, which also boasted a spectacular Mediterranean coastline.

We were staying at a small campsite on the west coast, close to the capital, Ajaccio. Our caravan, decked out with a bright orange awning down one side, was literally a stone's throw from the sea, and every day would be spent snorkelling in the warm waters in search of the wonders of the deep.

Equipment was pretty basic at this stage - a pair of Woolworth's best blue 'flippers' and an equally unsuitable mask, complete with snorkel with ping pong ball in the top, which was supposed to keep out the water when you went too deep. Unfortunately, it also had the alarmingly frequent habit of keeping out the air when it wedged itself into the small pipe, completely blocking it. A death trap by any standards, but at the invincible age of fourteen, it was the next best thing to a submarine.

It was on one of my routine excursions to the dizzying depths of ten feet that I had my first encounter with serious marine life. After taking several deep breaths, I had struggled down to a rocky outcrop, fins flapping and arms flailing, when suddenly a blob of greased lightning shot out of a hole, squirted something black and inky in my direction and disappeared. The shock was instant, since everyone knows that everything in the sea is out to eat you, including a six-inch octopus. Two seconds later, I made what must have been a world record ascent from the water, becoming the first airborne diver, and landed in the large orange dinghy my dad was paddling around on the surface.

Many years later I was to experience déjà vu while diving under Swanage pier. Fifteen feet down, in fairly murky conditions, a duck shot out of the gloom doing several knots and coming straight for me. We saw each other at the same instant. With a garbled 'quack', the duck shot off in a confusion of feathers and bubbles, and I had a flashback to Corsica. More control was in evidence this time though, no doubt due to the gaggle of students I had in tow, who were gamely following their fearless instructor into the unknown, ducks and all!

Following my exploits in Corsica, I was convinced that diving was what I wanted to do. The thrill of being able to see the wonders of marine life close up, coupled with the frustration of the brevity of these aquatic excursions, made me all the more determined to find a way to stay longer in this new-found world – but it would have to wait. The holidays were nearly over, and it was time to return to school.

It was then that one of those fortuitous coincidences that can turn your life around just fell out of the blue.

During my first week back in the hallowed corridors of Malvern College, nestling at the base of the Malvern Hills in Middle England, I spotted a poster on one of the noticeboards:

ANYONE INTERESTED IN SCUBA DIVING - SIGN BELOW

Someone, somewhere, was trying to tell me something. That someone turned out to be a fellow student by the name of Paul Towel. Paul had recently completed a diving course in Plymouth and thought it would be a good idea to start a club at Malvern. He will never know how timely his enthusiasm and intervention was to prove to be. I immediately signed up, and a few days later, after avidly checking the noticeboard every few hours, a new note appeared, proclaiming the first ever meeting of the Malvern College Sub-Aqua Club.

From here on, there really was no turning back. It even reached the stage where passing the British Sub-Aqua Club (BSAC) Third Class Diver exam became more important than O levels. Definitely a case of 'You'll never amount to anything doing that, laddie!'

An influential factor in anyone's training is their

instructor, and for me it was no exception. Your introduction to any new skill can often determine how proficient and enthusiastic you will eventually turn out to be. In my case, I was more than lucky to be under the committed guidance of a certain Mr Rocky Hill - as craggy as the name - whose dedication to the school club went beyond the call of duty. As far as I'm aware, Rocky was never employed or paid for his services, yet he would gladly give up his spare time to lay on private lectures for us excitable rookies before setting out on a long night shift at the nearby Dowty Meco engineering works. I owe a lot to those long hours of coaching, and Rocky is someone to whom I am deeply indebted.

During the following years I dedicated my time to passing the basic diver grades and more importantly consolidating the qualifications by diving around the UK and in Menorca in the Mediterranean.

After leaving school, six months were spent eating, sleeping and living diving at Fort Bovisand in Plymouth.

Bovisand, with its impenetrable stone walls and fearsome reputation, stood guard at the easterly entrance of Plymouth Sound and had been built over successive periods of unrest in the UK's illustrious history. As a fort, complete with canons, it had protected the strategic and vital safety of the Sound from marauding enemy ships. Since that role had no longer been required, it had become a bastion of British diving, providing one of the most respected centres for training sports and commercial divers anywhere in the world. Being on the doorstep of some of the best UK diving was a bonus, and at the time there were probably few British divers who hadn't made use of its extensive facilities.

For me, this was where the craft of diving was really hammered home. Here you would see every right and wrong way a skill could be performed, and the experience was invaluable. Someone can have all the qualifications under the sun, but if they haven't actually put the skills into practice in real situations, they may as well be confined to a swimming pool.

Following a summer of total contentment, it was back to education, which meant heading north to Heriot-Watt University in Edinburgh to immerse myself in a four-year marine biology degree. The choice may seem obvious, but it was centred more around dreams of mermaids and dolphins than a burning desire to stare down a microscope at copepods and crinoids. There was also a 'Diving Science' module within the curriculum, which was basically an excuse to spend an extortionate amount of time playing around in the water, and to be honest it was probably my main reason for taking the course in the first place.

While daytime was spent learning the science of the sea, evenings and spare time were spent beneath the surface. Not just getting wet, but gaining instructional qualifications that could be put to good use back at Bovisand during the holidays, by preaching the wonders of the underwater world to those who would be converted.

However, it was towards the end of the four years that reality started to set in, and it suddenly became very clear that very soon I was going to have to earn a living in the real world. After considerable research, it seemed that the best marine biology jobs in the UK were with the oil companies, looking at the environmental impact of new installations and developments in the North Sea. The other main option was the fish farming industry in the Highlands, but this seemed to entail being shacked up for long periods of time with a group of individuals that looked like they'd walked off the set of *Deliverance,* and the prospect was not appealing.

So I made the fateful decision to take a risk and try something I'd always dreamed of - working in the movies. Hardly the most logical step, you might say, and I wasn't even sure which area I wanted to work in, but the image of 'stuntman' kept appearing. And so, with thoughts of derring-do and swashed-buckles, I packed my bags, said farewell to the lochs and open splendour of Scotland and headed south for the urban sprawl of London, the only real centre of the film industry in the UK at the time.

The big city was a big shock after the comparative tranquillity of student life in Edinburgh. Not least because there were bills to be paid and no grant to cover them, and with money rapidly running out, that meant I needed gainful employment. Since the thought of jumping into the Thames looking for lone fish wasn't high on the list of things to do, I searched around for somewhere I could put my other qualifications to good use and teach diving.

At the time there was really only one option - the London Underwater Centre (LUC), run by Reg Vallintine. Reg, a one-time director of the BSAC, started sport diving before the term had even been conceived, and he had run dive schools all over the world. He knew virtually anyone who was anyone in the diving community and was one of the true grandfathers of the sport. A cross between Neptune and Father Christmas, with a small white beard and bright twinkly eyes, he kindly took me on board to work as a part-time freelance instructor in his expanding dive school. I couldn't have been in better hands.

As the LUC was the only school in London, we were frequently asked to help out with the safety on underwater film and TV projects, as well as teaching actors and presenters how to dive, including Anneka Rice and Jim Davidson. This not only provided an invaluable insight into the industry but also an increased enthusiasm for a future I was now determined to pursue. Also, being in London, we had the occasional well-known personality wanting to learn to dive just for fun, which was always interesting.

However, it does help if you know they are well known.

On one occasion I had been asked by Reg to take a trainee up to Stoney Cove, an inland dive site in Leicestershire, to complete some open water training. I was given a name - Mr Rodgers - and an address in Kingston-Upon-Thames. He would drive us there and back and I should report on how things went.

Now, I would say that my knowledge of movies is pretty fair, but when it comes to music, I have heard of the Beatles and Michael Jackson, and my own tastes probably extend as far as Pink Floyd, Genesis, and some great film composers, Hans Zimmer, Harry Gregson-Williams, Steve Jablonsky and John Barry. But beyond that there is pretty much a musical vacuum - and if you want to hear me scream, to quote Bruce Willis in *The Last Boy Scout*, 'Try playing some rap music.' So I put this out in my defence before I continue.

On the way up to Stoney, we chatted about a number of things, and the conversation turned to what Paul, as he had introduced himself, did for a living. He replied that he was a singer in a band. So while semi-tuning out, I said I guessed it was probably pretty hard to make a living like that, and I asked if they had managed to play any pubs and clubs. He said he had played in a few places. 'What's the band?' I asked out of politeness.

'Well there have been a couple,' he replied. 'There was one called Free, and another, Bad Company. Right now I'm in The Firm with a guy called Jimmy Page.'

I suddenly realised that things certainly weren't 'All Right Now' and that it was fortunate that it wouldn't be long before I was swallowed by a very large hole in the ground, which would at least be full of water!

Paul took it all in his stride, performed flawlessly with regards to the diving, and was even kind enough to give me a ticket to see The Firm at the Hammersmith Odeon, where he again performed flawlessly. I assumed it would be a last-minute seat, squeezed in somewhere at the back? Er, no - it was in the front row of the circle sitting next to his wife.

Many thanks, Mr Rodgers - you are a gentleman, sir.

On the film side of things, my first experience of a major underwater shoot through the LUC was certainly a case of being thrown in at the deep end. It involved working as a safety diver on a commercial for Ridley Scott Associates. Here, an actor, dressed in a suit and tie, had to simulate taking a Mu-cron decongestant pill underwater, complete with giving the appearance of drinking from a glass. He then had to rise up and break through the surface of the water, where the tag line would say that you should take Mu-cron 'to help you breathe more easily'!

It was directed by Tony Scott, brother of Ridley, and he would go on to make such blockbusters as, *Top Gun*, *Beverly Hills Cop 2, Crimson Tide, Enemy of the State* and *Spy Game*. The location, however, wasn't exactly the bright lights of Hollywood. Rather, it was the less than auspicious concrete and brick complex that made up the Barnet Copthall Leisure Centre in Hendon, North London.

But this taste of filmdom was enough. There were lights, there were cameras, and there was the buzz that only a film set can produce. I knew then that this was the path I wanted to take. Where I would end up I had no idea, but with the winter months providing minimal teaching work at the LUC, I had to accept an offer of more permanent employment from the Diving Locker, a dive shop on London's Fulham Palace Road. Here, at least, I could be assured of a more regular income, and there was also the prospect of helping to develop and build up a diving school from scratch.

Then, a few months later, something happened that would change my life forever…

2

Big Break

It was a depressing, soggy Monday morning that didn't bode well for the rest of the week. It started out pretty much like any other in the early part of March 1986 – to the urgent, irritating buzz of an overeager alarm clock and the persistent rattle of heavy rain against the old box sash windows of the room I was renting in a rather run-down Victorian flat in Clapham, South London.

In fact, the thought of an imminent life-changing experience was furthest from my mind as I realised the delinquent alarm had decided, yet again, to make its presence felt twenty minutes too late.

After a hurried breakfast that did little for my digestive system, I was greeted on the third attempt to start the car by an annoyingly cheerful Capital Radio traffic reporter stating that there was gridlock on Putney Bridge - something to do with the heavy rain coupled with a broken-down bus on Fulham Palace Road. The result - tailbacks across the famous river crossing that for one day a year was home to the start of the Oxford and Cambridge Boat Race but for the rest of the time was a vital artery in the commute to work.

I was going to be doubly late.

There was indeed gridlock on the bridge. The old stone structure supported a car park of vehicles, jammed nose to tail in lemming-like lines waiting for someone to move. A cacophony of horns sounded off sporadically like incoming fire on some ancient battlefield.

Looking out through the steamed-up windscreen, my entire view was blocked by a white Transit van that was so dirty the only way you could tell the colour was where people had scrawled lewd messages in the grime. With nowhere else to look, my gaze wandered to the misty grey ribbon of water that flowed beneath the bridge and on through Central London.

Water – the environment divers feel naturally at home in, and one that had played an important role in my life so far, but today there was enough of the stuff coming out of the sky to keep even the most enthusiastic indoors. As more irate horns blared out, I wondered what on earth I was doing here, nine-to-fiving it in a London basement, when what I really craved was a world of adventure, diving the planet and somehow being paid for it.

Work at the time was helping to develop the aforementioned dive school in West London. The aim, somewhere down the line, was to build a brand new centre in Kew, complete with training pool, shop, holiday bookings – you name it. At present though, things were in the 'development stage', a term that would become all too familiar over the years. Basically, a lot of ideas were floating around but not a whole lot was actually happening.

A particularly sharp blast on a horn jerked me out of my reverie, and in a desperate bid to move forward and claim ownership of the six-foot gap that had suddenly appeared, I almost collided with a Routemaster bus. It had materialised out of nowhere and wasn't going to give way. The driver glared at me with the smug confidence and sure knowledge that I probably didn't want a red stripe down the side of my car and muscled his way into the space. I turned off the engine. This was going to take some time.

Twenty minutes later, with the car crammed into a space that was guaranteed to earn the attention of any passing traffic warden, I hurried out of the driving rain and down into the small underground room that doubled as an office and equipment repair shop. It was the sort of place a hobbit would have felt at home. The steep, creaky stairs and narrow opening masquerading as a doorway merely added to the effect.

I was greeted by the raised eyebrows and barely audible Monday morning grunt of the engineer colleague I shared the space with. He was currently lost in the seemingly fascinating internal workings of a Poseidon regulator and was clearly unimpressed with my lack of time-keeping.

My desk was covered with paperwork from the previous week, and just looking at the pile of folders and unopened mail, you could tell it was going to be one of those days. As if in resignation, I shook the pollution-filled raindrops from my jacket, threw the sodden coat over the back of a chair, and headed reluctantly for the desk.

And then the phone rang.

The shrill clamour almost made me jump – it was still

early after all, and it certainly wasn't welcome. Thinking if I maybe left it for a while it would go away, I started to scan through the papers on the desk – but it kept on ringing. It was probably some prospective trainee expecting to be filled with the joys of diving, and it really was too early for all that sort of thing. Unfortunately, after receiving threats of bodily harm from the corner, I reluctantly lifted the handset. Gathering as much enthusiasm as possible, I took a deep breath and asked the caller how I could help.

On the other end of the line was the somewhat gruff yet somehow kindly voice of someone I would get to know fairly well. His name was Harvey Harrison, and his first question was the usual one – did we run intensive diving courses? At this, I switched into autopilot and launched, surprisingly enthusiastically, into a description of the wonders of the deep and just how it would change his life. As I waited for the expected barrage of questions, I could hardly have known that it was my life that was about to change.

There was a slight pause... then, 'Yeah, but can it be done fast? I'm on a tight schedule here.'

Weren't they all?

'I'm working on a feature film and need to work an underwater camera,' Harvey continued.

This they certainly didn't all want to do. Gone were thoughts of piled paperwork, disgruntled engineers, rain and drizzle. It could have been a blizzard outside for all I cared. He had my undivided attention.

As I prised every scrap of information I could from Harvey, it transpired he was the lighting cameraman for a film adaptation of Lucy Irvine's book *Castaway*. It was the true story of two people, Gerald Kingsland and Lucy Irvine, uncomfortably married out of convenience so they could live together on a desert island and try to survive for a year. The film starred Oliver Reed and Amanda Donohoe, and those familiar with the story will know it took place on an island off northern Australia. However, as Harvey explained, for filming purposes, they were going to be using a number of islands in the Seychelles – for seven weeks. His voice suddenly seemed to fade into the background. It was as though he was speaking from another planet, as my mind clicked into overdrive.

I had been trying to find a way to work in the film industry for some time, and here was a golden opportunity landing right at my feet. If only I could work out how on earth to get myself onto the shoot. I was of course way ahead of myself here. I mean, I had only been talking to the guy for five minutes and already I was part of the crew, but there's nothing like positive thinking.

Harvey's dilemma was that he needed someone who could shoot underwater, very much on the whim of the director, and who had the time spare to be around for about two months. He had contacted most of the underwater cameramen in the UK, none of whom had been available, suitable or amenable to the budget. He was resigned to using a local diver in the Seychelles to operate the camera while supervising underwater himself - hence the need for the course.

I had a better idea.

While at this point I knew nothing about camerawork, there was a man who did. A year or so earlier I had come to know a budding underwater filmmaker, Mike Valentine, who at the time had been working as a sound recordist for the BBC, but whose dream had also been to work in features. He was an accomplished underwater stills photographer and had put together a number of stunning audiovisual shows, even taking over the London Planetarium for one of them. He had also made a couple of short 16mm films. He was hugely enthusiastic and I was sure would jump at the chance to work on *Castaway*, and he would, of course, hopefully need an assistant.

What Harvey needed was someone who was imaginative, enthusiastic and cheap.

I rang Mike that evening.

Thankfully, and predictably, his response was the same as mine, and I could almost hear the gears whirring as he realised the opportunity here. Not only was this the chance of a lifetime to work on a feature film in an exotic location but also there was the very real prospect of it being a springboard to further jobs in the future.

The film industry is notoriously difficult to get into, but as they say, one thing leads to another, and once in, it's a very small world. You just needed that first break, and while this could be it – we certainly weren't there yet.

After I relayed Mike's enthusiasm to Harvey, he agreed to take a look at his films and audiovisuals. A date was set for the following week, and that was the easy part. From here on, it would be like thinking you had won the lottery but needing to find the ticket to check you had the right numbers – it wasn't going to be fun.

On the night of the meeting, I remember having that pit-of-the-stomach feeling you only get at extreme moments in your life – exam results, first date, driving test - and it wasn't going away.

After Harvey arrived at Mike's flat in the aptly named

Hollywood Road, and the pleasantries were over, he settled down in one of the deep sofas with a mug of coffee and Mike pressed the 'play' button.

It was a tense time while Harvey sat assessing the images bombarding his eyes. During the show there was the occasional shuffle, a nodding of the head, even a few raised eyebrows, but we were having a hard time reading his expression; there was so much riding on the verdict.

'Very nice,' he said finally, still clasping the now empty mug after the final reel, but then he would, wouldn't he?

After Harvey had left and the door had closed ominously behind him, we just looked at each other – there was nothing really to say. We could now only wait for the response from *Castaway*'s director, Nic Roeg, who would make the final decision.

Nic Roeg is one of the UK's most highly acclaimed creative directors, having given the world such masterpieces as *Walkabout* and *Don't Look Now*. It would be down to him whether we would be going back to the day jobs or having our dreams realised. Things, as they say, were out of our hands.

Waiting for A Level or degree results was nothing like this. There the outcome was just a staging post on the way to an undetermined somewhere. This was potentially 'somewhere'.

When the reply came, it was in the form of a short phone call – though I don't quite know what else I expected – and all of a sudden we were both going to the Seychelles for seven weeks, Mike as underwater cameraman, me as safety diver/underwater assistant. It was that simple. One of those unexpected, wonderful moments that makes the film industry such an exciting and surprising place to work.

It was an easy decision to give up a job in a dingy basement workshop for the sun and sand of the Seychelles, and although at this point I was only looking at a couple of months work, and I had no idea what I would do when I returned, you really can't turn opportunities like that down.

The next few weeks passed in a blur and were spent preparing for the trip and starting to understand the logistics of how a feature film worked. Even these days were eventful, including my first trip to a studio - Elstree - where the UK production office was based.

At the time, Elstree was a bastion of the British film industry. Situated almost in the centre of the town of Borehamwood, about ten miles north of London, it was a relatively small affair by international standards, but to me this was Hollywood. After all, this was where the original *Star Wars* and *Indiana Jones* sagas had been filmed, and as I wandered through the empty sound stages, you could almost hear John Williams' memorable scores leaping out of the walls at you.

There were also in-water preparations to be made, including test-driving an underwater sled designed to provide point-of-view (POV) shots and allowing the camera to glide effortlessly through the water. Looking more like something James Bond would escape on than a piece of filming hardware, it consisted of two large orange diver propulsion vehicles (DPVs) bolted to a metal frame, with the camera mounted between them. I'm not sure what the onlookers in the public swimming pool made of it all, but it was certainly starting to build my expectation.

The camera and DPVs weighed several hundred

pounds, requiring three people to lift them - not the sort of problem you want as excess baggage at the airport - so this, along with our dive gear and compressor to fill the cylinders, was shipped out ahead of the main crew. We were to join the party later on, after they'd set up the location production office and checked out who served the best tequilas.

So, on Friday the 2nd of May 1986, I boarded Air Seychelles flight HM 701 from Gatwick to Mahé, capital of the Seychelles. It turned out to be a flight of unrestrained excitement, tempered by more than slight nervousness. After all, this was my dream come true - what if I screwed up? What if it didn't work out? What if…?

But as the flight wore on I put any thoughts of failure behind me, along with the grey skies we'd left back in London, and drifted happily off into a woozy, alcohol-induced sleep, content with the thought that I was setting out on the adventure of a lifetime...

3

Stranded in Paradise

'Another drink, sir?'

It was like a voice from a distant planet. 'We've just passed over the equator.'

I rubbed my bleary eyes, squinting against the blinding rays that streamed in through the small windows down the length of the aircraft cabin, making the interior look like something out of a Ridley Scott movie. I suddenly realised this was the furthest south on Planet Earth I had ever been. For an instant, I had images of disappearing anticlockwise down a plughole in full scuba gear, rapidly followed by thoughts of... feature film... *Castaway*... and yes, you're really here... and then I was awake.

The interruption to my dream came sharply into focus and I eagerly took the glass of bubbly from the Air Seychelles angel smiling down from above, and then I settled in for the rest of the flight.

Stepping off the plane at Mahé, the largest island in the Seychelles, was like entering a sauna. The heat was like a blast furnace, and my clothes were damp with sweat before I even touched the tarmac, but who cared – this, as they said, was paradise, and it certainly was. The Seychelles was the first place I'd been to where the reality was better than the brochure. Everything is more extreme than you are used to. The vegetation is a vivid green, the sea and sky a cobalt blue, and all without the aid of Photoshop.

After the usual delays and frustration with immigration and customs, which you eventually accept as one of the necessities of international travel, we were whisked across to Praslin, one of the larger of the islands in the group and our base for the duration. The trip was made in a rather small, all too noisy, island hopper aircraft. On landing, a final taxi ride dropped us at the Praslin Beach Hotel.

We'd been given the rest of the day off, which, as we were to learn, wasn't as obvious as it might have seemed, even though we'd spent half of it cramped up in the confines of an aircraft and the rest acclimatising to the intense heat and hundred per cent humidity. The luxury of this free time, not fully appreciated when we had it, was spent swigging beers in the hotel pool, wondering if this was really happening or whether I'd wake up in a cold and windswept London any minute.

And so passed the first of four days off in seven weeks.

The following morning dawned bright and hot, and after an initial hesitation wondering why the heck palm trees were growing outside my London flat, my brain clicked into gear and the expectation of the day ahead filled my thoughts.

The drive to work was, well, rather different to jams on

Putney Bridge. No congestion charge needed here. A steep, winding pass crawled up into the Vallée de Mai, a luxuriant, mountainous jungle that enveloped the centre of the island like a green mantle. Once over the summit, a cool breeze led down to the ocean on the other side. Beyond this, we drove past the dirt strip, with accompanying straw hut, that masqueraded as the airport. Finally, the tarmac transformed itself into a dirt track that led along the sun-drenched coast to the production office.

The production office of any film is the nerve centre of the operation. It's where the campaign is planned, co-ordinated and implemented from. It's where battles are won and lost.

It's always in a state of controlled chaos.

On our arrival at the wooden two-storey affair, set amongst the cool fronds of the ever-abundant palms, the underwater team, basically Mike Valentine and me, were shown to a corner of the porch - our office.

The equipment had already arrived and was piled high into a mountain of silver boxes that almost reached to the roof. While Mike checked it over, I managed to locate the compressor and found a safe spot at the rear of the building where I could set it up and fill the dive cylinders. Fifty tons of equipment had been shipped from the UK. I'm sure we had most of it.

The compressor started its trip intact, languishing happily beneath a shady tree at the rear of the production office. It shared the location with a slow-motion tortoise of gargantuan proportions and age. The animal had been there for as long as people seemed capable of remembering, and the tumultuous roar of pumping pistons and flying fan belts seemed to do little to disturb its outlook on life. The same, however, could not be said for members of the production staff. Like a rejected pet, the compressor was banished to a more secluded site – further away. Quieter on the ears – but further to carry the cylinders. As if in protest, the machine systematically shook itself to pieces over the coming weeks. What had started life as a proud creation of Bristol Pneumatic Ltd ended the shoot like some sort of dismembered Robocop.

With the compressor pumping away and the camera gear checked, next on our list of priorities was to locate some form of transport to carry our equipment around the island. It appeared, courtesy of Terry English, transport manager, who had undertaken a logistical task Norman Schwarzkopf would have been proud of, in commandeering every serviceable vehicle on the island… and then some.

However, we got the 'and then some', having the dubious pleasure of sharing a dilapidated Suzuki jeep with our film and diving gear, and Nick Phillips, the production engineer. Nick was an invaluable addition to the crew. Not only was he responsible for designing and building camera-mount systems for some of the more complex shots, but he could also fix just about anything. Unfortunately, as far as the jeep was concerned, what started out as us giving Nick a lift when needed, turned into a major breakdown service, as equipment failed by the day and Nick had to speed off on yet another rescue mission.

By the wrap, the island roads, film crew drivers and special effects hit squad (more on that later) had taken their toll. The once proud army of vehicles had been reduced to battered wrecks cast strategically across the island. Profound apologies to any tourists requiring transport later that year.

With the transport sorted, we were now ready for anything - even the main unit.

Films, during their production phase, consist of a number of units. The main, or first, unit deals primarily with the lead actors and dialogue. The second, or specialist, unit, will normally cover action, aerial, or, in this case, underwater filming.

As the weeks passed, the novelty of shooting with the main unit seemed to wear off, and very quickly, the second unit was the place to be. Even our illustrious producer Rick McCallum took a sabbatical and made it out to the tranquil haven of the underwater team. While *Castaway* was one of Rick's earliest films, he would go on to greater things as producer for *The Young Indiana Jones Chronicles* on TV as well as the three *Star Wars* prequels.

And then it was time to go to work.

The palms parted and I walked down onto the location - well, a beach actually. The most perfect sliver of glistening white sand, lying serenely between luxuriant jungle and the azure waters of the Indian Ocean.

The shot being set up was half in, half out of the water - not what the underwater camera and its ten-ton housing had been designed for.

Cameras are obviously not watertight in their own right, so when filming in or under the water they have to be encased in a waterproof housing that still allows control over all the camera functions. For this particular shot, we had the luxury of a tripod to support the housing.

I was to set up the camera on the tripod and make sure

it was secure and wouldn't fall over. Natalie Henrion, the stand-in for Amanda Donohoe, who played Lucy, was lying in position as I helped line up the camera.

I was concentrating on the tripod, whose left leg had stubbornly become stuck under a rock, when a shout distracted me.

'Okay, ready!' yelled Nic Roeg.

I glanced up, back at the tripod, then back up the beach. The lithe figure of Ms Donohoe was walking slowly towards me - naked. After a while you got used to Amanda's body, it was just part of the set. But it was interesting to hear her talk later about her approach to the nudity in the film, which she had to endure for a large part of the shoot. Originally she had thought things would get easier as time went on and she became used to being naked in front of all the crew - mainly guys. In fact, she said things actually became far more difficult, as everyone started to become her friends. It must have been a particularly hard shoot for her.

The next few days saw more action with the main unit and our first encounter with a certain Mr Oliver Reed.

The trouble with meeting legends is that everyone has their own impression of what these people are going to be like, and, believe it or not, they are just like you or me − well almost. It's just that they've received far more attention, so they carry a confidence and expectation way above that of most people. The other problem with legends is you have to remember that they reached their status through media interpretation and moulding.

So it was with some trepidation that I was introduced to Mr Reed... or Ollie. He was sitting under a palm tree in true Robinson Crusoe garb, having his make-up adjusted. He promptly asked me the most natural thing in the world.

'Like a beer, mate? Got some in this cool box.'

Somehow, though, this took on a whole new connotation. I mean, this was Oliver Reed, after all. Press reporting had already implanted its negative expectations onto me.

Ollie was, in fact, the nicest, most polite, charming person you could wish to meet - when he hadn't been drinking. The trouble was that he did drink, and that was when you started to believe what you read. It's a shame that such a great actor had to take what is enjoyable in moderation to extremes and have his persona degraded by the vagaries of the press, but then, if you give them a weakness, they will exploit it.

Introductions over, it was time for lunch. Meals became an oasis of tranquillity in the desert of heat and sweat that made up the rest of the day. It was a chance to get out of the burning sun and relax.

It all sounds great - going to the Seychelles for seven weeks - but it doesn't take long for the novelty to wear off and the bugbears of any environment to become more important than the experience itself. Soon we were all dreaming of pasteurised milk and Marmite - the script was becoming reality.

About a week later, as we were finally becoming accustomed to the intense heat and humidity, and the compressor had lost an arm in the form of the drive-belt guard, Nick Phillips wandered over to the underwater crew's section of the porch.

'Give us a hand, guys!' came the innocent request.

What he needed help with was a waterproof box that

was to be mounted on the end of a thirty-foot camera crane.

The crane, which Nick had designed, had been shipped out from the UK and assembled on the island. Maybe we didn't have most of the fifty tons after all.

It consisted of a bridgework metal jib supported by a fulcrum. Balance was provided by metal drums filled with water to equal the weight of the camera attached to the end of the jib. These had to be filled by pumping seawater into them wherever the crane was used. Its *raison d'être* was for a stunning shot that would start underwater, close on the coral, pull up through the surface, and on up, twenty feet into the air.

In order for the shot to work, the camera mounted on the end would have to be controlled remotely, so our underwater housing wouldn't be suitable. Instead, the main unit's camera would be mounted in a special waterproof box, which was yet to be tested for its ability to resist water.

What seemed like a thousand hand-screwed screws later, we had the glass port in place on the front. Cursing and swearing, we set off in the jeep to find some water to sink it in, preferably for good.

The water happened to be the Indian Ocean, complete with pristine white sandy beach. What followed could best be described as a Laurel and Hardy classic.

Anyone walking their dog, turtle, or anything else for that matter, would certainly have wondered at the sanity of three grown men clambering on top of a metal box in the surf, trying to submerge it to see if it would leak.

But however hard we tried, it just wouldn't sink. The problem was the buoyancy - too much of it. After ten minutes of useless struggle, we crammed everything we could find inside - clothes, bits off the jeep, our lunch, our drinks. It was stubbornly defiant. Then… suddenly...

'Strewth! The bloody thing's pissing water in!' shouted Nick.

We stared incredulously through the glass side. Water was indeed sloshing around inside the box. It looked like it was back to the drawing board. There was a frenzied rush to haul the infernal contraption back up the beach. Our lunch was getting wetter by the minute and the whole thing now weighed a ton with the addition of the water inside.

After much sweat and the release of the thousand screws, we found the leak. The water bottles we had put in to help weigh it down had split. The box was waterproof. No one had told it that it was okay to let water out. Still, it had definitely seemed heavier when we hauled it out!

And after all that, the crane was never used for its stunning shot and is probably now propping up some dilapidated garage roof in downtown Praslin.

Our first meeting with the special effects department taught me something I was to learn only too well - just how fiddly and time-consuming a single shot can be. When audiences watch a film, they have no idea how painful and agonising an experience it can be to produce the footage, however good or bad the final result may be. A few seconds on screen can sometimes take hours, even days, to set up and shoot. It's no wonder productions cost what they do.

We were to shoot a scene that sounded fairly straightforward in the script. Virginia Hey, playing

Janice, a reporter sent out with Gerald and Lucy to cover their arrival on the island, walks through shallow water to a helicopter that is going to take her back to civilisation. En route, a number of stingrays fleet past and through her legs. Well, it's bad enough getting Lassie to do her tricks, so stingrays - forget it! Cue special effects (SFX).

These days, we are so used to seeing spaceships zap across our screens and dinosaurs rampage through jungles that we forget that SFX covers a multitude of sins, and back then there wasn't the digital process to help out. Basically, anything in a movie that is not obviously done by man or nature is a special effect of some kind. Our rays were no exception. They were exact in every detail, and even as a marine biologist I was barely able to tell them from the real thing. They had been designed by Roger Shaw, an animatronics expert, and operated by Alan Whibley, head of Ace Effects, the SFX company commissioned for the shoot.

The principle was fairly straightforward. The rubber rays would be pulled on two pieces of fishing wire alongside and through Virginia's legs. The action would be filmed close up and it was my job to aim the rays in the right direction while Alan pulled hard at the other end of the wire.

The first problem was the wind. It had whipped up the water, reducing visibility, so the footage wouldn't match that shot by the main unit on the surface a few days earlier. This would normally be a major continuity problem, but after much consideration it was decided that the murky water would add to the menace of the creatures. It would also help hide the wires.

The great appeal of working on films is that you always

end up doing things you never get a chance to do in real life. I mean, I had never aimed a rubber stingray through a girl's legs before, so what experience can you draw upon to get it right? Probably the closest is throwing a paper dart, but it's not that close.

Finally, we were set up and ready to go. In shallow water, I held onto the ray. Mike yelled a garbled 'Action!' through his mouthpiece. Alan pulled hard, and I hurled the ray towards Virginia, aiming for her legs. The difficulty was persuading the ray to turn on its side to get it through. The final solution was to film a number of versions and let the editor sort it out. After all, that's where films are really made, in the cutting room with that infamous floor.

Twenty takes later we had something in the can, but the visibility wasn't great. It definitely looked murky, and there was no time to reshoot. It would have to do, and as is so often proven - film-making is the art of compromise. The shots are in the film.

The following day we set off to prepare for a slightly more dramatic sequence.

It involved a shark, caught on a line, supposedly being hauled in by Gerald and Lucy. To facilitate this, we headed out to a shark cage that had been moored just offshore. This sounded like good news. At least they were thinking of our safety.

How wrong you can be.

As we approached the cage in our Zodiac, there were a number of local fishermen milling around in their boats. We bumped gently against the pontoon and moored up. The cage itself was about ten foot by ten foot with a walkway around the edge. We jumped onto it and crossed over to the hatch in the middle to get a look at the space inside. Mike was about to lift it up when we noticed the fishermen crowding closer. It was one of those moments where people are reacting and you don't quite know why.

'I'm climbing in to check the space,' Mike explained jovially.

At this, the fishermen came even closer. We were slightly puzzled but put it down to natural curiosity over these idiot film people.

We were right.

As Mike lifted the hatch, he was met by several rows of teeth coming the other way. The fishermen had put the sharks inside the cage, ready for filming. We beat a hasty retreat and resorted to snorkelling on the outside to inspect our prospective stars from the safety of the open ocean, wondering how Seychelles logic would show its unlikely face next.

Our next task would be slightly more complex to set up.

There is a sequence in the film where Lucy, frustrated and frightened by Gerald's attempts to force himself upon her, keeps a knife close by her in their tent. The sequence had to impart the menace she felt, together with the lethal thoughts that accompanied her dreams.

It was to be our first night shoot and Mike, Nick, Natalie and I made our way out to the shark pontoon, now blissfully free of any of the toothsome creatures. To illuminate the sequence, a film lamp was set up to cast shafts of light into the water.

The first shot involved Natalie, doubling for Amanda, thrashing at the water with a carving knife. In the movie, the action is accompanied by the sound of splintering glass to great effect. Throughout, I was about ten feet below in the murk with a diving cylinder, letting off bursts of air to surround Natalie with bubbles. It didn't take much to remember what the cage above had been designed for as I peered into the darkness between takes. Much of the night was spent whirling round, glancing at shadows, while trying to keep an eye on where the bubbles had to go. Not the easiest of tasks with several thousand watts of light pouring into your eyes and no form of communication.

For another shot, Natalie had to swim upside down through the light rays, just below the surface. With the camera also turned upside down, this would provide the eerie illusion of Lucy swimming over the surface of the water surrounded by an ethereal glow. It took a while for Natalie to get the hang of the unusual swimming position, but once mastered, the shot looked as though it would be quite spectacular.

Many of the following days were spent scouting locations for suitably different shots, and although the Seychelles are in tropical waters in the southern hemisphere, the visibility wasn't what we had expected, nor was the amount of marine life.

We were lucky enough to see a turtle on one occasion, but the run-off from the land, caused by heavy rainfall, resulted in a general lack of suitable filming conditions. While the weather is a big factor here, and everywhere has its good and bad locations, things were looking pretty grim until our travels took us to the small island of Coco, about five miles from Praslin. As a location, it was almost perfect, being the ultimate image of a desert island - a pile of boulders, a couple of hundred feet across, covered by palm trees and lapped by crystal-clear water. But what was more important was that the underwater life was the best we had yet encountered, with a mini-reef fronting the southern side and just teaming with fish.

We were so relieved to find favourable conditions that we were spoilt for choice as to what to shoot. Over the next few trips, Mike filmed 'upside-down waves' crashing against the rocks, fish dining on the morsels of sea urchins crushed on the camera lens, silhouetted against the sun - that one made the movie - and general fishy background shots.

It was on Coco that we spent much of our time, and we were frequently joined by those of the crew who were able to escape the main unit, which always seemed to have an air of pressure and tension about it.

It was also on one of these trips that the paradise syndrome started to wear a little thin and a number of technical problems with the camera housing came to a head.

Most of the problems had been relatively minor and put down to the quirks of the system, but modifications over the years had taken their toll and the internal mass of wiring was forever getting itself crossed. On this particular occasion it caused untold frustration.

We had just arrived on Coco, an operation that, all in, took three to four hours. The shots had been worked out. Mike was underwater and I was venting my buoyancy compensator (BC) ready to join him. Suddenly he erupted through the surface with a barrage of expletives. The camera wouldn't turn over. It had jammed internally. Even with Nick Phillips' investigative skills, it couldn't be fixed. A day wasted, no film shot and a return to shore was all the reward for our efforts. There were a number of days like that.

A camera that refuses to turn over is annoying but not catastrophic. Something that is in an entirely different league is a housing that leaks or floods. Our worst nightmare was realised in only a few feet of water.

Mike was trying to get shots of the island through the breaking surf and the camera was being continually knocked around by the waves that repeatedly bashed it into the sand. When we opened the back to change rolls, we were greeted with a torrent of water – not good. Sand had entered the O-ring seal, allowing water inside.

The O-ring is probably the most important component of any underwater camera system. It was a failed O-ring that brought the Space Shuttle *Challenger* down - albeit a somewhat larger one. It is very simple in design and principle, being merely a seal between two areas of different pressure. In the case of our equipment, it was a rubber ring sealing the back of the housing to the main body. It's this piece of magic that keeps the water out. However, if even the smallest grain of sand, grit or hair interferes with the seal, you can potentially say goodbye to the camera. With modern film cameras costing tens, sometimes hundreds of thousands of pounds, not to mention the logistics of getting hold of another one in a far-flung location, it's not a problem you really want to encounter.

With this in mind, the O-ring is always double-checked and greased to ensure a perfect seal prior to any dive, but there is probably not an underwater camera crew alive that has always achieved perfection.

So it was with some nervousness that we took our 'damp' camera to Norman Godden, or 'Nobby' to the crew.

Nobby was one of a fading breed of camera technicians, rarely seen on locations these days. His sole purpose was to maintain and repair damaged camera systems. Usually the hire company will be responsible for repairs, either by sending their own technicians when necessary, or by replacing the damaged kit and repairing it at their own facilities. When you are thousands of miles from any workshops, standard procedures do not always apply.

Nobby lived in his own corrugated iron and wooden shed, surrounded by mechanical gizmos and equipment. His verdict on our little problem was relaxed and soothing.

'Well I'm sure we can do something about this, lads.'

A visit to Nobby's was always an experience, as it usually became a storytelling session, with Nobby recounting evocative tales from the past. Like the time he had been left by David Lean with a flare gun and a bottle of brandy in the middle of the desert at midnight. His task - to signal the approaching crew as to the location for the next shot of *Lawrence of Arabia*. These were the myths of the industry - the reason for the allure.

Sure enough, Nobby managed to work his magic, and the camera was soon cleaned, dried and readied for use. We were back in business.

But not for long.

The trouble with life is that when problems come along they seem to hunt in packs. There had been a bug going round the crew, dramatically diagnosed as dengue fever, and people had been dropping like flies. Inevitably, my number was up.

It was probably a combination of the heat, humidity

and fever that did it, but I was floored for three days - confined to my room. I have never felt so drained of energy in my entire life. Numerous trips to the bathroom to throw up was the sum total of my physical achievement for seventy-two hours.

It was during this time that my flat back in London, along with the rain and cold, seemed like a new definition of paradise to me. But, seemingly as quickly as it had arrived, the fever passed, and with new-found strength my updated dictionary was soon discarded and it was back to work. But before that, it was time for the event of the shoot.

At some point in every soap, the plot calls for a wedding to keep the interest - and ours was no exception.

Alan Whibley, SFX supremo, had chosen the middle of the shoot to tie the knot. It turned out to be a memorable occasion, followed by the inevitable late-night party that was bolstered by the enthusiastic antics of Leni Peihopa and his guitar.

Leni, a large, bubbly New Zealander from downtown Birmingham, England, played Ronald, Gerald's island friend in the film. He had been commandeered, along with his family, for his native looks and accent. I don't think he ever quite got over the experience and constantly lifted everyone's spirits with a permanent grin and a, 'nothing is too much trouble' attitude, while his skills on the guitar wreaked havoc, with renditions of everything from old tribal compositions to 'Good Golly, Miss Molly'.

The day after the wedding we were thankfully not required to go to work. It was no doubt carefully planned by the production staff, who realised little would have been achieved anyway. It was spent doing as little as possible.

The following days were filled with numerous fiddly shots, some in the water, some out, such as balancing the housing on the side of the Zodiac, filming waves crashing a few feet away on the rocks, while trying not to become part of their spectacular show.

These shots were repeated from the land with two cameras. The main unit, high up on the rocks - the underwater unit, low down on the rocks. Here we could again use a tripod, but the reason they needed the underwater camera was because the shot was close to the result of the wave's impact - like in it.

I was watching the waves crash in and around Mike, when suddenly he was knocked for six by a particularly large one. The tripod and camera fell on top of him, pinning him to the rock beneath. If the next wave was as big, he would be swept into the sea and smashed on the rocks below.

I glanced around briefly to see who was nearest. Everyone was watching the waves - the main unit's camera was still running. Mike was struggling with the tripod and the waves were building.

Blow their shot, I thought, and charged down the rocks. We had almost righted the camera by the time any of the others had moved. The favour was to be returned during the filming of our next feature together, *The Fruit Machine*, but more of that later. It does however emphasise that to work safely in any filming situation you need to be aware of when something serious is happening and when help is needed.

A few days later I pitched up at the production office to find the place in uproar. The staff were pinned to the walls, beholden to a rather large crab that had wandered into the middle of the floor. On the far side of the room, Roger Shaw was leaning against the wall, one of his animatronic radio control units in his hand.

This was too good to miss.

'Okay, Roge, bring her over here!'

Roger immediately caught on, moving the joystick forward on the control box and slightly advancing towards the crab. The crab, alarmed at the sudden move, walked away from Roger. The girls were now watching in amazement. As the bewildered crab scuttled around the room, Roger twisted the joystick in time with its movements. It ended up between two of the office desks. The girls were less wary now.

'That's incredible, Roger,' said Clare. 'Take long to make?'

'Not really,' came the nonchalant reply.

The girls crowded closer, about to pick up the hapless animal, but the crab wasn't having any of it. It raised its claws, darted its beady eyes around, then shot between their legs, sending them screaming behind their desks. The crab finally made it to the safety and sanity of the outside world, relieved to be free from the madhouse within. Roger soon followed, with some choice language following him through the door.

Several days later, the weather, which had up to now blessed us with constant sunshine, decided we needed some variety. For the next two weeks it barely stopped raining.

Apart from the obvious problems of working in the rain, it meant that any shots would not cut properly with those filmed earlier.

When we watch a film, there is a tendency to think everything is shot in sequence and just stuck together at the end - not so. It's quite conceivable that the parts of a sequence lasting a few seconds on screen have been shot weeks, even months apart, and sometimes, with large blockbusters, even on different continents. So things like whether it's overcast or sunny can significantly affect continuity and thus, shooting schedules.

As we built up to one of the major sequences in the film, a tidal wave demolishing Lucy and Gerald's hut, it was rather ironic that, given all the rain we'd had, Ace Effects had shipped out several tons of wind- and rain-making equipment. True to form, on the night of the shoot, the heavens opened. Maybe the good Lord was trying to show us that he was the ultimate SFX creator. However, it all added to the drama and realism, and for me it resulted in a couple of seriously exciting nights.

I got a hint of the bizarre nature of what was to come while reading the call sheet for the first night. It said:

TIDAL WAVE SEQUENCE: LOCATION - PRASLIN AIRPORT.

I mean, where else do you film a tidal wave, but at the local airstrip?

The underwater camera was involved, as it was to be placed close to the hut to catch the wave of water crashing through the windows.

At the side of the airstrip, the construction crew had built a replica of the hut, but we still needed the tidal wave. In front of the hut, a huge scaffolding structure supporting four tip tanks, twenty feet in the air, had been constructed. The tanks, like giant skips, held several tons of water, and when tipped over, they released the water down chutes, giving the illusion of a massive wave hitting the set.

However, for the scene, a tidal wave wasn't enough. A full-blown storm had to be raging. To create this, five powerful pumps and fire hoses would shower the area with heavy rain, while three wind machines, consisting of aeroplane engines mounted on small trailers and driving propellers, would provide the gale force winds. As if all this were not enough, the reason why we were at the airstrip in the first place finally became evident. A Twin Otter aircraft, using its two engines at full blast, would also be used to generate the strength of the storm. We were in for an interesting night.

While I was trying to take in the awesome events about to unfold, I overheard Selwyn Roberts, production manager, former British Army and overall co-ordinator of the logistics of the production, complaining that they needed a couple of dummies to put in the hut so it would look as though Lucy and Gerald were inside when it collapsed. Not realising he meant 'mannequins', my ambition suddenly got the better of me - after all, nobody else would be stupid enough to want to go inside the hut, so I volunteered.

Selwyn actually liked the idea, and as a result I spent an hour in make-up, having Gerald's scraggy wig and beard glued on.

The question of the hour, though, was who would take Lucy's role? The glamorous task fell to Alan Whibley. The transformation was truly an Ace Effect! We hardly made Seychelles couple of the year, but nevertheless, we headed for the set in anticipation.

It was now nightfall.

On the journey over, I had time to stop and think, which was quite a dangerous thing to do at a time like that. I mean, was this really sensible? It seemed not, but it was one of those moments where you have to seize the opportunity and worry about the consequences later. Not the best of philosophies, you could rightly argue, but one that's worked for me over the years and certainly makes for an interesting life. As we drew closer, the film lights at the side of the airstrip caught my attention and the feeling of trepidation passed.

Then it started raining.

There was something quite magical about the bizarre scene that greeted us. The hut and tip tanks were bathed in an eerie glow from the lights, and steam rose from the metalwork as the rain cascaded down.

The underwater camera was tightly secured by the hut and all the SFX machines were in place. The occasional banshee whine would make everyone jump as one of the aero engines was fired up to speed, sending palm fronds and loose material scuttling into the air.

On any set, you'll always find a large number of people who seem to be doing an awful lot of nothing. The trouble with film-making is that it's a collaborative art form, requiring many skilled people to make it all come together. It's just a fact of life that they can't all be busy at the same time. While the prop department are ensuring the set looks right, the lighting department are setting the lights, and the camera department can rig the camera, but once everything is ready, you still need all these people on hand for any adjustments or changes that might be required. This is the time-consuming part of film-making - fine-tuning all the components to make that final, breathtaking moment that makes a great movie great.

Eventually, all of our components were in place, and Amanda and Ollie, naked to the bone, were put through their paces.

Although the Seychelles is blessed with a naturally hot climate, particularly in the summer months, at night, with the rain bucketing down, wind machines blasting you and hoses spraying water on you, the body and soul can soon forget the latitude. With numerous problems arising, it didn't take long for the actors to lose their cool.

It was a long night, even for me, huddled in a tent against the driving rain, waiting for the final shot, which now seemed less like a good idea with every passing minute.

The evening's boredom was broken when the Twin Otter, engines at screaming pitch, broke away from its chocks and headed straight for the production tent. The pilot, who had been seemingly otherwise distracted, finally managed to control the careering aircraft before it chopped the tent and half the crew inside into mincemeat. I quickly forgot about dozing quietly, waiting for my call to the set, and concentrated with renewed enthusiasm on the unpredictable world of moviemaking.

The tidal wave sequence was the last shot of the night. You can't exactly rebuild the set in five minutes to do a retake once you've flattened it with several tons of water. So after waiting all night for my moment of glory, and with the rays of dawn edging their way into the brightening sky, the shot was finally called.

Then - disaster!

At the eleventh hour, it was decided that it would be too dangerous to put either Alan or me into the hut. The art director, Stuart Rose, couldn't guarantee what would happen when the water hit.

It's one thing to be inside an SFX hut that has been designed to collapse in a particular way, using rams, weakened walls and such like; it's quite another to be inside a hut constructed of corrugated iron and palm fronds that is about to be hit in haphazard fashion by tons of water from a great height.

As it turned out, Stuart was right. When the water hit, the whole hut fell like a deck of cards. Anyone inside would have been flattened like a pancake.

By the time the shot was called, everyone was well into a sense of humour failure with the weather and looking forward to hitting the sack, when a moment of light relief broke the tension. As the water subsided around the hut and everyone was applauding a now bedraggled Alan Whibley, still resplendent in his Lucy wig, a loud moaning was heard coming from the pile of collapsed metal and wood. Immediately there was uproar.

Who was in there?

After general panic all round, Reg Prince, Ollie's stand-in, was hauled from the wreckage, grinning foolishly. He had crawled in after the water had hit. Well, it made us laugh and lifted our dampened spirits.

After sleeping most of the rest of the day, we were back at the airstrip the following night. They needed to reshoot from different angles. We had four cameras, a rebuilt hut and numerous set-ups to get through.

Free of my Gerald hairpiece and beard, I was commandeered by the SFX crew to help with the complicated evening's proceedings.

It's rather an unnerving experience to be standing a few inches from an aeroplane propeller spinning at a zillion revolutions per second, but that was how the evening started.

It only got worse.

After a while, I got used to the scream of the engine and the howl of the wind. What I didn't get used to was the occasional burst of water that appeared from the sky as one of the fire hoses lost its target, accidentally or on purpose. Since I was only wearing a T-shirt, the frequent drenchings simply added to an accumulating numbness that was slowly creeping into my body.

There were three of us on the wind machines, and while we aimed the manic contraptions at the set, assistants would throw palm fronds and bush scree into their path, to be hurled dramatically against the hut.

If we thought it was bad outside, inside, Amanda and Ollie were trying to have sex! This is the only sequence in the film in which we are inflicted with a full-frontal, naked Mr Reed. Amanda, of course, was wearing her usual costume - nothing - but that was unashamedly easier on the eyes.

With shouts of 'More! More!' from the director, it became a competition between the three of us in the brass section to knock down part of the hut first. There was no time for boredom this evening.

As the night progressed, everyone was again preparing for the big event - the tidal wave, but as the shot approached, Alan Whibley had a problem.

The four tip tanks had to be released at precisely the same time for the wall of water to look effective. This was normally done by running a piece of metal across a line of electrical contacts that fired the release mechanisms that tipped the tanks over. Tonight there would be no auto-release. The contacts were waterlogged. The tanks would have to be released manually.

Four of us climbed to the top of the twenty-foot tip tank gantry. Up there you didn't need any wind machines, nature had provided her own. The wind and rain lashed down and I began to wonder more and more just what the heck I was doing there.

Alan explained the task, shouting over the roar of the elements and the machinery below.

'It's really very simple, guys. The tanks are held in place by metal hawsers. These are linked by World War II Wellington bomb releases. Now, at the side of each release is a narrow slit, see?'

I saw.

'In the middle of the slit is a hole. Bit difficult to see, like, cos it's well down the slit and it's bloody dark up here. To release the hawser, all you gotta do is ram a nail into the hole at the bottom of the release and the tank'll go over. Simple, eh? Oh yeah, you gotta make sure we all do it together, else the whole effect's screwed!'

I felt better already.

A 'dry' run with everything working, except the bomb releases, was enough to prove we didn't stand a raindrop's chance in hell of communicating with each other. It was just too noisy.

The answer came in a flash.

To simulate the lightning strikes, the SFX crew had a series of powerful flashbulbs that ignited in unison.

'Got it!' yelled Alan. 'Release the water when you see

61

the fourth flash, okay?'

Okay. It was getting simpler by the minute!

I climbed back up the tower, my heart pounding. I held within my hand the power and likely probability of blowing the whole shot. The adrenaline started to flow.

Down below, the wind machines started up. Four fire hoses suddenly erupted, narrowly missing the gantry - but what the heck, I was soaked already. I tried to look across at the others but the wind and rain obscured my view. Suddenly, a screaming banshee wail added to the bedlam.

'What the hell's that?' I yelled. No one heard me. Then I remembered the Seychelles Air Force was in on the act. The Twin Otter revved and screamed, threatening to break its leash, but I was above it this time - no problem.

Things were happening fast below. Palm fronds were flying. The Otter was shaking alarmingly, then FLASH... There was the first one... FLASH... the second, or had there been two together? I started to panic. If I screwed this up, that was it - *you'll never work in this town again!* The other tanks hadn't gone yet, so mine stayed. FLASH... that was surely the fourth. I hesitated - the tanks still hadn't gone, then... FLASH. Right, this had to be it. I forced the nail in.

'Shit!'

Nothing happened.

Everything was happening in slow motion. To my left I could see Alan's tank going over, but why was it so slow? I rammed the nail in again. The howling and screaming faded into the background as the nail drove home. The tank was tipping. The water thundered down, joining the other hundreds of gallons on their collision course. The surge of adrenaline and euphoria hit at the same time. I yelled with excitement and relief. Along the gantry the others were whooping with joy. I managed to peer over the edge. The hut was flat. I could barely believe it had worked.

There were beers all round.

After the airstrip experience, the rest of the shoot was relatively mundane by comparison. The last week was merely a wind-down, tidying up loose ends.

Not put off by my failure to get on screen in the hut, I had a second chance that came even closer.

Some close-up underwater shots were required of the horrendous sores on Ollie's legs, seen while he was walking through the water. Since Mr Reed wasn't needed for the shot and was shooting elsewhere, I volunteered. This meant a day walking through shallow water with 'blood' pouring from the expertly made-up sores that now adorned my legs. The shots were great - they made the rough cut - but they didn't make the final print. Someone somewhere was trying to tell me something.

You knew it was close to the end of the shoot because people started getting silly. At a time like this, it's not a good idea to allow the SFX guys to have very little to do - the result was the SFX hit squad. What started out as a harmless bit of fun ended up in all-out war between departments.

Cars were ambushed with fire hoses... ignitions were connected to thunderflashes... wheels were removed... and McCallum came within a two-foot tide of having his car floated on a pontoon in the middle of the bay. The resistance finally put a stop to all the nonsense by parking Alan Whibley's car on the roof of the SFX shed.

The final shots of the film were at the airstrip, but this

wasn't the dirt strip we had landed on seven weeks earlier. Gone was the rickety old hut that had acted as arrivals and departures. In its place was a brand new terminal building complete with tarmac strip, paid for no doubt, by the liquor consumption of the crew.

The scene, appropriately, was Lucy contemplating her final thoughts while flying over the island that had been her home and life for a year.

It was while we were all gathered together for these last few hours that a strange feeling started to creep over me. I'd felt it many years earlier at the end of a school term, only this was more final. When you went home for the school holidays, you were usually going back. This time, you were breaking up for good. Sure, you would see many of the faces again - the film industry is a small one - but not all together as a unit.

It was really very sad. Everyone had been through a tough shoot and the crew had knitted together as a team. Amanda summed it all up as she stepped from the plane, her final scenes complete. She burst into tears of relief, sadness and happiness, all rolled into one.

All that was left, having packed up the tons of equipment and gathered the pieces of the compressor into its wooden coffin for burial, was the trip home and time for reflection.

For me it was an unforgettable experience, my dreams come true. There had been rough times and extremely good times, but the sadness at the end was tempered by the expectation of what might be to come.

I needn't have worried.

4

Tooty Fruity

For several weeks following my return from the Seychelles, I was still on a high from the experience. I must have become the archetypal film nerd party guest, constantly recounting my 'Hollywood' adventure. But gradually, as the euphoria wore off, which didn't take that long, the spectre of reality started to rear its ugly head and it began to dawn on me that I didn't actually have a job.

Since I had given up teaching at the Diving Locker to work on *Castaway*, I now had to find work to pay the inevitable bills, which were starting to mount up and rapidly depleting my fairly minimal earnings from the film. At the time it had seemed like a good chunk of money, but as my naivety about the industry wore off, I realised just how poor a deal we had been on. It didn't matter though, as the experience itself had been payment enough, and if at the time you had asked me to do the whole thing again on the same deal, I would have absolutely said 'yes'.

I was starting to experience the rollercoaster lifestyle that is the film industry – never knowing where the next job is going to come from. This early realisation was a wake-up call, and from that moment on I knew I had to be pro-active with regard to work and not just hang around waiting for the next job to come in, but to always be looking for new directions and avenues from which to earn money, while at the same time pursuing my central goal.

The logical step was to start my own diving business. The aim would be to teach sport diving as the bread and butter work, while pursuing film contacts for the more exotic adventures. I was soon to find out though that not all films were made in the Seychelles with warm water and pristine sandy beaches. When the next feature did finally come along, it was about as far removed from *Castaway* as you could possibly imagine. However, it did involve water, working with dolphins, and Robbie Coltrane in drag! It was called *The Fruit Machine*, and on reading the script, it soon became clear this was not your average mainstream blockbuster.

The story followed the adventures of two gay kids, Eddie (Emile Charles) and Michael (Tony Forsythe), running away from their homes in Liverpool. They become involved in a race for their lives, after seeing Annabelle (Robbie Coltrane), the transvestite owner of *The Fruit Machine* nightclub of the title, being murdered. The killer (Bruce Payne) follows them to Brighton, where Eddie becomes obsessed with freeing a dolphin from the local dolphinarium - a metaphor for his own captive lifestyle as a gay teenager. Interwoven with this are Eddie's dreams of a mysterious green-eyed dolphin-man

(Carston Norgaard) releasing him and setting him free from the imprisonment of his world. After breaking into the dolphinarium, Eddie is attacked by the killer and seriously wounded. Michael arrives and, in a confrontation with the killer, knocks him into the water, where he drowns. The next day the killer is found dead in the dolphin pool and the suspected 'dangerous' dolphin is loaded onto a truck for removal. Following this, Michael wants to free the dolphin for Eddie, and he steals the truck with the dolphin on board. In the resultant police chase, he careers along a pier and crashes into the sea. As the truck sinks with Michael trapped inside, the dolphin, now released from the rear, changes into the green-eyed man and helps Michael escape. Michael returns to Eddie, only for him to die in his arms from his wounds.

Certainly not your standard Hollywood fare, but it turned out to be a moving and hard-hitting story, and pretty much what the British film industry was about in the late eighties. More importantly, from my point of view, there were some fairly challenging underwater sequences and the prospect of working with dolphins, albeit in a dolphinarium in Yorkshire. This was one of the reasons I had originally spent four years at university studying marine biology, but I could hardly have imagined this would be how I would eventually end up working with these amazing animals.

On closer inspection, the underwater scenes were VERY challenging and it would take a fair amount of ingenuity, thought and preparation to bring them to the screen.

One of the first priorities was to make sure we had the right crew for the job. It would need to be larger than

Castaway, as the work was more involved, and this time there was more of a budget to play with.

Mike Valentine would again be the underwater cameraman. I was supervising the safety and training of the actors, and there were two new additions to the team. Phil Barthropp, a super-fit former England hurdler, had worked frequently with Mike when he had been at the BBC. Phil was there as camera assistant, and he was also happy to help out in the water if required. He has since gone on to become a highly talented and successful cameraman in his own right. The second addition was Emma Crewdson, a flaming red-headed model who had appeared in a couple of Mike's homemade productions and would act as a general assistant. She had filmed at the dolphinarium with Mike before, so they were well used to the requirements of working with the animals. In fact, these particular dolphins had featured heavily in one of Mike's short films that had helped secure the job on *Castaway*.

As for the underwater sequences in *The Fruit Machine*, there were quite a few, but two in particular stood out as being of concern. The first involved Eddie in a bedroom underwater in one of the dream sequences. The second, and by far the most difficult, was where Michael was trapped inside the sinking truck and was rescued by the dolphin-man.

As ever in film production, sequences that appear seamless on screen are often shot days, if not weeks, apart, and often at different locations, which may even be on different sides of the country, as well as in a studio. *The Fruit Machine* was no exception, with exteriors of the dolphinarium and the truck chase being shot in Brighton and the dolphinarium interiors and underwater sequences shot at the *Flamingo Land* theme park near Kirby Misperton in Yorkshire.

One other important aspect of film production, which is frequently overlooked, is the preparation time. Most people think of the time spent making a film as merely the 'production' or actual shooting stage, with a bit of 'sticking together' at the end. In reality, the pre-production stage is often as long, if not longer, than the whole of the rest of the process put together, and for big-budget extravaganzas, it may even be up to a year or more. My involvement began several weeks prior to shooting, working with Emile, Tony and Carston on the underwater sequences.

Normally, this sort of potentially dangerous action would be carried out by stuntmen, but director Philip Saville wanted things to be as real as possible. If you can see the actors doing the action for themselves, the whole story becomes that much more believable. The obvious example of this are the stunts Tom Cruise does in the *Mission Impossible* films, which are easily as dangerous and breathtaking as any done by a stuntman, and make the films that bit more thrilling because you know he is actually doing them himself.

Back on *The Fruit Machine*, the boys, of course, wanted to go for it, so they had to go through an intense training period to get them into shape for the challenging times ahead. The training was particularly important for Tony, as he had the dubious pleasure of being the one trapped inside the sinking truck.

One advantage of working with teenagers is that they adapt very quickly to new ideas and new skills. To them, it's really all a big adventure and they are often quite fearless. This can be a double-edged sword, as on the one hand it means they will try anything, but on the other you often have to rein them in and make them realise that some of the things they are doing are potentially quite dangerous.

Whenever you train artists to carry out this sort of work, you have to remember the chances are they have probably never dived before and will therefore know nothing of the procedures and dangers they will encounter. They will also have none of the instincts normally required for safety and survival should something go wrong.

Most people would probably think that an extensive diving course would be necessary before even the most basic stunt can be undertaken. However, this isn't the case. Often, the more theory and skills thrown at someone, particularly in a short space of time, the more confused and worried they become. The trick is to concentrate on only the specific things that are absolutely necessary, not only for them to be able to complete the sequence to the satisfaction of the director but also to be totally safe in the process. You must also remember that you can't hide things. If you are asking someone to do something dangerous, they have a right to know what those dangers are and to make their own decision as to whether they wish to go through with it or not. It also means that hopefully they know when to stop and will tell you when that moment comes. Actors are notorious for saying they can do something in order to get a part, but when working underwater, we're not talking about looking ridiculous on a horse if you can't ride properly.

There's a little more at stake than that.

The best approach is always to work up slowly and repeat everything regularly. This way, new skills are continuously being learned, while at the same time reinforcing those that have already been mastered. It can be a fine balance, and it largely depends on the individual as to how fast you can progress.

To this end, the training started in a small six-foot-deep pool, just to get an idea of everyone's relative swimming ability. As it turned out, it didn't look as though I was going to lose anyone swimming lengths. The next stage was to see how adaptable they would be with the basic diving skills they would need for filming.

Apart from becoming familiar with breathing from an aqualung, the first serious skill the boys had to master was breathing underwater without a mask. This is something every diver should be able to do without hesitation but is something less experienced divers often struggle with. It is probably the one skill trainees find the most difficult and one that requires the most concentration. If you can't understand why, just get hold of a snorkel, fill up a sink, and try to breathe through the snorkel with your face in the water, without holding your nose – you'll soon get the idea. It was something Emile, Tony and Carston would have to do as second nature if they were to be confident enough to complete the filming. In Tony's case, his life could well depend on it.

The reason this skill is so necessary is that there will often not be time for an artist to replace a mask between takes. They may not even be able to wear a mask at all if make-up is being used, as a mask could smudge something that had taken minutes, sometimes even hours, to apply.

This means the actor may have to breathe from an aqualung, with no mask on, for extended periods of time. If they have a problem with this, they could end up panicking and racing to the surface in a hurry. This could have severe consequences, potentially leading to damage to the lungs depending on the depth the ascent was made from.

For those not familiar with diving, as you go deeper the pressure becomes greater. In order for your lungs and other air spaces in the body to withstand this increase, the air you breathe from the aqualung is provided at the same pressure as the depth you are at to ensure equalisation of the pressure. It should therefore be fairly clear that when you come back up and the pressure is reduced, any excess gas has to be released. If it isn't, it can expand and cause damage in whichever part of the body it happens to be in. If this is a lung, it can inflate just like a balloon, and burst just like a balloon if overfilled. This is why divers have to breathe out when they come up to ensure any excess volume is released. If someone panics and rushes to the surface, there is every possibility they will forget to do this, hold their breath and damage their lungs.

Once in the water with all the kit, Tony, Emile and Carston soon mastered breathing without a mask. With this hurdle out of the way, it was then simply a matter of making them as at home underwater as possible in the given time. The best way to do this is to turn the training into a game. It not only makes things fun and enjoyable but it also makes the learning process quicker and easier.

We started with an aqualung at each end of the pool. They would have to swim from one to the other, first with a mask, then without a mask, and finally with their eyes shut. One of the aqualungs would then be taken away and they would do it with just the one - blindfold.

From here, we progressed to a larger, deeper pool and repeated the skills, always stretching them that little bit further. Overall, they did a great job. The purpose of the games is to build confidence, so should something go wrong, or if they had to wait for a safety diver to reach them, they would know they could survive comfortably without air for a reasonable period of time, and when they finally did receive a mouthpiece, they could confidently clear the water, start breathing and relax − all in a day's work.

Once I was happy they had done all they could, it was time for them to get back to their day job − acting - and for me to join the crew on location.

All the underwater footage was to be filmed at *Flamingo Land* in Yorkshire, so on the 15th of October 1987 I set off north up the A1 with a buzz that can only be felt at the start of a new project. Ahead was an up-close encounter with dolphins and the beginning of another feature film. If the date rings any bells, it was the night of the great hurricane of '87, but that was several hours away at this point, and a lot would be packed in before the storm hit.

Arriving at the gates of *Flamingo Land* late that afternoon was slightly surreal. The park was closed for the winter, and where normally there would have been hundreds of kids and families enjoying the facilities, there was nothing but empty roads and shut-up enclosures - a bit like a ghost town. Even the resident animals seemed to be put out by this intrusion into their downtime. The park itself was a cross between a zoo and a fairground, and at the time it was one of only four locations in the country where dolphins were kept in captivity. Now there are none.

The dolphinarium was at the far end of the park, and as I approached in the fading light, first impressions were not great. I mean, it certainly wasn't *SeaWorld*. There was a large semicircular open-air arena surrounding what looked like a fairly small pool. The far side of the pool disappeared into a large covered area, which had a scruffy corrugated roof with a brazen *Flamingo Land* logo in bright red letters on faded white walls. It was also damned cold.

Having travelled up alone, I had arrived before the rest of the team, but already there was the growing paraphernalia of a film crew making its presence felt. All too quickly, memories of *Castaway* came flooding back as I parked behind a large generator truck and walked past lighting and props lorries towards the entrance of the pool building.

As I approached, the distinctive squeaks and whistles of the dolphins could be heard coming from within, and my earlier misgivings were hastily put aside. The way in through a side extension was actually the food prep room, and as I made my way through, the smell of fish was overpowering. It was something we would all have to get used to over the coming weeks. Once inside, the squeaking and whistling only intensified.

The pool itself was shaped in a large filled-in figure of eight. The design had been well thought out, with half the pool inside, undercover, while the other half, as I had seen earlier, was out in the open. With seating for audiences both inside and out, it enabled the show to go on whatever the British weather could throw at it. For most of the shooting we needed the controlled lighting of a studio, so a divide would be built between the two sections, creating a sealed interior. As we were filming over the winter, this would also help keep out those severe northern gales.

The main pool was already a hive of activity, with the construction crew building small parts of the sets and the lighting department checking out the electrics and positions for the main lights. One problem round any pool environment is that there is always water and moisture, which tend not to mix too well with high voltage electricity. It was something I showed a particular interest in, as I would be spending much of my time in the water. I had barely had a brief look round when Mike, Phil and Emma arrived.

It had been a long journey for all, but the presence of the dolphins more than made up for any feelings of tiredness, and as if drawn by a magnet, everyone spent the first half hour or so constantly throwing balls and generally acting like demented kids.

The dolphins, all female, were called Sharky, Betty and Lotte, and were looked after by their trainer, Peter Bloom. In fact, 'looked after' wasn't quite the right description for Peter's approach to 'the girls', as he called them. He was clearly utterly devoted to them, and they seemed to be equally enamoured with him, which was a good thing, as they were going to have to learn a whole raft of new tricks very quickly if we were to put half of what was required onto film.

When you touch a dolphin, the first thing you notice is its skin. You might imagine it's just a solid, hard surface. Actually, it feels like a hard-boiled egg that's been peeled - hard, yet soft at the same time. The skin surface is one area scientists are specifically researching, as the muscular structure within it allows the dolphin to minutely vary its profile and so reduce friction, thereby increasing its speed through the water. This would be an invaluable property for the coating of submarines if it could be reproduced artificially.

After being bewitched by the dolphins for far too long, a time that seemed like only seconds, we remembered we were here to do a job, and so went to check out the underwater unit production base. In the Seychelles it had been a porch beneath cool palm fronds - here it was a basement below the food prep room, but at least it had a shower and heater and was warm and dry. Given the time of year and the temperature outside, that was all we needed. It was also the closest room to the pool, so there was minimal distance to travel with dive kit or the cumbersome camera housing. On closer inspection, the shower rattled and grated when in use, but at least the water was hot, and there was a good work area where we could lay out all the gear and prepare the housing and underwater lights. There was also an additional feature that came at no extra charge.

Since it was off-season and *Flamingo Land* was closed, we had to share the room with some guests from other areas of the park: eight more than inquisitive parrots and cockatiels. At least our new-found friends were talkative, which was more than could be said for the tortoise in the Seychelles. In fact, their ability to mimic and 'reply' to conversations drew expressions of amusement and exasperation in equal measure.

It is common knowledge that dolphins are highly intelligent creatures, but just a brief word on this before we continue. Clearly the animals have a brain larger and more attuned than your average animal, and over the years, through films and myth, the ability of this brain has been compared favourably to our own. However, it should be remembered that they are still just animals, albeit very approachable and open to interaction with humans. A perfect example of this was when, often late at night, after a long day shooting, you could always find members of the crew crouched by the poolside talking to the dolphins or throwing them a ball. Now this could be taken a number of ways. As Peter Bloom would say, any animal that could happily sit there all day long throwing a ball back to you can't exactly be challenging Einstein - but then, for the dolphins to throw the ball back, someone had to throw it to them in the first place...

The first time in the water with Sharky, Betty and Lotte was a truly magical moment, but it was tempered with caution following a talk from Peter.

Dolphins are large, strong animals, consisting primarily of muscle, and the one thing a shark fears most underwater is a dolphin. They have been known to ram into their underbellies at full speed, stunning, sometimes even killing them. So the illusion of 'Flipper', all sweetness and light, is one to be put aside. That smile is there by design, not from emotion. It's not that they are inherently aggressive or vicious, but they are excitable, boisterous and very strong.

The main thing is to always keep your eye on where they are and what they're up to. To them you are a plaything in their environment that just has to be investigated. It's also important to keep your hands to your sides, as they see these strange appendages as something they can use to get you to play with them. Since a dolphin doesn't have hands, the only way it can really interact with you is through its mouth. That's not to say it's going to bite you, more like hold onto you and take you where it wants you to go. Of course, a dolphin's mouth is full of teeth, so you're likely to get scratched, if not actually bitten, during this process. The rule is that if an animal shows more than a healthy interest, keep your hands to yourself and turn your back. They soon get bored and go and find someone else to bug. This, of course, is far harder in reality. Once you are in the water, you are so overcome with excitement you just want to enjoy the experience, but you have to remember you are sharing the water with a 'wild animal' that's in its natural element and is far stronger and faster than you will ever be.

As I jumped in, all this and more was spinning through my head. The first thing that happened, even before the bubbles of my impact had cleared, was that three streaks of greased lightning raced past me. Any new visitor to their world had to be investigated with the greatest urgency. Once over the shock of three projectiles hurtling towards me, I eased myself down the side of the tank and stood on the bottom in awe, watching the dolphins fly around like aquatic cruise missiles, their sheer grace and speed even more pronounced than it had appeared from the surface. It made you feel totally inadequate. If we could even match half their ability in our own world, we would all be Olympic athletes.

It really was quite humbling.

Once I'd collected my thoughts, I headed out to the

centre of the pool. As everything appears about a third larger underwater, due to the refraction of light through the mask, the tank didn't really look that small. However, if you take into account the speed of the animals, it was pretty confining, and it was hard not to imagine them swimming free on the crest of a wave in the open ocean. A romantic notion, and one that's a contentious issue.

Having recovered from the initial shock of the first underwater encounter, I had a general swim around to get a feel for the environment we would have to work in. While this trip was merely a recce to test everything out and film some simple background shots of the animals in the water, there were many more complex set-ups to be completed at a later date.

Once we had completed everything to Mike's satisfaction, it was time to retire to the pub after what had been a quite memorable day.

That night the great storm hit.

We awoke to a virtual TV blackout. Trees were down on every road. There was general mayhem and carnage across the country.

Most of the rest of the morning was spent at the dolphinarium to finalise details for the main shoot. Then, with a final look round, we left the construction and lighting crews to finish off prepping the sets and lights while we returned to London.

A week later, on the 25th October, we travelled back up to Yorkshire for the beginning of an intense and exciting eight days filming.

When we arrived, the circus was in full swing. All the

departments were there, with their accompanying support trucks parked around the complex. The dividing wall was now in place, separating the exterior from the interior of the pool, and once inside, the effect was to dramatically reduce the size of the pool.

The key shots for this trip were the surface sequences of Eddie in the dolphinarium (Brighton in the film) watching the show in disgust and wanting to free the dolphin, followed by the sequence where Eddie and Michael are attacked separately in the dolphinarium. Actually, Eddie's attack is seen off-screen, but Michael has a prolonged fight with the killer, including some in-water action. The more complex shots of Eddie's dream sequence and Michael trapped inside the truck would be saved for later in December – when it was even colder.

Shooting the dolphin show was fairly straightforward, and as it was all above water, I was really there just in case anyone fell in, so I had plenty of time to watch the filming process, which, after a while, as most people will admit, can become slightly tedious. But I was still in that enthusiastic learning phase and so absorbed everything that went on. The interest level did rise for one shot however. It was when the dolphin trainer, played by Paula Ann Bland, leans over the pool from a small platform and one of the dolphins leaps up and plucks a ribbon from her bikini top, causing it to split open revealing her more than ample breasts. A great gag, you might say, but one that wasn't as simple as it sounds to execute.

First off, Paula wasn't happy to allow the dolphin to do it for real, and so a stunt double had to be used for the moment when the dolphin actually grabs the ribbon. Paula would then be back on camera for the reveal of the breasts. Clearly there were no stunt breasts available! In order to see her top flying open, there had to be a mechanism to release it. To achieve this, stunt co-ordinator Peter Diamond, a veteran of *Star Wars* and *Indiana Jones*, and a legend in the stunt game, had to sit in a plastic dinghy beneath Paula, and at the critical moment pull a piece of fishing wire that released her breasts. Tough job, but someone had to do it!

The final sequence for this trip was the attack by the killer, played to chilling effect by Bruce Payne. Bruce seemed to have cornered the market in menacing characters at that time, and he would go on to probably his biggest role in *Passenger 57* with Wesley Snipes some years later. He is one of those actors who throws himself wholeheartedly into his part, and the sequence called for him to chase Michael (Tony Forsyth) around the pool, then attempt to drown him by holding his head beneath the surface. Michael escapes by swimming underwater into the dolphin holding pool. He climbs out then knocks the killer into the water with a paddle, where he drowns.

The problem of filming something like this, where an artist is acting as though he's in trouble, is that it's difficult to know if he really is in trouble. In this scenario, things weren't too bad, as we were close to the surface and safety, but the signals I worked out with Tony were to become invaluable when we were working with him later inside the sinking truck. The best approach is to have the artist do something completely at odds to the action being portrayed, such as putting a hand on their head, or some other equally out of place movement.

The filming went well, and with Bruce bringing a frightening air of menace to the role and Tony throwing himself into it with his usual enthusiasm, the shots were safely in the can. It had been an easy few days for me, but with the more difficult shots looming, there was no time for complacency.

Before that, though, the whole production decamped to Brighton, where the exteriors of the dolphinarium would be filmed, along with shots of the actors walking past fish tanks in the aquarium. The final shots in Brighton were the most spectacular - the truck chase along the seafront and the finale of the vehicle flying off a pier into the sea.

As the underwater crew were really only there for the shot of the truck crashing into the water, we had half a day watching the exploits of the stunt drivers racing down the seafront with a camera truck in hot pursuit. Once they were happy, and they had to be, as they weren't going to be able to use the truck later as it would be at the bottom of the English Channel, it came time for the big stunt.

As this was potentially extremely dangerous, with many variables, there was no way even a stuntman was going to drive the truck into the water. We were using a small brick-built pier about a quarter of a mile east of the main pier at Brighton. The truck itself was a pickup version of a Ford Transit with a canvas cover over the rear.

For the first part of the sequence, it would be driven down the pier by a stunt driver. When it reached the end, everything would stop and the special effects team would take over. In this case, another of the true legends of British action films, Dave Bickers, would set up and fire the Transit off the end of the pier. Dave was a former motocross champion and had been rigging action sequences on films for longer than most people could remember. However, when Mike asked him precisely where in the water he should be to avoid being hit, 'France' wasn't exactly the reply he had been looking for!

The Transit would be fired by an air-ram up a short ramp and into the sea. A full-size dummy dolphin would be placed strategically in the rear, in the hope it would emerge as the truck sank below the surface. This could then be cut into the film, showing a real dolphin swimming around the Transit, which would be filmed in the dolphinarium at *Flamingo Land*. Since it could only be done once, it was in the lap of the gods as to how it would all pan out.

With everything in place, we set off in a small rigid inflatable boat (RIB) to take up station, hopefully a safe distance from the end of the pier. Mike climbed into the water with the camera but was attached to the end of a rather long rope, ready to be hauled out of the way if it looked like the truck was headed in our direction.

Everything was set. 'Quiet' was called for. There was a brief pause. All cameras ran up to speed.

Then 'Action!'

There was a loud bang and the truck shot into the air. Fortunately, it never made it to France, but it seemed to hang for an eternity before crashing into the water in an explosion of spray about thirty feet from where Mike was nervously floating.

It was truly spectacular, but the shot wasn't over. The most important action was yet to happen. As the truck slowly started to sink, there was a sudden spurt of air from the far side, and miraculously the dummy dolphin flew out of the back. When finally edited and cut to music, it produced one of the most poignant and emotional moments in the film, one that could hardly have been bettered, and as is so often the case when you're out in the field and things are beyond your control, it was really all down to a great deal of luck.

Sometimes, nothing seems to go right, however much effort and preparation goes into a set-up, yet at other times, such as here, the simplest of things can happen to perfection and the magic of cinema is there for all to see.

With the shot in the can, our job was over and we watched as the local commercial dive team had the unenviable task of dragging the sunken Transit out through the waves. The next time we would see it would be at *Flamingo Land,* ready for the climactic sequence of Michael trapped inside.

And so, on the 6th December, with winter drawing its ever-tightening clutches around us, we made the long haul back up to Yorkshire for some excitement, drama, and a few heart-stopping moments I could well have done without.

Unfortunately, in our time away, the construction crew had seen fit to remove the divide between the exterior and interior of the pool, so we would now have to work in the full force of the icy blast of a northerly wind. The Seychelles it was not!

Finally though, it was time to get down to business, and time for Emile, Tony and Carston to show off what they had learned over their many hours of training. The easiest scenes would be attempted first, which would help ease everyone into the more difficult sequences to follow.

For the scene where Eddie/Emile dreams about seeing the dolphin-man, Green Eyes, at his bedroom window, the room had been built as a set on the bottom of the pool. It consisted of two walls, one of which contained the window Eddie would look out of. The action involved one of the dolphins coming up to the window and looking in at Eddie, who then swims to the window, sees the dolphin and swims out through the window, which had no glass in it, and off with the dolphin.

Simple.

While preparing for each shot, Emile would be on the bottom, breathing from a dive cylinder, and I would be close by, checking he was okay. We had done enough training to ensure he was up to the task, but the unknown factor was whether the dolphin would act her part within the time that Emile could hold his breath. This would be down to Peter's skill and the use of a tennis ball.

When training dolphins, it's a gradual process to get them to learn certain commands and act upon them, always rewarding a correct action with a fish, so they associate getting food with getting things right. It's also necessary for them to have something to focus on, particularly if they are expected to go to a particular position and do something when they get there. This is done by using a tennis ball on the end of a short stick. The dolphin associates the tennis ball with the place she has to go to, then any other action can be developed from there. In the case of the swimming-through-the-window shot, it was down to holding the tennis ball in position, just out of shot, for the dolphin to swim to when Peter gave the command. With the right camera angle it would appear as though the dolphin was swimming to the window to look in at Emile. In fact she was merely going straight to the tennis ball, and once there, on cue, Emile would swim out of the window and off into the gloom.

There were of course times when the dolphin wouldn't quite go up to the window, or would be startled when Emile suddenly swam out, but it was the first time we had all really been working underwater together, and all things considered, it went surprisingly well.

There's a shot towards the end of the film when the dolphin, having escaped from the Transit, turns into Green Eyes in order to help Michael, who is trapped in the cab. This was one of the earliest uses of computer graphics in a feature film to transform, or 'morph', a person into something else, and although very clunky by today's standards, at the time it was fairly groundbreaking, and it heightened the drama and spectacle of the finale of the film.

The shot was achieved by having Phil Barthropp, who doubled for Carston, and one of the dolphins, swim past the camera separately, in as close to the same position as possible. One of the shots would then be matted on top of the other in the computer to create the transition. Overall, the effect was impressive, but you would never realise the number of freezing man-hours spent in the water to achieve those few seconds of film.

We had been pleased and pleasantly surprised at how well things had gone so far, but there was still an air of trepidation as we approached the final sequence.

In a nutshell, it called for the Transit to sink with Tony/Michael inside, struggling to escape. Once the truck had settled on the bottom, the newly released dolphin, now transformed into Green Eyes, would crash through the driver's door window and Michael would swim to freedom.

It was as difficult as it sounded, but as ever in filming complex and potentially dangerous sequences, it can be broken down into safely and tightly controlled sections.

When approaching anything like this, safety is paramount. You have to have backups to the backups, which is precisely what we had in this case, particularly as Tony Forsythe would be performing all the action himself, with no use of a stuntman for any of the shots.

The sequence would require two set-ups. One would be the sinking of the Transit, which would be done by lowering the whole truck into the water by mobile crane. The second would be the truck fixed to the bottom of the dolphinarium and angled over so the driver's side was uppermost. In this position the key action of Green Eyes breaking through the driver's window and releasing Michael could be best captured.

The most important aspect was the safety redundancy for Tony. The plan was that, in an ideal world, if nothing went wrong, he would be able to breathe freely right up to the point where Green Eyes smashed through the window. To achieve this, Steve Fila of Commercial Diving and Marine Services in York sealed the Transit cab, so when it was on its side, the upper part was completely airtight. A massive air cylinder with a large bore outlet was then fed into the sealed cab. This would provide air and maintain an air pocket in the upper side of the cab (the driver's side when it was on its side) so that Tony could always breathe. In an emergency, the volume of air could be drastically increased at the turn of a valve, completely expelling any water from inside the cab.

If this failed, Plan B was an aqualung, hidden under the driver's seat, with a mouthpiece that Tony kept close to him.

Should this fail, Plan C was me outside the cab with an extra-long secondary regulator that I could pass to him if he couldn't find his own regulator. As the cab had been made airtight to maintain the air bubble, the rear window had to be clamped shut. This would take a few seconds to open, so it was preferable that Tony went for his own mouthpiece first, while I was getting to him, hence the importance of the training we had gone through in the pool.

Plan D - the fourth and final backup - was the crane. If there was any problem at all, or the main air bubble failed for any reason, the crane could lift the whole vehicle clear of the water in a matter of seconds.

We thought we pretty much had it covered.

People often think that stuntmen and stunts are incredibly dangerous and are carried out by foolhardy individuals. Actually, the reverse is true. Stuntmen and those who co-ordinate and perform stunts are the most careful, considered people you are ever likely to meet, and as described here, the skill is to think and plan for every conceivable eventuality, and even some inconceivable ones. There is of course always the unexpected – but then that's life.

The lowering of the truck into the water for the first shot was the simple bit, or so we thought. Before we started filming we wanted to test out the way the Transit would move when being lowered into the pool and to make sure everything happened as expected. To do this, I climbed inside the cab in full scuba gear to run though any potential problems. This, in theory, was the safest part of the operation. The Transit was raised into the air and moved over to the lowering position. Mike was in the water with a number of other people, and the operation started. I was keeping an eye out for any weak areas in the structure as it was being lowered, as well as any potential leakage points.

Suddenly there was an almighty CRACK and time stood still.

One of the straps attaching the truck to the crane had broken and the Transit fell into the water. It immediately sank to the bottom. From my point of view, apart from the initial shock, there was no real problem. I could breathe, I wasn't trapped, and it was hardly very deep, but it was interesting to note that Mike was the only one who bothered to come and check if I was okay. Everyone else merely made their way back to the side, waiting for the truck to be reattached.

Things were checked and rechecked, and when it came time to do the actual shoot, everything went according to plan. As a result, I cannot have enough praise for Tony. Although he had no real problems when doing the training, and had enjoyed the whole process, it's quite another thing to be in cold water, sealed inside an enclosed space, and sunk to the bottom of a pool. In the event, there was no requirement for any of the backup procedures, and Tony was able to breathe from the air pocket in the cab throughout.

For the moment when Green Eyes breaks through the window, breakaway glass was used for safety reasons. This is a material, often known as sugar glass, which is easy to break and results in no sharp edges or splinters that can cut or cause harm. It worked perfectly first time, resulting in an effective shot looking up past Michael struggling in the foreground to Green Eyes crashing through the window at the top of frame and Michael then escaping - all in one shot. It's great when a plan comes together!

Once we had completed a few pickups of the dolphins underwater, that was it for my second feature. It had been very different from *Castaway*, partly because of the nature of the shoot and the subject matter, but also because it had been more challenging from a diving point of view, though there had still been the same camaraderie that exists on any film when you all come together to produce this far from normal creation and end up with something rather special at the end of it.

However, if I thought this was as challenging as underwater filming could get, I had another thing coming...

A final word on my encounters at *Flamingo Land*.

I returned with a few friends several years after working on *The Fruit Machine*, just to dive with the dolphins for fun. There were four of us, and we spent several wonderful hours interacting and playing with the girls and realising just how boisterous they can be.

We were all quite surprised, though, that they took a particular interest in Angie, one of two girls in our group. They seemed to spend a disproportionate amount of time with her and were particularly gentle when approaching her.

Now, it's known that dolphins can use echolocation to see inside objects in three dimensions, and it's why they are often intrigued by the internal movement of an underwater camera. However, Angie didn't have a camera.

We were all rather stunned though to find out shortly afterwards that she was actually several weeks pregnant.

5

Terrors of the Deep

Coming off *The Fruit Machine* didn't produce quite the same high as *Castaway* had done – things weren't as new and unexpected as they had been then, but they were still exciting and challenging, and if nothing else, it made me more eager than ever to carry things further forward. It also meant that *Castaway* hadn't been a one-off and that there was a realistic chance of developing a career within the industry.

One thing I was starting to learn, though, was that from an underwater point of view, the various jobs threw up interesting challenges in the way you had to adapt normal diving techniques to achieve things you would never normally have to do. It was something I found particularly rewarding. But nothing could have prepared me for what was to come next in the summer of 1988, where I was to act as the underwater co-ordinator on what was to be the most technically challenging shoot so far.

The film was called *Leviathan*, a $22 million dollar sci-fi thriller, which for 1988 was big budget. It had a total shooting schedule of seventy days and was being produced by the De Laurentiis clan. It was directed by George P Cosmatos, who had directed *Rambo - First Blood Part 2, The Cassandra Crossing* and *Escape to Athena,* amongst others.

It was basically *Alien* meets *The Abyss*.

However, at the time, that would have meant very little, as *The Abyss* hadn't even been released. It was part of one of those occasional Hollywood trends where you have a number of similar films all coming out in the same year - two asteroid films, two Mars films, two Robin Hoods, etc. - only this time it happened to be underwater films that were flavour of the month, with *The Abyss, Leviathan* and *Deepstar Six* all being released around the same time. Rumour had it that the makers of *Deepstar Six* had originally had some claim over *Leviathan*, which never came off and so they put their own production on a fast track to beat *Leviathan* into cinemas. However, with all this interest in underwater projects, it was just good to be involved in one of them.

While *The Abyss* was without doubt the most complex and technologically advanced underwater film ever made, and may well remain so for all time, if only due to the fact that computers will most likely create underwater environments in the future, *Leviathan* certainly had its fair share of accolades, with several academy award winners working on the technical side and a good cast and budget to match.

The principal actors were Peter Weller, hot off *Robocop*, Amanda Pays from *Max Headroom*, Richard Crenna from the *Rambo* films, Ernie Hudson from *Ghostbusters*, and

Hector Elizondo, who will forever be remembered as the long-suffering hotel manager who takes pity on Julia Roberts in *Pretty Woman*.

The story revolved around a group of deep-sea miners living in Shack 7, an underwater habitat ten thousand feet down. They worked outside the habitat using one-atmosphere diving suits, which protected them from the extreme pressures.

The miners were made up of the usual disparate characters one would expect in this sort of Hollywood fare, led by Peter Weller as Beck, and Richard Crenna as the burned-out Doc, who more than puts a spanner in the works as things progress. Amanda Pays played the feisty Willie, a prospective trainee astronaut and potential love interest for Beck.

As they search for metal ore deep underwater, they stumble across an old Russian shipwreck: the *Leviathan* of the title. It turns out to have been sunk on purpose to prevent the escape of a grotesque genetic experiment that had gone horribly wrong. The substance that had caused the genetic aberrations had been given to the unsuspecting crew in a bottle of vodka, and sure enough, the bottle finds its way into Shack 7.

You can probably guess the rest. Needless to say, chaos and horrors ensue as the aberration manifests itself in the form of a creature that proceeds to kill and absorb the crew members one by one, resulting in heads and limbs of the individuals appearing as parts of the creature's body.

Reading through the script, I noticed there were an awful lot of underwater sequences. However, many of these we could discard immediately. These mainly involved scenes where the miners were walking around on the seabed. Why weren't we needed? Basically because they weren't filmed underwater. The massive one-atmosphere suits used during filming were actually props that hadn't been designed to go anywhere near the water, let alone keep somebody alive beneath it. The sequences were filmed dry-for-wet, which means they were shot in a dry studio and techniques were employed to make them look as though they were underwater.

These techniques, including the use of careful lighting, filters and suspended particles in the air to simulate the underwater look, have been used many times before and, to be frank, are often less than convincing. However, the *Leviathan* crew pulled off some the most realistic dry-for-wet sequences ever filmed, and I would defy even experienced divers to be able to tell all the scenes that were shot in this way. Clearly some worked better than others, but credit must go to the crew for pulling off a very difficult effect and for sustaining it for the duration of the sequences in the film.

The main reason for shooting this way is ease of working and cost. Something they were all too aware of on *The Abyss*, where virtually everything was done wet-for-wet. While the final result is undeniably impressive, the problems and escalating costs made it probably one of the most difficult shoots in film history. If anyone doubts this, they should watch the hour-long 'making of' documentary, which is available on the two-disc DVD version and is one of the most extraordinary documentaries of its kind ever made.

With so much being shot dry-for-wet, you might ask why an underwater crew was needed at all.

As is usually the case on any water-related project, there are always plenty of small pickup and insert shots that have to be done for real, so we were needed for these. But the main reason was for a major escape sequence towards the climax of the movie.

To explain what had to be achieved, we have to return to the story.

Once things have turned for the worse in Shack 7, the habitat starts to implode. In order to escape, the remaining survivors, now down to Beck, Willie and Jones, escape by attaching lifting bags to the one-atmosphere suits, which pull them all the way up from ten thousand feet. As they near the surface, explosive charges blow off the legs, arms and main body of the suits, leaving the divers holding onto the helmets. These are still attached to the lift bags, which they ride up until they are shallow enough to discard and swim the remaining distance to the surface and safety.

This is what we had to commit to film.

The location for the underwater work was to be Malta. Set in the south-eastern Mediterranean, the island is an interesting mix of Euro/African culture and topography, and is a haven for sports divers wanting to learn to dive. The water is some of the clearest I've ever dived in, and that includes the Caribbean, Red Sea, and Pacific and Indian Oceans, and is one of the main reasons why many film projects find themselves in this part of the world. The water temperature is also conducive to filming, requiring only a thin wetsuit for comfort during the summer months. The only thing the environment lacks is the marine life associated with coral reefs or more tropical locations. However, there are many caves to explore, a number of shipwrecks, and that fantastic visibility, which makes Malta probably the premiere diving destination in the Mediterranean and why it has one of the densest population of dive schools anywhere in Europe.

The other significant reason for going to Malta was the Rinella tank at the Mediterranean Film Studios near the capital, Valetta. There are only a small number of fairly basic sound stages at the facility, but it does boast two massive water tanks, which made it the best water filming facility in Europe, if not the world, at that time. Films such as *Orca: The Killer Whale, Popeye* and *Columbus* had been filmed there, as well as *Cutthroat Island* and *U-571*. Nowadays, the Fox Studios built in Mexico for James Cameron's *Titanic* provides larger and more up-to-date facilities.

The main tank in Malta is 300-foot by 400-foot, 4-foot deep and looks out over the sea. The second tank is completely different in design, being round and conical in shape. It was built specifically for *Raise the Titanic*, is 39-foot deep, and holds 9,750,000 gallons of water, which can be filled in ten and a half hours by a series of massive pumps powered by four, 250 horsepower diesel engines.

The special aspect of both tanks is that they have 'infinite horizons'. This means they are positioned in such a way, overlooking the sea, that when full, the design allows water to overflow at the seaward side. This overflow is continuous, as pumps are constantly pumping water into the tanks. The result is that, if you are at water level, looking across the surface, over the infinite horizon, the water blends seamlessly with the sea beyond, even though the tank is a fair height above sea level. The effect is quite startling, and if you watch the film, or any film where there are ocean shots with the main actors in frame, the chances are they were filmed in a tank of this sort, and I very much doubt you'll be able to see the join.

With considerable time spent trying to work out how we were going to co-ordinate all the complex shots safely, I was reassured by the fact that we had pretty much the same crew as *The Fruit Machine* - Mike Valentine, Phil Barthropp and me. We were also going to be joined by Francoise, Mike's wife, who would act as unit nurse and general liaison with the production. As Francoise was a qualified nurse and understood the problems of diving, she was incredibly useful to have around, and she would often prevent the powers that be from becoming too demanding after we had been in the water for six hours already that day and had no desire to make any more ascents.

Prior to the start of the shoot, I had been teaching a group of sports divers in Malta, so it made sense for me to transfer to the crew hotel and kick my heels for a couple of days before the others turned up. By the end of the year, I had spent several months in Malta with film shoots and training duties, and it had almost become like a second home.

Our hotel was the Dragonara Palace in St Julian's, a stone's throw from the only casino on the island, which, in hindsight, for certain members of the crew, was probably not such a great idea, as most of their wages were likely gone before they had even earned them!

The hotel was pleasant enough, but the crucial thing was that the air conditioning worked. Malta is pretty arid in the summer, and there was none of the humidity there had been in the Seychelles – a good thing, but that year the temperature was up around 100°F/38°C, the highest the islands had encountered for many years.

While killing time before the others arrived, I hitched a ride up to the studios to take a look at the facilities and see how preparations were going. As the taxi dropped me outside the studio gate, I was hardly impressed. The facility was built on a small, scruffy hill overlooking the sea just to the east of Valetta, but other than that, all there seemed to be were a few run-down buildings and a lot of scrubland. It was only when I drew closer and the two massive tanks came into view that it became clear why we were here.

Just below, and slightly to the right of the entrance, was the smaller, but deeper, circular tank, and away to the left was the main three-hundred-foot by four-hundred-foot shallow tank. It was currently drained of water, so the bottom could be painted a patchwork of pale and dark blue colours. This was to reflect the colour of the sea up off the bottom and so give an impression of depth in the shallow water.

The first thing that strikes you is just how shallow it is. This is in common with similar tanks at other studios, such as Cinecittà, Pinewood and many in the States, though these have horizons that look onto painted or green-screen/blue-screen backdrops, rather than the sea. Most are only around four feet deep. If you think about it this makes a lot of sense. The action being filmed is normally taking place on the surface, so if actors have to act as though they're in the middle of the ocean, and if the crew have to be all around, holding reflectors, props, mikes and cameras, it's rather counterproductive if people can't stand up. There is usually a deeper section in the middle of the tank that allows for things to sink into, or, as in our case, for the creature to rise up out of.

It's quite interesting to watch the machinery used in these facilities, as a large amount of equipment has to be able to be moved around when the tank is full of water. This includes the army of special effects gear employed to create sea and waterborne effects, which can be anything from small swells to full-blown storms. They even had 'icebergs' in the tank for *Orca: The Killer Whale*! In order for all this machinery to be put in position, it is pulled by vehicles, which have to be able to move through water four feet deep. When the tanks are drained, it's quite weird to see tractors and trailers on four-foot extensions trundling around the dry concrete.

The piece of equipment most commonly used for creating storm effects is the tip tank, like those we used on *Castaway* to create the tidal wave. At the Rinella tank though, they were on a completely different scale. Here, the water is held in two large skip-like tanks at the top of what looks like a small ski jump. When the water is released at the pull of a lever – no bomb releases here - it shoots down the slope to flood the set, or whatever is in the tank below. Other useful pieces of kit are wave machines, which are specially formed blocks, here about ten feet by five feet by five feet, though they could be virtually any size, which move up and down on hydraulic rams at various speeds. The result is controllable water movement, from a small swell to breaking waves.

For *Leviathan* we wouldn't need the tip tanks, but we would need the wind and wave machines and a major prop in the form of a US Coastguard rescue helicopter. This was for a sequence at the end of the film, where the chopper lands in the water to pick up the survivors in the middle of the ocean and the creature surfaces and attacks them. The chopper was a Sikorsky Sea King and was being built on-site. When it was completed you really couldn't tell the difference from the real thing, at least from the camera side. The other side was an ugly mishmash of iron framework and metal plate.

Although the main tank was impressive, the studio itself was rather run-down and dilapidated. When building the helicopter, for example, there were thousands of metal rivets that had to be put in place. Instead of having a simple tool to do this quickly, every single one had to be put in by hand. However, the workmanship of the local craftsmen was second to none – albeit somewhat slow.

The second, or 'deep', tank was, if anything, even more impressive than the main one. Nowhere near as large, area-wise, it was conical in shape and resembled the cone of a volcano, with the bottom area far smaller than the top. This was to allow the weight and pressure of the water to be supported in the soft, sandy soil of the location. When I arrived it was half-full, and although we wouldn't need it for filming in, apart from the odd close-up shot, it was an ideal place to check out and test equipment. It was also amazing to think that the whole thing had originally been built for *Raise the Titanic* and was probably one of the reasons Sir Lew Grade, commenting on the film, said, 'It would have been cheaper to lower the Atlantic!'

It was even more amazing to see the model of the *Titanic* used in the film. It was sitting there, parked at the side of a ramshackle shed. But this was like no model you've ever seen. Fifty-five feet long, and with detail down to the smallest porthole, it was an incredible work of art, recreating in its entirety, one of the most famous ships in history. In fact, it was fairly in keeping with the whole studio, slightly broken-down and having seen better days, but impressive, nonetheless.

A couple of days later the rest of the underwater team flew out.

After everyone had settled in, it was time to go to work.

The first sequence involved the major escape at the end of the film, with the one-atmosphere suits racing for the surface. At the time, the suits were still being used on the sound stages at Cinecittà in Rome, where all the interiors were being shot. That gave us time to check out some of the other toys the special effects department had dreamed up for us to play with, and to meet their supervisor, Nick Allder.

Nick was an unassuming, down-to-earth sort of guy, whose frequent use of, 'All right, my luvly!' soon endeared him to all of us. He was also very good at his job, being in charge of all the major mechanical special effects, which included the coastguard helicopter, collapsing sets, explosions and pyrotechnics. He had won an Oscar for his work on *Alien* and had been responsible for one of the most shocking, iconic moments in film history, where the chestburster form of the alien erupts through John Hurt's chest.

On the day we met up, he was working out how he could get the local set-builders to put the rivets in the helicopter a whole lot faster, but he broke off to show us some of the props he'd come up with, including a number of motorised shark fins. These would be used in a sequence that truly demonstrates the way pieces of film, shot miles and days apart, can be edited seamlessly together to produce tension and drama.

At the end of the film, when the three survivors have reached the surface and are waiting to be rescued by helicopter, not only do they have the creature to contend with, they are also encircled by sharks that proceed to attack them. The material for this sequence was shot all over the world.

First, the aerials of the chopper arriving for the pickup were filmed off the coast of Italy.

Second, to get the wide underwater shots of the sharks attacking the heroes at the surface, stunt doubles were filmed in the Bahamas, with real sharks swimming between their legs.

Third, close-ups of the actor's faces, with the shark fins in the same shot, were needed to show the danger they were in. This would be filmed in the tank in Malta. Using real sharks was out of the question, not only from the safety point of view but also from the performance point of view. It isn't exactly easy to get a shark to perform to order – a bit like stingrays really - so cue the motorised shark fins.

Nick had built five of these creations out of fibreglass and mounted them on short poles on diver propulsion vehicles (DPVs). The idea was to have the fins sticking just above the surface and drive them around the actors in the water, simulating the movement of an attacking shark, all in perfect safety.

It might have been perfectly safe, but it wasn't as easy at it looked, though testing them out proved to be a whole lot of fun. It involved racing around the half-full volcano tank, trying to work out the movement that would look most realistic. Two basic actions were required - a menacing weaving motion on the surface, and surfacing and submerging. The main problem was that the structure of the fins ended just below the base of the fin itself, so any excess movement upward would reveal the pole the fin was mounted on and ruin the effect. The trick was to keep the bottom of the fin as close to the surface as possible without pushing it out of the water. It was even more difficult to raise and lower the fin, as you had to keep it as level as possible to again prevent the underside from being seen. Actually, this was quite good discipline, as shark fins tend to rise and sink in and out of the water in a horizontal position. The thought also sprung to mind that when the shoot was over, the fins would be the perfect accessory to take down to the local beach, cruise around awhile and watch the reaction. I'm pretty sure the production got wind of this, because as soon as the shoot was over, the shark fins disappeared quicker than you could say 'Jaws!'

The next day, some of the parts of the one-atmosphere suits arrived at the hotel and we were able to start to piece together just how we were going to film the dramatic escape sequence.

The suits themselves were made up of a number of sections, which made them easier to put on. As the actors had to wear them on the sets, they were designed so they could be worn like a set of clothes, with a 'trouser' section, a front and rear section, two arms and the helmet. All the components were made of fibreglass, but on screen you'd never know it wasn't inch-thick metal. The main difference, apart from the lack of functionality, was the weight. Whereas these could be worn relatively comfortably around the set, a real version, made of metal, would have required a crane to lift it in and out of the water. The inside of the helmet even had detail down to the smallest gauge, showing the remaining breathing gas supply and other readouts.

Once we had checked out the pieces of the suit we had to work with, it was a matter of deciding which parts of the sequence could be filmed with what we had. Since the main SFX crew weren't arriving for several days, as they still had work to complete in Rome, we would have to wait for the full suits and backup before we could film with them. What we could do, though, was start to check out the dive procedures and capabilities of the stunt doubles we would be working with.

Whenever any sequence like the escape sequence is filmed, it first has to be broken down into easily filmable chunks. As always, the prime concern is safety. What is the safest way to do something? Can it be made easier by changing anything without compromising the action and drama? The conclusion you come to will dictate both the experience and number of people you need, as well as the location and equipment required to complete the job safely and effectively.

The escape sequence would be broken down into four separate sections.

1) The full suit, with lift bag, rising from the deep.
2) The suit 'exploding' off the divers.
3) The divers riding lift bags/helmets to the surface.
4) The divers free ascending to the surface.

Clearly, this sort of wet-for-wet action is beyond the

scope of most actors, unless you have the time and budget to spend training them over a considerable period of time. At least on *The Fruit Machine* we were only ever in about twelve feet of water in a confined pool. Here we would be in the open sea, working at depths down to sixty feet, with the seabed as deep as a hundred feet, so the risks and potential dangers were far greater.

The main problem is having the artists rising up through the water from depth with no discernible air supply and no one within easy reach of them. It's one of those situations where you need to work with professional divers who know what they're doing, know their limitations, and are quite prepared to tell you when you are asking them to exceed them.

On the whole, the divers the production had hired were very good. Massimo Giovannucci was a dive instructor from Italy who would double for Peter Weller/Beck. Paola Giacomini, another instructor, would double for Amanda Pays/Willie, and Bobby Rhodes would double for Ernie Hudson/Jones. While Massimo and Paola were experienced divers but had done no film work, Bobby was a veteran film stuntman who had done a lot of gladiator movies, was big, black and looked like Ernie, but he had very little diving experience.

The individual sections of the sequence would have to be scheduled to fit in with the availability of the props. As we initially didn't have access to all parts of the suits, we had to start with the point-of-view shots (POVs) of the divers looking up at the surface.

A POV shot is where the camera simulates the point of view of an artist in the film; in this case, what the escaping divers would see as they were coming up. The idea being to try to put the audience in the protagonist's position and feel part of the action. As the filming only required Mike and the camera, it was the perfect opportunity for a shakedown dive and to make sure the housing was functioning properly. This time we fortunately didn't have the hotchpotch of a housing we'd had on *Castaway* and *The Fruit Machine*, but a sleek, new white housing designed by Hydroflex. This was like using a sports car after clunking around in a Lada, and it had none of the intermittent failings of the old red box.

Most of the dives for the escape sequence were filmed off the small island of Comino, which lies between Malta and its sister island of Gozo to the north-west. It provides some of the best diving in Malta, offering clear water with great drop-offs, as well as numerous safe and easy caves to explore.

We headed out from the small harbour at Marfa on Malta's most north-western point for the short trip across to Comino on board the good ship *Nireus*. We had hired the boat, a charming wooden sail-cum-motor vessel from Maltaqua, one of the premiere diving schools on the island who were providing us with all the dive gear for the shoot.

The first days on any production are always a getting-it-together experience and moulding everything for the days ahead. The *Nireus* was a great little boat for our purposes, having a large open fore and mid-deck where all the props and dive gear could be stowed, as well as a covered section at the rear for work on the housing and for Phil to change the film rolls. He undoubtedly had the worst job, being stuck in the aft cabin for much of the time with his hands up the aptly named 'Nun's Knickers,' or blackout bag, reloading the film magazines for later use. The weather conditions were so extreme that summer that he always seemed to be more soaked than we were whenever we poked our heads into the cabin, and he hadn't even been in the water - it was all perspiration.

Once out at Comino, the skipper moored up on the southerly part of the island in around twenty feet of water and we jumped in for the first dive at eleven forty-eight on the 8th July.

Everything went to plan, and four dives later, the POV shots were completed, as well as some additional footage of waves and light rays, which could be cut in at opportune moments in the credit sequence or other parts of the film.

It's always a relief to complete that first day and make sure everything and everyone is on the same page, particularly as there were more challenging times to come and not much time to get into high gear.

The second day was spent checking out Massimo, Paola and Bobby for the free ascents. As we hadn't dived with them before, we would now get a chance to evaluate their ability in the water. If possible, it's always preferable to work with people you know as you can instantly tell if there is a problem, because you know the way they react to things. But, as here, you often have to work with unknown divers, and the ability to quickly assess someone's experience in the water is essential if you are to get the best out of them without putting them, or any of the rest of the crew, at risk.

As explained previously, coming up from depth and holding your breath having breathed compressed air is not a good idea. The air expands and can burst your lungs if you don't release it, so it was with particular care that we conducted the tests with the stunt doubles. It soon became clear that Bobby wasn't confident enough to perform this from any great depth, so we concentrated on working with Massimo and Paola. This was the final part of the sequence, as seen in the film, which, as can often be the case, would end up being the first to be shot. It was where the escaping miners let go of the helmets and lift bags to swim the remaining distance to the surface.

As we were happy Massimo and Paola were up to the task, we started the shoot with a real sense of optimism. I would swim each diver down to the start depth with them breathing from an extended secondary regulator. When they were in position and Mike was happy, they would let go and swim to the surface, breathing out as they went. For safety reasons we could only film this a few times each day, so we had to make sure everything was exactly right before each take. The most difficult thing was ensuring the divers' bubbles were clear of the shot before they started the ascents, but with thorough planning and carefully chosen camera angles from Mike, all was achieved with little problem. Paola and Massimo carried out the ascents from around fifty feet, and much of the credit for the tension and danger seen in the final sequence must go to their professionalism and skill.

The next section involved the more complex task of working with the suit, or at least part of it. Since most of the suit still hadn't arrived, we had to get on with the helmet shots. Here, the artists are hanging onto the helmets, still attached to the lifting bags, which are pulling them up from the depths. The main problem here was continuity. Since we were obviously nowhere near the actual depths described in the script, and as many of the shots would be filmed on different days and at different depths and would be cut together to make up the sequence, we had to ensure the lifting bag was always an appropriate size in each shot.

The long way round would have been to film everything in sequence at specific depths, as happened in the story. In practice this just wasn't possible, so in the end we worked out the best way would be to use a fixed-size lift bag made out of fibreglass and control the buoyancy separately. This was done by fixing two buoyancy compensators (BCs) inside the bag, which could be filled or vented depending on the situation. In order to achieve maximum lift, and so give a greater sense of speed, the BCs were filled to capacity. As they ascended, the air would expand and vented through the blow-off valves. Since they were already at full capacity when they vented, the volume would remain the same and so the amount of lift would remain constant, giving a uniform speed throughout the ascent. The released air was then allowed to escape through a few small holes drilled in the top of the fibreglass lift bag, which would hardly be noticed in all the confusion and excitement of the action.

The process worked amazingly well, and the next task was to work out a procedure to enable the shots to be easily repeatable to ensure we would get a number of usable takes.

Since the divers were supposed to be rising from ten thousand feet, we had to make sure we didn't see any of the seabed while we were shooting (something that wasn't entirely achieved if you watch the movie closely). We also had to have control over the starting position. This was so

Mike could line up the camera and, as Paola and Massimo would be doing the whole shot on one breathe of air, so they could be completely happy and settled before we began.

To achieve this, we rigged a heavy-duty shot weight on the seabed at a depth of a hundred feet and suspended a buoy at around forty-five feet. The helmet and lift bag were then attached to the buoy by a quick-release fastener that would release under tension. The chariot now only required a rider. They were swum down, breathing off a diver's secondary regulator, and positioned beneath the helmet.

You always have to work to the artist in this sort of set-up, as they will be the ones without air and can only go when they are completely ready. Once they had a secure grip and indicated they were happy, I would check that Mike was ready. He would give the 'action' signal, and I would indicate to Paola or Massimo to remove their mouthpiece, which they would do after a couple of final breaths. As soon as the mouthpiece was clear, the fastener that held the lift bag and helmet to the buoy would be released and they would just have to sit back, breathe out and enjoy the ride all the way to the surface.

It took a fair amount of preparation, but it produced an easily repeatable and, above all, safe way of working. Throughout all the stunts that had to be performed, there wasn't a single incident or case of decompression illness, which really all comes down to good planning and preparation.

A break in the dives came with a trip to the studios to meet up with the American special effects crew who had built the creature and who had been responsible for the design and construction of the one-atmosphere suits. We were quite in awe of these guys, and if we could have known what they would go on to achieve, we would have been even more so.

Stan Winston and his team, including Tom Woodruff Jr, John Rosengrant, Shane Mahan, Shannon Shea and Richard Landon, were without doubt the best in the business when it came to animatronic special effects. At the time of *Leviathan* they had already completed *The Terminator*, *Aliens* and *Predator*, and they would go on to even greater heights with *Terminator 2* and the *Jurassic Park* series. Praise for these guys could not be high enough, and the sheer artistry that went into the design and creation of the creature in *Leviathan*, right down to the blood vessels in the teeth, will give you an idea of the dedication and hard work that made them the best Hollywood had to offer.

However, when we first met them, they appeared to be quite shell-shocked from their experience at Cinecittà. It transpired they had been cooped up for days on end in dark, hot and smoky sound stages, and the bouncy, holiday-like attitude of the newly arrived underwater crew seemed oddly out of place to them. But with the bright sun, sand and sea of the Maltese location, the cobwebs were soon blown away and they ended up having as great a time as any of us.

After a brief visit to Stan's makeshift workshop, and after picking up some additional pieces of the suits, it was back to our own little world off Comino to film the section where the suit detaches from Willie on the ascent.

Like with most sequences though, film is the art of illusion - the camera definitely does lie.

In order to simulate the suit detaching from Paola, Amanda Pays' double, it would all be shot in close-up, which would be edited into a fast-paced sequence to make it appear dangerous and happening deep below the surface.

However, we only ever filmed on a sandy seabed in twenty feet of water.

Each part of the suit was shot separately. There would be a close-up of the arm sections blowing off, her body coming out of the torso, and the helmet and lift bag pulling her up.

To simulate the arms coming away, Paola wore only the upper part of the suit, consisting of the front plate, rear plate and helmet. Air was provided between takes by a safety diver through a long secondary regulator, which was removed while shooting.

To make it look as though explosives had broken up the suit, a low-pressure air hose, attached to a dive cylinder, was looped inside the torso of the suit with holes strategically placed where the arm sections were attached. All that had to be done was for a diver off-screen to pull the relevant arm away while a second diver opened and closed the dive cylinder valve quickly. This let a burst of air 'explode' out of the holes near the arms, thus simulating an explosion. When cut together with sound effects, it provided a simple, elegant and safe way to make it look as though the arms had been blown off the suit. This technique was repeated for the other sections of the suit.

Again, for something like this you need careful planning and preparation. In the end, five of us spent many hours underwater to achieve a series of shots that in the finished film last no more than a few seconds.

After this all too brief shallow interlude, it was time to head back down for the more tricky shots of the full suit making the ascent. With us this time were John Rosengrant and Shane Mahan and Shannon Shea from Stan's team. These were the guys who had originally designed the suits, so they could hopefully deal with any problems we might encounter.

The first issue was actually trying to make up a complete suit from all the used pieces they had in their workshop. As the suit had never been designed to stand upright on its own without someone inside it, the whole thing had to be cobbled together with piano wire. They then had the unenviable task of making sure it all stayed together through the forthcoming abuse it would undoubtedly receive underwater. The main thing was to ensure bits didn't fall off when we weren't looking, resulting in continuity problems later on, not to mention the issue of finding them on the seabed a hundred feet below.

The full suit was no small piece of kit and proved tricky to work with. Once in the water it was incredibly ungainly and heavy. To ensure it didn't sink like a stone, there always had to be positive buoyancy in the BCs in the fibreglass lift bag, which was holding the whole contraption up. It took quite some time to balance the lift of the BCs with the weight of the suit. After a while, we managed to get the suit to be perfectly neutrally buoyant suspended beneath the lift bag, and it made an impressive sight.

Neutral buoyancy is the condition when an object, or diver for that matter, stays in one position in the water without floating or sinking. To achieve this, the object must weigh exactly the same as the volume of water it displaces. If it weighs more, it will sink. If it weighs less, it will float. When neutral, it stays exactly where it is and is effectively weightless.

The suit ascent shots represented the really deep ascent from Shack 7 up to the point where the suits detach from the miners. Since the suit didn't really work, no one could be inside. It would have been possible to do this if time and budget had permitted, but for the shots required, there was no need. We covered the faceplate with a spray of black paint so you couldn't see inside and we were ready to go.

We were adopting the same procedure as before to achieve uniformity when repeating a shot, where the suit and the lift bag would be taken down to the buoy, which was now at sixty feet to give us more shooting time, and then attached through the quick-release mechanism. The main problem was controlling the descent speed on the way down, using the BCs inside the lift bag. This was done with a second direct feed hose (a small hose attached to the air cylinder, through which you can inflate a BC at the touch of a button) from my regulator's first stage. With two direct feeds, I had full control of my own BC but could easily connect to either of the BCs in the lift bag and fill them accordingly.

In practice it was rather more difficult.

First, the whole rig had to be positioned directly above the buoy, sixty feet below. In order to descend, you then had to reach into the lift bag and pull the vent valve on one of the BCs. Before the descent became too fast and out of control - which would start to happen when the air in the BCs was compressed by the increased pressure with depth - you had to nip under the lift bag, swim inside, attach the direct feed and inflate the BC in a controlled manner so everything didn't suddenly shoot back to the surface.

After a while, we managed to get things down to quite a smooth operation, but there were a couple of concerning moments when the suit/lift bag rig threatened to plummet to the seabed a hundred feet below.

Once attached to the buoy, which was weighted to the bottom, the BCs could be fully inflated and the whole rig primed like a greyhound, straining at the leash, ready to leave the trap. On, 'Action', I'd squeeze the quick-release, hold my breath to minimise the bubbles in shot, and wait for the rig to shoot to the surface before retrieving it and repeating the whole process again.

The only potentially serious incident that occurred came from something completely beyond our control. We had just jumped into the water and were starting our descent with the suit, when we heard an urgent metallic banging. Since working underwater means you can't talk to each other, unless you have sophisticated communications gear, any sort of rhythmic tapping usually means somebody wants your attention. After a few seconds looking around for the source of the sound (as sound travels five times faster underwater, you can hear it a long way away, but it's difficult to locate the direction it's coming from), we glanced up at the *Nireus*. It seemed perilously close to the rocks, and we realised that perhaps we should go up to see what was going on.

On reaching the surface, we realised the boat WAS perilously close to the rocks – like, another five minutes and there would have been the sound of splintering wood. There was a lot of shouting, and the tapping was still continuing madly underwater.

Eventually we found out things were not good.

During the most recent lunch break, the wind had picked up enough to put a chop on the water. It was now quite rough and the boat had started to drag its anchor, pushing it towards the rocks. This wouldn't normally be a problem as it could easily be rectified; that was, if the skipper hadn't decided that now would be a good time to go for a dive all on his own. When one of the crew had tried to start the engine, the prop shaft had promptly fallen off!

There followed several minutes of not so controlled panic on board, during which time we stayed well out of the way, floating calmly in the water, which was probably the safest place to be. At least if the boat sank we were already wet. Finally, with a triumphant yell, the prop shaft was successfully refitted and the boat slowly began to move away from the rocks.

The problem we now had was what to do with the suit. It was in the water and the skipper wanted to get as far from the rocks as possible due to the worsening weather. We only had one choice – take the suit down to the seabed and leave it there. As this was around a hundred feet, and with the weather and visibility steadily worsening, it was unlikely anyone would come by during the time the suit would be left on the bottom.

To cap it all, this had been the one day that a journalist from the *Times of Malta* had come out to report on the making of the film. Needless to say, the copy in the paper the following day made the filming expedition sound somewhat more exciting than the film itself!

It was several days later before we could return to retrieve the suit in a RIB. It was still there, and after a major struggle we managed to heave it on board and speed back to base – mission accomplished. What anyone would have made of seeing the 'spacesuit' lying across the middle of the RIB was anyone's guess, but we never did receive any frantic phone calls from NASA.

By the end of the second week we were all fairly waterlogged, so Sunday's R & R round the pool was most welcome before the following week's action in the main tank. Although there was still a lot of work left to do, it was all in four feet of water and so wasn't too heavy on the diving side.

By the time we returned to the studio for the final week's shooting, the place had been completely transformed. Everywhere was a hive of activity, with all departments working at full stretch to pull together the complex and highly involved sequences on the water.

The main tank was now full, with water continually overflowing the seaward side, creating the infinite horizon, and it was really quite weird, being at water level and seeing people walking along the far side of the tank as though they were walking on water in the middle of the sea.

Across the centre of the tank, a walkway had been constructed in the shape of a large 'T' to allow the crew and technicians to walk out over the water without getting wet. At the end of the walkway was the main shooting area, and to the left, the now fully complete US Coastguard helicopter was in all its glory – rivets and all. Close up, it really did look perfect.

The scene to be shot was the climactic confrontation between the creature and the remaining miners, Beck, Willie and Jones. Just when they think they've made it to safety on the surface and the helicopter arrives to pick them up, they are attacked first by the sharks, followed closely by the creature, which appears dramatically out of the water. It proceeds to kill Jones, then turns its attention to Beck and Willie, who are struggling to make it to the chopper. At the last second, Beck throws a grenade into its mouth, which detonates in a massive explosion of rubber and latex.

It was going to be an interesting few days.

Before the actual shooting, we had another chance to take a close-up look at the creature. There were a number of versions of the beast. The main one was basically a suit worn by Tom Woodruff, who seemed to have cornered the market in creature parts. He was completely hidden, with only a small air hole to breathe from and minute eyeholes to see out of. It must have been incredibly difficult working inside, as the whole head assembly, which was positioned above Tom's actual head, weighed a considerable amount. This weight, coupled with the heat in Malta that year, must have been unbearable at times. A second, more static version of the creature, or 'stunt creature', would be used for the rise out of the water and blown up for the finale.

The main problem with monsters in movies is that they always appear to look like a guy in a suit. In the original *Alien,* Ridley Scott worked around this by only showing glimpses of the creature and photographing it from strange and obscure angles. In *Aliens,* James Cameron had five guys in suits to recreate the alien hordes, but again he used specific camera angles and different movement techniques to try to disguise the fact that at the end of the day it's still a guy in a suit. Nowadays, digital effects can create realistic living creatures that can be made in any shape and do anything the director desires, but at the time, the technology wasn't quite up to speed, so we had to make do with Tom in the suit.

The way Stan Winston and his team tried to fool the audience was by making the overall profile, shape and actions of the creature as unhuman as possible. In this case, it was done by adding appendages and growths to the suit, and making them move by remote control. Inside the suit, Tom was really there just to provide basic body movement from a fixed position and the main arm and claw movements. A number of operators would then be off-camera working the many appendages by cable remotes, and a further three would work the mouth and facial expressions using radio control – truly amazing.

Before moving onto the real meat of the helicopter sequence, we had to complete the 'shark attack' shots using the motorised shark fins.

After the rehearsal in the deep tank, I felt there wouldn't be too much problem with this sequence, but what we hadn't counted on was just how shallow the main tank was. It left very little room to manoeuvre. The problem was that even though the camera was at water level, looking out across the infinite horizon, the silver dive cylinders on our backs reflected up under the surface and the camera was picking them up. Also, some of the guys driving the sharks weren't able to keep the fins low enough, so the bases kept coming out of the water.

The technique that seemed to work best was to hold the

DPV to the side of your body and continuously check the fin to ensure the base of it never broke the surface, while at the same time trying to make the 'performance' of the fin mimic that of a shark in a feeding frenzy. We ended up constantly scraping ourselves along the floor of the tank, ripping our wetsuits to shreds in the process.

Many exhausted hours later, they had the footage and we moved onto some slightly less tiring insert shots of Ernie Hudson, having been infected by the genetic aberration, turning into a monster.

Ernie is a big strong guy, but he wasn't too happy around water, so to get him into the dizzying depths of four feet for these initial shots was a task in itself.

First, the make-up on some skin distortion prosthetics was touched up, and then a large tentacle was wrapped around his waist. A cable from this led off to an operator who would make it thrash around furiously in the water. We then all climbed into the tank to witness Ernie half drown while being 'attacked' by this lone tentacle. A second shot had Ernie wearing a prosthetic covering to his leg, which concealed small air pipes, fed by a bellows, which, when activated, would make it look as though his skin was pulsating and changing in form. The guy was a real trooper... until it came to the final shot...

...which was to have the full-size creature rise out of the water and then proceed to drown him. For this he would have to go underwater and stay there for quite a while, breathing off a regulator, with the creature thrashing around above. This was to prove quite an experience for both Ernie and me, as I would be the one down there with him making sure he could breathe and not end up drowning for real.

121

The first part – getting the creature to rise out of the water – was a mechanical effect co-ordinated between Nick Allder and Stan Winston. The deep pit in the centre of the tank was used to house a mechanical platform that used a hydraulic ram to push it, and the creature, up, out of the water. This was the static 'stunt creature' that would be blown up at the end of the shoot.

The difficult part was how to get the Tom-in-a-suit creature to attack Jones/Ernie without killing him.

From the look on Ernie's face, this clearly hadn't been in the contract, but after a quick run-through of what he needed to know to keep him alive – which wasn't much as we were only in four feet of water – we headed into the hot zone.

The action would be covered by two cameras – one up on a platform above the water, and the other, the underwater camera, in the water. This would move in and out of the action but point up at the creature in the waves, to avoid seeing Ernie and me cowering below.

Once everything was in position, I submerged next to Ernie's legs, ready for - as he no doubt saw it – his descent into hell, and waited. I knew when 'action' had been called as Ernie started thrashing around above me. Then, suddenly, out of nowhere, this massive claw ripped through the water. I didn't have much time to dwell on this as a second later Ernie ducked below the surface, arms flailing madly, desperately in search of something to breathe from. I grabbed his costume and pulled him down to me, thrusting a regulator into his mouth. After checking he had cleared it, and giving him a reassuring pat on the back, I returned to check where the claw was.

The action Tom had to perform in the suit was to look

like he was drowning Jones below the waves, so the claws were crashing into the water with alarming regularity and ferocity, and as I watched this surreal mayhem above me, I slowly realised they were coming closer and closer. Since the tank was only four feet deep, there was nowhere for us to go, and those claws would rip straight through Ernie's costume or my wetsuit if they made contact. If I'd been an actor, I wouldn't have needed much motivation to get the adrenaline pumping, and it brought back the exhilarating moments on top of the tip tanks in *Castaway*. What I didn't know at the time was that Tom was in severe difficulty. To understand why, you need to think back to how the creature works.

Guy in a suit, right?

Now, you take that suit, which weighs a few hundred pounds with all the mechanics, etc., and you put it in the water and have it thrash around. The problem is that the suit is made of foam rubber and latex, which absorbs liquid, so suddenly the whole thing is waterlogged and becomes twice as heavy. Tom could barely stand up and was becoming more exhausted by the second. Apart from the problem of the claws coming ever closer, there was the additional danger that Tom could topple completely over. Although there was an emergency procedure to get him out of the suit quickly on the surface, if he was underwater there could be any number of problems, not least of which that he wouldn't be able to breathe. When 'Cut!' was finally called, I helped to get a rather dazed Ernie above the surface, and I'd barely done this when it became clear that Tom was in trouble. All I could do was rush over and literally stand beneath him so he had something to lean on while Stan and his team extracted him from the suit.

A few more minutes and he wouldn't have been able to stand at all.

As it should be, the finale went with a bang!

The final shot was to blow up the creature. To make sure this one-time-only shot was caught on film, a number of cameras were used. These would be locked-off (left unmanned) at various points around the tank, including the underwater housing close in.

Because any explosion is highly dangerous, with a degree of unpredictability, there was an understandably cautious approach to the shot. The line *'You're only supposed to blow the bloody doors off!'* came to mind, and so we were all pulled back about a hundred feet from the creature. All the cameras were running at high speed to capture the action in slow motion, and all were operated from remote control or with the operators behind protective shields.

On 'Action!' from George, there was an almighty BOOOM, and what had once been a terrifying creation of Stan Winston Studios was now a million fragments obeying Newton's first law. It took several seconds for all the pieces to splash back down to Earth, which was followed by 'Cut!' and a round of applause.

It was all over.

At the end of every film shoot there is wrap party where everyone can let off steam. When this is in the UK it's usually huddled indoors on some freezing sound stage, but at least being in Malta it meant we had the luxurious surroundings of the Hilton Hotel and swimming pool. The other good thing was that we actually made it to the end of shoot party. Often, being on the underwater unit means you are only working for a few days out of the weeks or months a production can take, so to be there at the end was a rare luxury and a welcome bonus.

The party went with the usual release of steam associated with any end of term party, only here you were dealing with grown-ups who drank - a lot! Needless to say, many people ended up in the pool, and at one point the director ended up on the floor in a rather bemused state.

Usually this time is just spent relaxing and unwinding after the hard and exhausting work, and thoughts of 'what comes next?' are furthest from your mind, but halfway through proceedings Mike received a phone call that put the icing on the cake.

The week after we got home we were going to be working with Steven Spielberg.

6

Best of the Best

There are times in any career when you have moments you remember above all others. For me, one such moment occurred in August 1988. This year in particular was turning out to be pretty memorable, but the call to work on the third *Indiana Jones* instalment, *Indiana Jones and the Last Crusade*, really topped them all, despite turning out to be a fairly short affair.

There was one overriding factor as to why I had originally wanted to work in film and television, and that was the excitement and buzz of undertaking unusual and adventurous projects, which the industry provided in spades – and what better example than *Indiana Jones*?

Unfortunately, the location didn't quite match the exotic promise of the film, being merely one of the stages and the backlot at Elstree Studios in Borehamwood, but that hardly mattered – this was the best of the best after all.

It was also rather ironic that the largest and most

exciting blockbuster I would work on also had the least amount to do on it. Initially, the only requirement was to provide support in the water during a brief tank shot on a sound stage, and that was it. Fortunately, as the day progressed, things became slightly more interesting.

If you remember the film, the first sequence we were involved in was where Harrison Ford is stuck in the catacombs underneath Venice with Alison Doody. The bad guys set fire to petrol that has leaked into the water in the tunnels, and the pair escape by turning over a coffin onto the water, giving them somewhere to breathe and shielding them from the flames. In the film you then see Harrison looking around underwater as though he has found a way out. The next shot is of him popping out of a manhole in the middle of a café and saying, 'Ah, Venice!' Doesn't sound like a whole lot of underwater work, but this is where you find discrepancies between the final film and the original shooting script.

As is so often the case on these large-scale projects, far more material is shot than is actually used. This may be due to the scene not quite working, the material being deemed superfluous to the story, or there being time restraints as to the length of the film in order to cram more showings a day into cinemas.

Quite why this sequence was cut down is anybody's guess, but it was probably felt the timing was too long, and the cuts made provided a neat segue to the next sequence without slowing up the story.

What was shot was far more involved, with Harrison and Alison swimming through the flooded tunnels, Harrison looking for and finding an exit to the surface, and the pair then climbing up a ladder out of the water.

All this was filmed in a flooded set in a small tank sunk into a stage floor.

When filming underwater in studios there usually aren't any purpose-built facilities. There are exceptions to this, such as U-Stage at Pinewood Studios, but what you normally find is a section of floor that can be removed to reveal a dirty, dusty old tank or pit, which then has to be filled with water and heated and filtered with portable systems hired in separately. Quite a palaver, but all necessary if the water quality is to be maintained for filming and the temperature is to be sufficient for the artists to work without the need for thermal protection. Having to wear wetsuits or drysuits can seriously hinder the type of costume an actor can wear and often the range of movement and performance they can deliver. The ideal temperature for this is around 90°F/32°C, which may sound a lot, but as water conducts heat twenty-five times faster than air, a particular temperature in the water soon becomes a lot cooler than a particular temperature out of the water. At a temperature of 90°F/32°C in the water, the body won't lose heat faster than it can create it. As there is usually a lot of hanging around while equipment, etc., is adjusted, changed or repaired, the water needs to be at a level comfortable enough for the artists to be immersed in it for considerable periods of time.

This temperature thing can sometimes be taken too far though. On one occasion I was working on a pop promo in a small pool in a studio in south-west London and I had asked the studio manager how far they could raise the water temperature. I was told they could get it up to around 85°F/29°C. I suggested they take it as hot as they could go, in the hope they might get it just above that level and closer to the preferred ninety degrees. When it came to jumping in, I was prepared for the worst and was wearing a thin 3mm wetsuit just in case. As I hit the water, I knew I had made a mistake. Desperately trying not to pass out, I asked the pool guys to check the temperature. It was well over 100°F/38°C! There followed frantic attempts to cool it down before everyone gave out to excessive dehydration and their blood started boiling.

Back on the sound stage at Elstree, Mike Valentine and Phil Barthropp were setting up the camera housing while I checked out the set. It looked remarkably cramped in the small, six-foot-deep tank, and as I looked down into the murky green water that was steaming slightly from the temperature, I could easily make out the tunnels, which had been built along two of the walls. For safety reasons and ease of shooting, only one side and the roof of each tunnel had been constructed, so there was no chance of anyone becoming trapped and the camera could move freely around. Some amazingly realistic skeletons had been added by the props department to enhance the ominous atmosphere.

The open design also meant that lighting was easier, with large ten-kilowatt film lights being able to be positioned back from the whole set, rather than having to be strung along a confined, narrow tunnel. Nowadays, lights that are totally sealed and can work down to extreme depths are used, but here we had to make do with simple, non-waterproofed movie lights. I must admit, at the time they looked particularly dodgy, as though if you dipped your toe in the water you would be instantly electrocuted. However, after a reassuring brief from the gaffer - the chief spark/electrician - he insisted the lights were running off DC current and we would be fine. Although your natural tendency is to be sceptical of people at moments like this, these guys do know what they are doing and the stars were also going in the water, which is always a good sign. If the lead actors still have a fair chunk of the film left to shoot, you can be pretty sure they wouldn't be going anywhere near anything dangerous. We were confident we would survive.

When things finally got going, my role would be relatively straightforward. I was there simply to make sure no one got stuck underwater and to help out if any assistance was needed – quite an easy day really, but it was the occasion that made the whole thing exciting and special.

In fact, things had been going fairly leisurely. Mike and Phil had the camera ready. I had swum through the set to make sure I was aware of any obstructions and potential dangers. We were just thinking that this blockbuster lark was slightly tedious as we kicked our heels on the vast stage with the small tank, when all of a sudden things started to happen – fast.

Robert Watts, the producer of the film, suddenly appeared out of nowhere with a couple of assistants. 'Okay, everybody, look lively. Steven will be here in five minutes!'

'Yeah, right,' we thought, starting to get ready, knowing full well we had ages, as things on sets never happened right on time. But exactly five minutes later, the bearded one, complete with baseball cap, sneakers, jeans and an *ET* T-shirt appeared – together with an entourage of about twenty people.

Suddenly the empty sound stage was full. There was noise, excitement and an air of tension that was palpable.

Then everything happened in a blur.

Before I knew it, Harrison Ford and Alison Doody were in the water. Spielberg was barking out the shots. I was moving around keeping an eye on things. A few changes were made. Harrison went back under again. Alison had some trouble holding her breath. Harrison knocked his head on the camera, drawing blood. No one was sued. I managed to establish that he had done some diving in Belize, but he didn't have any spare time to do much. They went back down for a couple more takes. Everyone said they were happy – and they were gone. It was as though a whirlwind had swept through the stage and we'd been left spinning in its path.

I've heard of films being described as production lines before, but I had never fully appreciated the degree to which this could be true. As film projects are such creative and collaborative processes, you would normally expect directors to wander around the set in real time working out the best angles, lighting, etc. Not here. This operation was so slick that three units were working together at the same time. Two would be setting up while Spielberg would shoot with the third, then it was onto the next one – Henry Ford would have been proud.

This might sound like the whole thing was rushed and that there was little room for the creative element to breathe. In fact, the creative element was probably out of breath. On films of this scale, where possibly hundreds of thousands of dollars are being spent every day – time is definitely money, so if the creative aspects can be worked out beforehand, with just a number of key people, all the other expenditure of working on a set can be saved for the time when it is most needed.

Having said that, there are alternative ways of working. On *Castaway*, Nic Roeg would turn up on set, look around, and make decisions as to how and what he wanted to shoot, even to the point of the whole crew being set up at one end of a beach and Nic looking around and saying, 'No, the other end.' But this works for him and is part of the genius of his directing. This would not really be practical on as large a film as *Indiana Jones*, where so much money is at stake. Spielberg would have every shot storyboarded and worked out and only deviate from the specific plan if something amazing or disastrous happened at the time of shooting.

Once the whirlwind had died down and I'd had a chance to collect my thoughts, it was time to pack everything away. It seemed like we had only just arrived. As we were doing so, Robert Watts returned to ask us if we would help out with a sequence they were shooting later that evening. It was in the exterior tank at the back of the studios, and, of course, we immediately agreed to do so. We could never have realised quite what we were letting ourselves in for.

What happened later certainly put the hurricane and tidal wave scene in *Castaway* to shame.

In the early part of the film, Indiana Jones is on a ship in the middle of the ocean, where he steals a priceless artefact from his arch-enemy. The ensuing confrontation results in the ship blowing up, Indy jumping in the water and the enemy's hat floating past him as he struggles in the waves clutching the artefact.

In true moviemaking fashion, no one ever went to sea

during any of this sequence. The ship was a dry set on a gimbal on a soundstage at Elstree, with small tip tanks providing the water crashing over the deck. The sea scenes, with Indy floating in the water, were filmed in the open-air tank on the backlot. The tank itself was quite small, a mere fraction of the size of those in Malta, and it also held the mock-up of the stern of a ship, complete with working propeller half out of the water. This had been used for the sequence where a speedboat is sucked backwards into its churning blades and systematically chopped into matchwood. As we were filming at night, this part of the tank wouldn't be seen. All we needed was a wall for Indy to jump off, over the top of the camera and into the water, to simulate being blown off the ship. The jump was performed by veteran stunt co-ordinator Vic Armstrong, who is regarded as one of the best action co-ordinators in the business, and in 2002 he received an honorary BAFTA for his services to film over the years. Harrison would then take over for the in-water shots, which were all in standing depth.

This might, on the face of it, seem rather dull, but in order to achieve the reflected glow of an exploding ship in the water, there had to be something to GLOW. What they used were two exploding dustbins and five flamethrowers. The flamethrowers are fairly self-explanatory as they were simply devices that shot flame from gas cylinders into the air and created a reflection in the water. The exploding 'dustbins', on the other hand, were potentially more hazardous, allowing debris from the ship to rain down on the water around Harrison. To achieve this, various bits and pieces of 'wreckage' were packed into specially prepared bins, which in turn were attached to gas cylinders. When the gas was ignited, the resulting explosion shot the debris across the tank to rain down in the water behind the star – very spectacular – particularly as all this was happening at night. In fact, the excitement of it all almost took away the fact that the water we were standing in was freezing.

We had come prepared for a shoot in an indoor heated tank, and so only had 3mm wetsuits. Unfortunately, the backlot tank was full of cold, unheated water in the middle of the night. We did manage to get hold of some drysuits for the sequence, but they were only membrane suits, which means that the insulation normally comes from a thermal undersuit, which we didn't have.

Just how significant this was going to be, I realised as soon as I jumped into the water. 'Bloody hell!' was a loose translation of what escaped my lips, but after that my teeth were chattering so much hardly anything intelligible came out.

The water was only about four feet deep, similar to the tank in Malta, and above us the sky was black. It was around eight in the evening and the whole unit was gathered around the tank to watch the spectacle. We'd been briefed on what was to come, but actually being there, we had the excitement and tension of expectation.

We were in our start position, backed up against the wall of the tank. Immediately above us were three other cameras with different lenses to provide wide and close shots of the action. There was also a VistaVision camera, which had 70mm film running sideways to provide an enormous print area on the negative, which in turn allows for more special effects work to be carried out with minimum loss of quality during the special effects process.

Nowadays, with the advances in digital effects and editing procedures, this sort of camera would be used less, but in those days it was invaluable to keep the quality up for certain shots that would receive a lot of treatment in optical post-production.

Behind these stood Spielberg with a bank of TV monitors showing him the view from all the cameras, including ours. To the sides, the SFX guys were ready with the exploding dustbins, and above were the five flamethrowers ready to spout flame thirty feet into the air over our heads.

After a final pep talk from David Tomblin, the first assistant director, we were all set.

The job wasn't exactly difficult – with Phil on one side of the housing and me on the other, merely supporting it at water level, while Mike operated the camera and moved in and out on the action to show Indy struggling in the waves, with the water lapping at the camera lens. The problem was that it had been such short notice that we hadn't come prepared for this type of shot, and there was no buoyancy for the housing. Since the camera would have to be predominantly out of the water, it was a huge effort to keep it high enough up and also steady enough for Mike to be able to get his shots.

Suddenly, 'Quiet!' was called. Then came the cry of, 'Action!' from Mr Spielberg.

Immediately things started happening fast. The wave machines threw a large chop across the tank. The wind machines revved up to max, blasting a minor storm across the water. The flamethrowers suddenly roared above us – we felt the heat – and then the exploding dustbins did their thing, blasting debris and wreckage into the water.

At the same time Vic Armstrong was airborne over our heads, to land seconds later in front of camera. The jump he made was hardly earth-shattering, but it was into only four feet of water, and he had to make it look as though he had disappeared below the surface, so the potential for a broken leg was too great to risk Harrison on it, though he undoubtedly would have been able to make the jump.

Seconds later there was a shout of 'CUT!' over a megaphone, and normality gradually returned as the whine of the wind machines slowed to a halt and the waves and fire were turned off.

After a repeat of the action and things were calming down again, I suddenly realised the adrenaline had been pumping so hard I hadn't had time to feel the cold seeping in through the T-shirt and jeans beneath the drysuit, but with the lull in proceedings it now started to make its presence felt.

I didn't have long to ponder my temperature inadequacies though, as the end of a tape measure landed abruptly on my head. 'Can you just walk out there about ten feet, mate,' came the request. The focus puller wanted me to pull the tape measure out to the position where Vic had jumped into the water and where Harrison would be acting in a few minutes.

The focus puller's job is a strange one if you're not familiar with the workings and make-up of a film crew. The focus on a film camera (or modern digital cinema camera) is not done by any autofocus mechanism, or indeed even by looking through the camera and manually focusing. This is because the final image is going to be blown up onto a massive cinema screen, so the focus has to be perfect. Any out of focus areas will be exaggerated on the screen, resulting in obvious flaws and possibly even with the film being unusable. To this end, even today, all focusing is carried out by a focus puller, who stands next to the camera and manually adjusts the camera focus during a shot. The initial focus point is worked out by stretching a tape measure from the camera to the subject that needs to be in focus. This position is then marked off on a focus wheel on the controls of the camera. If the focus is to be changed during the shot, either for effect or because the camera is physically moving and the focus has to stay on one point or move to another point, then these other areas of focus will also be marked on the focus wheel and it will then be up to the focus puller to ensure the correct points are turned to at the correct part of the shot – a highly skilled position where any errors will be glaringly obvious in the final film. You can't hide or blame someone else when you're a focus puller.

I grabbed the end of the tape and walked out into the tank, moving to the position I thought Vic had been in, and waited. No one commented for a moment or two and I started to watch all the goings-on around me. In the distance I heard a 'No, over there!' followed by a more urgent 'Oi, you in the tank! Two feet to the right!' I snapped out of my reverie to see who the hell had interrupted me. After realising it was the director, I hastily moved - but was that to his right or my right? I carried on in the direction I'd chosen, glancing back nervously, waiting for the inevitable. I must have made the right choice as no more messages came bellowing across the water. Funny how the simplest of tasks can put the weight of the world on your shoulders!

Once all the measurements were out of the way, I took

up my position with Phil on the opposite side of the housing and watched Harrison as he made his way into position in the tank – two feet to the right.

The whole process then started again. Harrison went through his action, the wind blew, the explosions exploded, and we moved in and out of the waves. Above all the bedlam going on around us, Spielberg was shouting instructions and comments over a loudhailer. In the middle of these came the words that probably made Mike's career up to that point.

'Underwater camera, that's great!'

One thing that struck me about Harrison Ford was his total dedication and professionalism. While I was quietly bemoaning the lack of an undersuit for my drysuit, he was in and out of the water with just his Indy kit on and no thermal protection of any description, and all without a single complaint. Also, he would be constantly trying to help out with any problems encountered during shooting. For example, the scene at the end of the sequence is where the bad guy's hat floats across the water in front of Harrison, but with all the wave machines at full blast the hat was simply tossed around and wouldn't behave on cue, so he suggested tying a nylon line to both ends and having stagehands pull the hat in and out of frame. Very simple, but it showed his commitment to getting the job done. It could of course have been that he was freezing his bollocks off and just wanted to get the hell out of there as quickly as possible!

Although actions like that help to humanise someone like Harrison Ford, there are also other moments when you just have to accept the guy's a big movie star and that's that. One of those was described to me a while later on a shoot for *London's Burning*. We were sinking a truck in a tank at Shepperton Studios with a stuntman trapped inside. The stuntman had also worked on Indy 3. Amongst the many gags he had done on the film, he had been the one fighting Harrison in the speedboat chase and who was eventually knocked off the boat into the water. Now, Harrison Ford throws himself into his parts wholeheartedly, which is great for the role, but not so great if you're opposite him during a fight scene, particularly if it's on a speeding boat. Any fight is extensively choreographed, with every punch being calculated to miss the opponent in relation to camera angles, stage of the fight, etc., but when you're on a boat doing forty miles per hour, things don't always go according to plan.

In this case, with the boat bouncing and lurching across the water at high speed, one of the punches 'missed'. In other words, it connected with the stuntman's jaw. The guy was almost knocked out, and when the boat finally pulled ashore to see if he was okay, he was pleasantly surprised to see one of the nursing staff rushing up with an ice pack. He wasn't so pleased, however, to see her run straight past him and put it on Harrison's hand!

The day on the Indy set had been one to remember, not just because of the action, but also because of the people and the environment. It was, after all, the pinnacle of movie making. For those that work in the industry on a daily basis this may seem to be overblown enthusiasm, but I have always looked at working in the film industry not merely as a job but as an experience. To many, it may just be a job, but you also get to do things no one else really does, and you are paid very well for it, so I make no excuses for enjoying those times, which are exceptional and looking at them for what they are - not just another day at the office.

The day ended with me having a broader grin than could have been achieved any other way, and at the time, I felt nothing could have topped the experience. In a way I would be proved to be right, but there were far more varied and challenging experiences just around the corner, and in their own way they too would be the best of the best.

7

Going with the Flow

As I have probably made only too clear, my love of film and the excitement of movies is what drove me to work in the film industry in the first place, but in March 1989 the chance came along to experience another completely different side of the industry, that of electronic news gathering or ENG.

If I had my time again, this is probably an area I would have liked to have worked more extensively in, as it's here that the real excitement and adventure of the media industry can be found.

It's all very well enjoying the slightly surreal world of film sets with multimillion dollar budgets and all the trappings of five-star hotels, but you are often left with a slightly hollow feeling at the falseness of it all. ENG, on the other hand, is the real thing. You are going into situations where you often have no idea of the outcome, and you are dealing with real issues, such as the effects of a virus on the UK's seal population, or the exploration of a treasure ship, or, as we shall see later, the discovery of the remains of Lucayan Indians in the Bahamas, and the plight of a beluga whale trapped in the rapidly rising temperatures of the Black Sea.

For now though, my concern was closer to home – in fact, it was thirty feet down in one of the world's most infamous ship graveyards – Scapa Flow in the Orkneys.

Most divers will probably be aware of the history of Scapa Flow. Situated at the very northern tip of the UK, just off the Scottish mainland, the group of islands that make up the Orkneys form a geographical ring around the huge inlet of water known as Scapa Flow. It is here that the British fleet has been protected on many occasions by this natural enclosure, enhanced by man-made barriers of block ships sunk in the entrances to prevent submarines from entering.

In November of 1918, Scapa Flow was used for a very different purpose. As part of the Armistice agreement, the German High Seas Fleet was interned and held hostage to prevent them from being a danger to the British fleet out in the North Sea. In all, there were seventy-four ships of different sizes and strengths, kept under loose guard in the Flow. They had skeleton German crews who would maintain a presence on the ships but who were not allowed to go ashore.

Seven months later, in the midst of further Armistice negotiations, Reuter, the German Rear Admiral in charge of the interned fleet, thought the negotiations were going badly and that the fleet would imminently be handed over to the British. Unfortunately, he was several days behind events as he had been given old newspapers to read.

He made the fateful decision to scuttle the fleet.

What he didn't know was that the Armistice had been extended, and no decision on the fate of the ships had yet been made.

In all, fifty ships sank in the Flow that day. A few had been able to be run aground by the British, who had acted quickly once they realised what was going on, but the majority were lost. In the years that followed, most were successfully salvaged, but eight remain to this day as a permanent monument to an extraordinary event in history. They make up one of the largest collections of submerged battleships anywhere in the world.

But why the interest now, you might ask?

The ships were sunk before any nuclear testing had released additional background radiation into the atmosphere. Although as human beings we feel no effects from this, following the tests, much of the world's metal has been contaminated. Since the metal on the ships was underwater at the time, it wasn't affected. This unusual property makes it extremely valuable for applications such as in hospitals for surgical machines and tools, and so it provided an interesting story for a news report.

The call had come out of the blue, as they usually do.

The previous year I had trained an ITN cameraman, Sebastian Rich, to dive. Seb had done some diving before but had never been formally qualified and he was looking to set up an underwater unit at ITN, to basically come up with interesting and exciting stories that would allow him to go diving around the world – can't argue with that.

We had both hit it off immediately, as our approach to things was very similar – if it's fun and exciting, it's worth doing, however difficult or unrealistic it might seem to be.

So, following a number of dive trips, which had included Malta and the Maldives, he called up to see if I was interested in looking at the wrecks in Scapa Flow.

I had never dived in Scapa, but its reputation had preceded it, and it was a dive location that had always been on my list since I had been at university in Scotland, so I started to look forward to an exciting run-of-the-mill dive trip.

Then came a 'but…'

'Mike, I need you to train up one of our reporters to be able to talk while he's actually down there on the wreck.' So far so good. 'Oh, yeah, he's never dived before, smokes like a chimney, and probably can't remember the last time he saw a gym.'

'Right,' I said. 'Who is he?'

'Lawrence McGinty,' came the reply.

I had seen Lawrence on many of ITN's news reports as he was their senior science correspondent. However, and I'm sure Lawrence won't mind me saying, Sebastian's description wasn't far off the mark. The plus side was that he was highly intelligent, and at one time he had held the position of news editor at *New Scientist* magazine, so he would take on board all the technical and scientific aspects of diving without any problem. Equally importantly, he shared our philosophy of always giving anything a go. I think it was this boundless enthusiasm and energy that carried him through what turned out to be a difficult and challenging experience.

In order to give Lawrence a fighting chance of being able to pull this off, we started with some basic dive training in the small pool in Putney where I'd trained the guys for *The Fruit Machine*. He sailed through this fairly confidently, but next up was the medical. We all held our collective breaths as the doc assessed Lawrence's physical ability to go where no ITN reporter had gone before. But we needn't have worried - he passed with no issues.

With the preliminaries out of the way, it was on to his first real test – a full rehearsal dive with cameras and communications equipment in the cold depths of a flooded dry dock in Woolwich.

The dock had been in use for some time as a water sports centre, including canoeing, sailing and diving. It was run by the local authority, and they had even gone to the trouble of filtering the water, resulting in remarkable visibility of around thirty feet - about the same as its depth. Unfortunately, a similar investment hadn't gone into a heating system, so drysuits were the order of the day. Sadly, some years later the funding ran out, the filters were turned off, and the whole dock was put off limits. What was quite interesting was that I had the opportunity to dive in it a few weeks before it was finally closed but after the filters had been shut down. The visibility had reduced to about six inches - pretty amazing filters if you ask me.

But back to Lawrence of Woolwich.

Not only had the poor guy to contend with this being his first ever open water dive, but we wanted to recreate the filming procedures to be as close as they would be on the day. We couldn't, of course, produce the inevitable waves and rain we would no doubt encounter, but the cold water was certainly there, and we did manage to find the thickest drysuit, a Poseidon Unisuit, to ease Lawrence into. I had also managed to track down a 'bubble helmet', which would be used for communications and allow us to hear and talk to Lawrence while he was underwater.

The bubble helmet had originally been designed by a French company to allow a three-sixty-degree angle of view. It was literally a Perspex bubble over your head that clamped to a metal collar with a dry suit neck seal and was secured in place with a strap between your legs. This was required to prevent the helmet, which was full of air – very buoyant – from breaking free and heading for the surface. As well as the strap there were large weights on the front and top to help make it neutrally buoyant. The trouble was that out of the water the weights made the whole thing incredibly heavy, and if you became at all unbalanced, they wanted to send your head on a trip to visit your feet. For this reason, the weights were put on at the last possible moment, just before you disappeared below the surface. We had one of only a few helmets in the country, provided by Jock Stuart of Glenvardon who would also supervise its use.

The helmet had initially been used for TV work by the BBC, who adapted the original design for use on a live transmission from the Red Sea. This programme later evolved into the *Sea Trek* series, where Martha Holmes and Mike Degruy were seen walking and talking underwater from all over the world. I say 'adapted' because the helmet was originally designed to be used with an oral nasal mask, which fitted over the mouth and nose and took away exhaled gas to the exhaust ports at the rear of the helmet. For TV work this was removed so the audience could actually see the presenter talking underwater, a change that greatly enhanced the presenter-in-the-field feel to the programme.

The problem with removing the oral nasal mask,

though, is that the exhaled gas, which includes 4% carbon dioxide (CO_2), quickly builds up, potentially causing unconsciousness unless the helmet is vented with fresh air every few seconds. If you ever watch any of the programmes where the helmet has been used, you will see the camera cut away from one presenter to another, or to a shot of a fish, etc., on a regular basis. This is to get away from seeing and hearing the presenter having to flush out the CO_2 - a process that makes a horrendous noise. This was just another thing Lawrence would have to contend with on top of everything else – like learning to dive and talk all at the same time.

It might seem like a really easy and pleasant way to go diving, having a 'goldfish bowl' on your head. The thought of there being effectively 'nothing' between you and the water is certainly very appealing. However, the reality is not quite as it seems. You don't see a completely uninterrupted view in three-sixty degrees. For those that have seen *The Abyss*, it is more like the POV of the water tentacle, where the edges of your vision are slightly out of focus, with only the centre part being clear and in focus. When you turn to look to your left or right, your eyes have to slightly readjust before they can see properly, which after a while can be quite a strain, even leading to headaches. Couple that with the potential build-up of CO_2, the fact that the helmet is forever trying to invert itself due to the weights, and you have a rather difficult piece of diving equipment to contend with.

The other area in which the helmet had to be adapted for TV use was in the communications department. In order to produce a quality of sound that would be intelligible to viewers, some serious work had to be done in noise suppression and filtration.

Normal communications equipment used for commercial diving work is fairly basic, and the sound received can often be open to interpretation. This may be acceptable in the commercial field, but for broadcast TV you need highly intelligible sound that is easily understood. I have seen some programmes where the equipment wasn't up to the task and they had to put subtitles on the screen. Not the point of it all really. We were determined this wouldn't happen to us, so Seb brought in Jon Hunt from ITN to help out.

Jon was Seb's long-suffering sound recordist who had accompanied him to many of the world's trouble hotspots in the past. Hopefully Scapa Flow wouldn't fall into that category, but Jon had been hard at work with the ITN technicians to replace the microphone in the helmet and tweak the recording procedure to record the best possible sound.

Something they would be unable to solve during the shoot, but could be dealt with later, was the regular rasping of air entering the helmet whenever Lawrence breathed. As the air inlet into the helmet was relatively close to the microphone, this produced an unacceptable screeching whenever air was injected during the breathing cycle. Even on *The Abyss*, where the helmets had been designed specifically for the film, they had to remove the sound in post-production, otherwise the noise would have been too intrusive and annoying over a long period of time.

We arrived at Woolwich on a fair, if not cold, day to check out the equipment and to make sure everybody was happy with their roles. The next time we would all be together would be jumping off the pitching deck of a boat into the cold waters of Scapa Flow.

The team was made up of hardened professionals, but not ones who had worked together before. Seb would direct as well as act as cameraman. I was overall underwater co-ordinator. Jock Stuart was responsible for the bubble helmet and looking after Lawrence. Jon Hunt was monitoring sound recording and the technical gizmos in the helmet. Malcolm Weaver, a stuntman friend of mine, would help out with lighting and general safety, and finally Russell Padwick, a colleague of Seb's, would prepare the lights and run the generator on the boat. As it turned out, everyone gelled quickly, being used to the ins and outs of film shoots, and soon the only unknown was how well Lawrence would perform once in the water with all the kit on.

It was Jock's duty to help dress Lawrence in his dry suit and helmet. I'm sure as he struggled with the cumbersome neoprene suit, immediately inflating his appearance to that of the proverbial Michelin Man, Lawrence was starting to have second thoughts, but no doubt a quick glance at our dubious stares made him grit his teeth and carry on. There was no way he was going to back out now.

Once Jock had him in the suit, he helped him to the side of the dock where he could sit down and be loaded up with the twin cylinders he would need to ensure he had enough air supply. He then had a moment to catch his breath before the unpleasant task of clamping on the helmet.

When the bubble helmet is in place, it's not like a normal scuba set where you can just take your mouthpiece out of your mouth and have a breather. Once it's on, it's on, and you're breathing from your limited air supply straight away, so we all made sure we were ready and in the water well before Lawrence made his entrance.

Once the helmet was strapped on, Jock went through the final checks to make sure Lawrence was happy and could vent the air with no problem. With a final 'OK' from a now rather nervous-looking news reporter, he eased himself into the water and we were off. Seb was already a few feet below with the camera ready for the descent.

Most people seem to think of video equipment as being small and lightweight, and it certainly can be, but we were using a professional Sony Betacam in a housing that was just as large as a normal film camera, if not larger, and equally as heavy.

As we needed Lawrence's sound recorded on the surface to maximise the ITN sound filters, there would be a cable feed from his helmet, as well as from the camera up to the surface, so the sound could be recorded straight onto the same tape as the video. The camera also had a tape inside to record visuals, just in case the ever fragile and temperamental video link should fail in the harsh environment of Scapa Flow – you can never have too many backups.

I was watching Lawrence, ready to give a hand if necessary, as he slowly lowered himself into the water, with Jock at his side, and then started to breathe underwater and head on down. It must have been a nerve-wracking experience for him, and even more so, when a few seconds later his feet headed skyward and his helmet did a slow-motion dive to the bottom, basically turning him upside down due to the weight.

Immediately we all leapt forward to steady him, slowly pulling him upright and helping him back to the surface. Once there, a rather frantic Lawrence indicated for the helmet to be removed, and we all learned a few new French words!

The problem was a lack of weight lower down his body, and as we added some more to his already crowded weight belt, it was probably at this moment that he started to realise that being so enthusiastic about something is not always such a great idea. But after a while, he calmed down, got his breath back, and, like the trooper he is, he was ready to go again.

This time things initially went more smoothly, but as he descended he started to have problems with his ears.

When diving, the water pressure increases with depth. At thirty feet it's twice the pressure it is at the surface. As we have seen, this has an effect on the airspaces within the body, such as the lungs. Another airspace that causes problems is the middle ear. The ear is made up of three parts: the outer, middle and inner ear. The outer ear is what you see on the side of someone's head and is open to the environment; the inner ear is where the sound waves are turned into nerve impulses for our brain to interpret and is full of fluid; but the area between the two, the middle ear, is full of air. This is blocked off from the outside world by the eardrum, and there is a passage leading from the middle ear down to the back of the throat called the Eustachian tube. This tube is usually in the closed position, so when you descend, the air in the middle ear is sealed off and the increasing water pressure pushes in on the eardrum, compressing the air inside. If nothing is done about this there will be pain at the eardrum as it is forced in. If you continue to descend, the eardrum will burst – not very pleasant. Divers get round this by blowing air up the Eustachian tube, which equalises the pressure in the middle ear. This is achieved by holding the nose and trying to blow out without letting any air out of your mouth, and is why face masks are designed with a nosepiece so you can grab hold of your nose.

In Lawrence's case, in the bubble helmet, he couldn't reach his nose as it was behind a solid Perspex dome. This isn't normally a problem, as with other types of professional dive mask or helmet there's a small rubber pad just below nose level, which you can move your nose onto and then seal off by pushing down. The problem was that Lawrence couldn't quite reach it, so after a bit of thought, ever the improviser, he placed a nose clip on his nose with a small piece of string dangling down in front of his mouth. As he descended, the clip pinched his nose allowing him to clear his ears. When he reached the bottom, he simply grabbed the piece of string with his mouth and used his teeth to pull the string, thus pulling the nose clip off. This would then drop to the bottom of the helmet, revealing a Lawrence *sans* nose clip to talk freely to camera. As the pressure effects are the reverse when you come back up, and the air expands, naturally venting itself, there was no need for the clip again during the dive, providing he didn't go any deeper – highly ingenious.

Once Lawrence was firmly on the bottom of the dock, thirty feet down, we manoeuvred him close to the wreck of an old rowing boat, which would have to stand in for a German battleship. It also gave him something to hold onto.

At the signal from Seb, Malcolm adjusted the light to make sure we could see our star's face properly. Then he gave a nod to Lawrence, who put on his best presenter's voice and tried to make the fact that he was delivering his lines thirty feet underwater in a suit and helmet sound as natural and normal as possible. The amazing thing was – he did.

With the words and pictures on tape and all technical and personnel problems sorted out, we returned to the surface well satisfied with the day's work. Doing a full rehearsal like this is worth its weight in gold, as it flags up any problems you are likely to encounter in the field, where the conditions will undoubtedly make it more difficult to sort out – but so far so good.

Seb showed the footage to the powers that be at ITN, and after some incredulous expressions at Lawrence actually talking at the bottom of the dock, clear as a bell, the trip was green-lit.

We took off for the Orkneys on 14th of March 1989 – the coldest time of the year for diving.

Although I had been to the Summer Isles on the north-west coast of Scotland during my marine biology years at Heriot-Watt, I had never been quite so far north as the Orkneys.

Coming in to land on this far-flung outpost of the UK was a spectacular sight. The evening sun glinted off the Flow like a jewel amidst the ring of islands surrounding it, and you could just feel you were arriving somewhere special. It must have been an amazing sight back in 1919 with the seventy-plus ships of the German fleet all peacefully at anchor, then suddenly all starting to list and dip into the cold waters of the Flow.

On landing at the small airport on the outskirts of Kirkwall, it wasn't hard to tell you were at a location on the edge of nowhere. As the wind threatened to bite through our thick protective clothing, we made our way, hunched over, to the terminal building. Away to the north-west the hills rose to a height of around a thousand feet, and there was a stark bleakness to it all - no tall trees – just squat windswept hedges, the mark of a true wilderness.

I am drawn to landscapes like this, as you are completely taken away from your easy, everyday existence and made to feel alive, being so close to the elements.

We bundled all the gear into a couple of hire cars and went in search of our accommodation. Once we were installed, it was time to find a boat for our trip. We had checked out a couple of names before leaving London, and the vessel we ended up with was called *Girl Mina*, run by the massively friendly and massively built Terry and his diminutive and homely wife Mo. Terry proudly explained that the boat had only sunk the once and she was perfect for what we needed. I looked at Seb with alarm, but we went to look her over anyway. We were assured she was as sound as they came and many divers had used her for trips in the area. She admittedly had the deck space we needed, some area below if the weather became too hostile, and an all-important compressor to fill the cylinders. I've been on many trips where you have to take enough cylinders to complete the job as there has been no compressor. As air is your main consumable, you need a significant amount of it, so it was this additional facility that made us give a reluctant nod of approval and charter the resurrected wreck to go in search of other wrecks.

For the key shot of Lawrence talking about the properties of the metal the ships were constructed of, it would have been preferable if we could have been on one of the large battleships. Unfortunately, all of those were too deep for Lawrence's experience. Even if we'd had an experienced diver, the amount of time we would have had on the bottom would have been so limited, given the restrictions of decompression and the potential for technical delays, etc., that we would probably have had to choose a shallower location anyway.

After much deliberation, Terry told us about a wreck called the SMS *Bremse*, a destroyer in about thirty feet of water, which had been partially salvaged. Ideally we would have liked a whole ship, but the *Bremse* was in a workable depth range, and amongst the pieces of superstructure and metal that had been left there was a spectacular six-inch gun from the foredeck. This sounded promising. We set off without delay.

There is always something exciting about heading out on an expedition of any sort, but this one was particularly memorable because of the location and the images we were trying to bring back, and the challenges that entailed. We had done as much preparation and testing as we could; it was now just down to seeing how things turned out on the day – and what the weather would bring.

As we ploughed across the Flow, our white-crested bow wave extending out in an ever-widening V, there was time

155

to take in just what a spectacular location this was. Ringed by mountains and islands on all sides, it was possible to reflect on the ships that had sat at anchor, only to be sunk deliberately on that fateful day. Fortunately there had been few casualties, unlike that other mass sinking of battleships, at Pearl Harbor, so there was the image of what it must have been like, but it was untinged with the sadness of great loss of life.

I was brought out of my reverie by Terry shouting out 'We're here!' and his mate dropping the anchor with a loud splash. Terry was pretty convinced we were on the site, but he felt he needed to drop in to check the anchor was close enough to the wreck, and secure. We needed to be close to the location as we only had a limited distance on the video and audio cables, and the thought of having to drag Lawrence miles through the murky water to find the wreck didn't fill us with joy. Also, if the anchor wasn't firmly embedded, there was the possibility of the boat shifting with the wind and tide – shades of the rocks off Comino - and Lawrence and Seb being dragged across the seabed by their cables. Something we certainly wanted to avoid.

I kitted up quickly and joined Terry, ready to jump in to check everything was okay.

As we descended, Scapa Flow greeted us with a green and very cold welcome. I could feel the water creeping into the thin latex hood of my drysuit and I knew I was in for a cool couple of days. But, true to Terry's word, we were close to the wreck. She was, as we had been informed, in numerous pieces, but the small section of superstructure and the majestic gun barrel pointing proudly skyward would provide the perfect platform and backdrop for Lawrence to stand on while doing his piece to camera.

It was the next stage that was going to be difficult. While Seb prepped the housing and Jon Hunt tested the comms gear, Jock Stuart and I helped Lawrence into the cumbersome Unisuit and helmet collar. It was at this point that I think Lawrence realised just what he had taken on board and the usual boyish enthusiasm seemed somewhat dampened - Woolwich dock was a long way away. We did our best to cheer him up, but it was going to be a tense few minutes.

After final checks, we manoeuvred him over the side, and it must have seemed a long few steps as he slowly eased himself down into the water. Once in, we checked he was happy breathing and flushing air through the helmet to clear the CO_2 - ultimately the most critical thing he had to do from a safety point of view. He gave us a rather hesitant OK signal and we started down.

As we descended, Lawrence cleared his ears with his improvised nose clip and everything seemed fine, but suddenly there was a concerned expression on his face and he made a rapid 'up' signal with his hand. We pulled him up the few feet we had descended and he clung desperately to the ladder at the side of the boat, seemingly unable to move. On closer inspection it became clear some water had entered the neck seal – not a major problem as the positive pressure would keep it at bay, but to Lawrence this must have seemed as serious as the *Titanic* hitting the iceberg. To make matters worse, air injected from the demand-valve at the rear of the helmet was making the water splatter against the inside of the Perspex in a misty spray. This must have been particularly unnerving and we were left in no doubt as to what he wanted to do next. As he shakily climbed back up the ladder, the weather added to the misery. It had started to snow.

This was only the first day and things were already looking bleak, but teething problems are to be expected on something as complex as this, with so many variables. It was all credit to Lawrence that we had even come this far. We just had to take a breather and sort out the obvious technical problem.

We also had to reassure one concerned ITN reporter.

Once we had hauled him back on deck and removed the helmet, the expression on his face didn't need words to explain the clear thought running through his mind - he wasn't going anywhere near the water again. His first action was to grab a cigarette and take a much-needed hit of nicotine. If it hadn't been so serious, he would have looked quite comical with his head peering over the rim of the neck clamp, cigarette barely balanced on the edge.

Gradually, though, this must have had some effect, because after a rest of half an hour or so and some gentle persuasion, he seemed to find the courage from somewhere and agreed to give it another go.

This time, with a triple-check on the neck seal before enclosing him in the helmet, and taking each stage one step at a time, we again heaved one of ITN's finest over the side and back into the cold and dark that lay below.

We took it very steadily on the way down. This time the neck seal did its job and Lawrence made it to the bottom - a little nervous, but a good deal dryer.

Once we had manoeuvred him close to his position at the gun and he had a secure grip on the wreck, he took a second or two to deftly pull the clip off his nose with his teeth. On the surface, Jon ran through a quick comms check; then it was down to business.

What followed was Lawrence, like a true professional, giving a virtually flawless rendition of his piece to camera, thirty feet down in Scapa Flow.

Although everything had gone well, Seb was convinced that with a little tweaking of lights here and performance there, it could be even better. There were also a couple of sound problems that needed sorting out, so it was decided the day would be looked on as an excellent 'dry' run and that to return tomorrow would give us all time to rest and work thorough the few things that needed addressing. At least Lawrence would know what he was in for, though whether that was a good or a bad thing we will never know.

The next day dawned bright, and though there was a light chop on the water, we headed out with renewed enthusiasm. Once on-site, we anchored even closer to the wreck this time, so Lawrence could literally drop straight down the anchor line to his 'number one position' and we could get right into it.

The first dive was spent placing lights to highlight the dramatic setting and ensure that once Lawrence was in position there would be no need to change anything.

With our man rekitted and with renewed energy, we lowered him into the water without a grumble or groan. Even the snow had disappeared, to be replaced by a warming sunshine that added to everyone's mood of optimism.

Things must have been far better for Lawrence this time round, as you could almost make out a smile on his face as he delivered his piece to camera, coming across with far more confidence and enthusiasm than the previous day.

After a couple of takes for safety to make sure we had it all in the can, Lawrence was hauled back up, like a used prop, and unceremoniously dumped on deck to be undressed.

To complete the report, we needed some shots of someone swimming round the wreck in the bubble helmet. These would be wide shots, just enough to establish the setting and that we really were underwater on a wreck and not in some dodgy tank in a studio. Clearly Lawrence wasn't up to free-swimming anywhere at the moment, so Jock donned the suit and helmet to double for him.

When we returned to the hotel that night and played back the footage, it really was quite spectacular. Seb had done a great job of lighting the wreck, Jon had made the sound completely intelligible, and Lawrence shone like the star he was, signing off his report with the killer line of '…Lawrence McGinty, News at Ten, IN Scapa Flow!'

The team had worked well together, and as soon as we were back in London, Seb, Lawrence and I started to think up more ways to relieve ITN of some of its cash.

It wouldn't be long before we were all off again into the blue on another expedition, but before all that, there was time for some *vanille fraise*!

8

Legwork

Ah... the glamour of the film industry.

You hear it all the time. Well, I can categorically confirm that any glamour is reserved for opening nights and congratulatory parties when films have won Oscars or broken the $100 million mark, not the normal run-of-the-mill production of a feature film. It also usually only includes the stars, producers and directors, and not many others involved with the actual making of the film. However, there was one occasion where I must admit it felt like some of the gloss had trickled down to the lower ranks.

It happened during the shooting of a French comedy adventure film in Italy, and as well as the aforementioned glamour, it was probably one of two instances in my life where I have come closest to drowning. Not, as you might imagine, at the jaws of some ferocious marine creature with rows of gnashing teeth, or because of a stunningly dangerous stunt or deep dive. No, it was down to a number of plastic left-footed artificial legs in only twenty feet of water.

It all started in April 1989 and turned into one of the most drawn-out, but pleasurable, shoots I'd been involved in so far.

The film was called *Vanille Fraise*, and it was a comedy thriller set around the characters of the French secret service who had sunk the Greenpeace ship *Rainbow Warrior* in Auckland harbour, New Zealand. The film follows the exploits of the agents in their bid to stop an arms smuggling ring in the Mediterranean. This meant, from the underwater point of view, some interesting Bond-style action sequences below the waves.

My involvement in the film was spread across three trips over a period of a couple of months. The first of these was to recce locations off the coast of Amalfi in Southern Italy and to check out some of the props that would be used in the film.

With the tasks ahead running through my mind, Mike Valentine and I flew down to Naples, that classic of Italian towns, neighbour to Pompeii, and forever in the shadow of Vesuvius, probably the most well-known volcano in the world. From here it was a lengthy minibus journey travelling inland through the magnificent Italian mountains to the south, returning to the coast at Salerno and then west to the picturesque town of Amalfi.

The coastline in this part of Italy must be one of the most beautiful and spectacular anywhere in the world, with small, precariously built towns almost hanging off the cliff walls, and the road a twist-back affair with towering cliffs on one side and vertigo-inducing drops to the sea on the other. The spectacle of the trip was pleasure enough, but the small town of Amalfi was a sheer delight. With its historical *Cattedrale di Sant'Andrea* and architecture dating back to the Roman Empire, the numerous alleyways and squares provided no end of opportunity for exploration and discovery.

On the southern side of the town, the large harbour was the focus of activity. Framed with the natural backdrop of the mountains behind, its waters were filled with fishermen and traders going about their business.

There were two reasons for the recce. The first was to check out a number of surface locations further up the coast, where spectacular islands with sheer walls and a massive rock arch would provide an impressive backdrop to some of the action. The second was to assess the harbour in Amalfi as an underwater location for a sequence that would take place beneath a motor cruiser. This would also give us a chance to make sure some of the props to be used in the film would actually work in the water. These included a missile that had to 'fly' through the water, nets that had to trap the agent divers, and an artificial leg that had to float.

The missile we thought would be easy. We'd just drop into the harbour and see if it would glide in an approximately straight direction as though fired from some high-powered launcher. Hopefully it would travel more than a few feet. What we failed to anticipate was just quite how well the thing would work.

With all our kit in place and a video camera ready to shoot some trial footage, Mike and I jumped into the harbour. Our immediate impression was that the visibility wasn't that great, but it was workable – around twenty to thirty feet. We edged slowly down the silty slope of the harbour wall and into slightly deeper water. The next problem was the myriad of ropes and lines that stretched out from the shore to moor up the many small fishing boats that provided the harbour with its spectacularly colourful backdrop but that down here were a lethal maze of potential entanglements.

We started to fin away from the wall and almost immediately lost contact with it. I took an approximate compass bearing to be able to find our way back and we were ready for the tests. It was round about now that I paused for a moment and had a thought that crops up every now and again on different projects: 'Only in the movies' – *OITM*. I mean, where else could you be twenty feet underwater in an Italian harbour and about to throw a missile like a dart to see if it flies properly?

A garbled shout from Mike through his mouthpiece brought me back to the present and I prepared for the launch. At his signal, I pulled my arm back like an Olympic javelin thrower going for the record and hurled the missile forward, completely expecting the thing to glide a few feet then limply drop down to the seabed below. What happened was that Mike had to duck as this hypersonic projectile flew past him and disappeared into the gloom behind. We both stood there speechless. We had just lost the only prop on the first attempt.

The next half hour was spent practising our best search patterns in a desperate effort to find the thing. Eventually it was located in thirty feet of water about twenty feet behind where Mike had been standing.

For future test flights we made sure the harbour wall was in the line of fire, and I went a little easier on the propulsion system. We ended up with some great shots to prove to the director that the missile would look highly realistic on the day.

The experiments with the nets were somewhat different. To any diver, nets are one of the most dangerous things you can come across underwater. Forget sharks and other potentially lethal sea life, a net has a mind of its own, and however hard you try to scare it away, it just keeps coming back. Their very nature means they can move easily and unpredictably in a current and they are purpose-built to entangle your equipment and not let go – and we wanted to put divers inside them.

The action in the film called for a number of potentially hazardous sequences. In the first, our two hero divers are swimming through the water. Above them, a net is fired from a boat. It lands on the surface then sinks rapidly, trapping them underwater. The boat then moves off at speed, pulling the net and divers behind it. If all that wasn't enough, a second sequence called for a net, again fired from a boat, to trap the female agent, who was attaching a bomb to the underside of the hull. The boat would start to pull away, but before it could, a second agent, without dive gear or face mask, had to swim down to the net, cut it open and release the girl - and it all had to be done at night.

These set-ups raised a whole series of potential problems, but what was of slight concern was when I heard that the second agent, who would swim down to cut the girl out of the net, was none other than Bobby, our wonderful gladiator stuntman from *Leviathan* - the one who had limited diving experience.

It was essential we worked out the safest way to use the nets for both sequences, which would each present their own unique problems. We would also have to develop some specific emergency procedures should anything go wrong.

As ever, the sequence would be broken down into individual shots, which could be set up carefully and safely. But even with this degree of control there would still be divers inside nets with mouthpieces hanging out, and in the one case, Bobby cutting the net open to release the diver.

Fortunately, the other two divers would be played by Massimo and Paola from *Leviathan*, who were both experienced instructors and whom I'm sure looked on this as a walk in the park after the exploits we put them through on the previous film. But the net sequences were unusually dangerous, and like with the Transit van in *The Fruit Machine*, we had to plan for every eventuality.

In many dangerous and dramatic scenes, the props and equipment seen on camera are often designed specifically for that scene to minimise any danger to the performers. However, for the sequence with the net being pulled through the water, it had to be strong enough to withstand the drag created by the movement of the boat, so it couldn't be made of any weak, easily breakable material. It had to be the real deal - a real net.

Our basic set-up would be to position safety divers along the route where the net would be dragged, close enough to get to the net if there was a problem. They would carry dual secondary regulators in case air had to be provided to both divers in the net at the same time. If this were necessary, a second safety diver would then come in and cut the net free.

For the night shoot, our main problem was that it

would be taking place in the harbour, where we didn't have much control. The only luxury we did have was that some of the close-ups/inserts could be shot later in a pool if we didn't get them for real in the harbour, but the pressure was on to shoot as much as we could for real. So it looked like Bobby was going to have to swim down, cut a real net with a real knife, just inches from Paola's face at night. The thought of that made me particularly uneasy, but it was eventually decided the best way to overcome this would be to shoot the close-ups of the net being cut without Bobby's face in frame. This would allow him to wear a mask and breathe from an aqualung during the shot - an altogether different proposition.

Back to our current recce trip, the final check on the props was to adjust the buoyancy of an artificial leg.

At the end of the story, the motor cruiser is finally blown up and sinks. A large number of the legs, which have been used to smuggle weapons in, have to float up from the sinking cruiser and shoot up out of the sea, so we needed to check whether they would actually float and just how they would look rising up from the depths.

There have been many jobs I've worked on where the simple things, like checking whether a prop floats or a set sinks, just haven't been worked out until on the day, and then you find it doesn't actually do what it's supposed to do – result: red faces and a lot of wasted time. For now though, this was a relatively easy task. We simply took one of the legs out into the bay and tested how fast it came back up to the surface. Since the shot would be cut from underwater to the surface to see them flying up from the depths, they had to be fairly buoyant. It was this factor that was to cause so much trouble later on.

After a few changes to the amount of weight we had placed inside to balance the legs and ensure they had just the right amount of lift, we found the optimum configuration. I'm sure the locals, and any tourists for that matter, wondered what on earth was going on as these divers emerged from the sea carrying an artificial leg – *OITM!*

Following a successful recce and assessment of the props, it was time to return to the UK for a month before the start of the main filming. During this period we had time to fine-tune the details and procedures for the more dangerous aspects of the shoot.

Before long we found ourselves airborne again, heading back to that most picturesque part of Italy. The thought of returning to the friendly little hotel at the head of the harbour in Amalfi was very appealing, but before we reached there, we had to make a small detour.

On our arrival in Naples, we were bussed down to the harbour and transferred to a small boat, along with all our gear, to make the rather bumpy hour and a half long journey out to the fashionable island of Capri, just offshore. The main unit would start their surface filming there the following day, so from a logistical point of view we would be staying with everyone else on the island for the first night.

Capri is everything you might expect it to be - beautiful, exclusive and definitely for the rich. In the harbour there must have been many millions of dollars' worth of floating toys.

We spent the first day accompanying the main unit on a shoot close to some of the local islands. This was boat-to-boat material, which is always fiddly at the best of times, but with the sun baking down and a cool breeze in the air, they could have taken all week for all I cared.

While this shoot was well organised, it constantly amazes me how often film crews go out on the water with a total lack of understanding and preparedness for the environment. Some of this can obviously be put down to inexperience when it comes to working on water, which is fair enough, but often it is down to a complete lack of common sense. The usual comments are along the lines of, 'Can you hold the boat there please... no, two inches to the left!'

People seem to be completely unaware of the forces working on a floating object such as a boat. There's the water movement, which could be caused by waves, tides, or currents. There's the problem of wind, which can spin or push a boat in any direction at a second's notice. However, when you explain this, there is usually a knowing nod, then, 'Okay, fine, but I still need it two inches to the left!'

So when you see close-ups of actors in a boat that isn't moving, the chances are there is some poor soul in the water holding it steady so that the light hits them at just the right angle and the sound boom stays just over their heads.

Back on Capri, it was time to pack up our kit and assemble in the harbour, ready for the short trip down the coast to Amalfi. We were travelling by sea, but not in some bumpy little day boat this time.

The main prop in the film, if you could call it that, was a boat called the *Falcon Maltais*. It was a hundred feet of stunningly sleek motor cruiser that looked as though it had driven straight out of a Bond movie. In fact, its real name was *Never Say Never,* and a large amount of the filming would be carried out from the boat, which meant we would have the hardship of commuting to work on it every day from Amalfi up the coast towards Capri. A forty-minute trip in an $11 million dollar gin palace feeling the wind in your hair on a warm Mediterranean morning certainly beats an everyday commute on the Tube.

Our first encounter with the *Never Say Never* was a moment of perfect timing. We were packing up our gear on the harbourside at Capri, awaiting the arrival of our ride down to Amalfi, when the *Never Say Never* appeared around the point. Looking like a sleek blue and white arrow, she cut through the wave-chopped water, spray erupting from her pointed bow. As we all watched this spectacle, relishing the thought of a week of unbridled luxury, a rather flash British expat, who'd clearly been watching us film types and all our gear, sauntered up rather nonchalantly. 'Hey, you guys making a film?'

'Yeah, sure.'

'Well, if you need anything, I know a few people round here. In fact I've got this great boat you could hire if you need one.'

We all looked at each other. 'I think we've got one thanks.'

'Yeah, but I bet she's not a patch on mine. I'll do you a really good deal.'

'Okay,' I replied. 'Which one is she?'

He pointed out a small white day cruiser, across the harbour, that by any normal standards was quite a nice boat, but hey, this was the movies.

'She looks great,' I said, 'but ours is just coming in.'

At that moment the *Never Say Never* steamed through the harbour entrance, and like a supermodel entering a room, all eyes turned in her direction. The expat looked up. His mouth fell open, and by the time I'd turned back to check his expression, he was halfway down the harbour. Don't you just love it when that happens!

With all the gear finally loaded onto the *Never Say Never*, we headed south with the rest of the crew for Amalfi. The sun was slowly sinking beyond the horizon, the wind off the sea was blowing across the deck, and we were doing around thirty knots in one of the most amazing boats I'd ever seen. It couldn't get any better than this.

Then one of the crew appeared.

'Champagne anyone?'

Once we reached Amalfi, we quickly settled back into the Hotel Aurora at the head of the harbour wall, which had now become home from home. The underwater crew had changed slightly since *Leviathan*. Mike was again cameraman/director, and I was on safety as usual. Francoise was unit nurse and interpreter, since she spoke fluent French, which was quite handy as everyone on the crew from the director down tended to converse in the Gallic tongue. Unfortunately, Phil Barthropp couldn't make the trip as he had other commitments, and he was sorely missed. In his place was China Thomson as camera assistant, Caren Moy as focus puller, and Carolyn Hooper, who would help out with continuity and stills.

The first underwater shots were of Paola and Massimo swimming with the bomb they would eventually place on the *Falcon Maltais*.

One of the key things here was continuity, not just from

a wardrobe point of view – it was fairly straightforward to work out which dive kit they both had on and which hand they wore their watches on – but also from the side by side swimming point of view. It's never easy, when shooting things on different days from different angles, to remember exactly where each person is in relation to the other at all times, and particularly more so when you are working underwater and can move in three dimensions. This had to be carefully logged so that in the final film, when everything was cut together, people didn't suddenly change sides from shot to shot.

With this in the can, we had to prepare for the sequence of Paola and Massimo trapped in the net. As ever, it would be broken down into a number of sections. First, the net was suspended in the water vertically. Small weights were attached to the bottom and small buoys to the top. This would hold it 'open' and allow us some element of control while orienting it correctly for the shot.

Once in position, Paola and Massimo would swim along, side by side, and Caren and I would pull the net from either side to provide the movement required to capture them. With Mike in the appropriate position with the camera, and moving through the water as well to give the impression of speed, the shot worked very effectively and was carried off with no real problems.

The next sequence was of Paola and Massimo struggling in the net with their mouthpieces hanging out while being pulled through the water. This was obviously fraught with potential danger, but again, with the magic of movies and clever editing and camera angles, it could be done in complete safety.

It would be broken down into two distinct shots. The

wide shot, where they could have their mouthpieces in their mouths, as they wouldn't be seen - though they would still have to hold their breath while the camera was rolling - and the close-ups, which would be used as inserts to the wide.

For the close-ups we could actually have the net on the bottom, not moving, and Mike would frame it in such a way that the seabed wouldn't be seen. This is of course far safer, as the divers are in a fixed position should something go wrong and help could be close at hand. Again, the illusion of them being pulled through the water would be created by moving the camera past them.

With these shots out of the way, the only one left in the sequence was the one that was potentially the most risky - pulling the divers through the water from the rear of the *Never Say Never*. As the motor cruiser wouldn't actually be seen in shot and as there would be very little control if we used such a large boat to pull them through the water, a smaller boat, one more easy to handle, was used.

Surprisingly, the most dangerous stunt turned out to be the smoothest to shoot. We placed safety divers along the route the net would travel. They carried backup twin secondary regulators in case both artists needed air at the same time. When it came time to shoot, the camera turned, the boat accelerated, the net moved through the water, Paola and Massimo struggled as though they were drowning, then, as they swept passed the camera, they relaxed their bodies as though unconscious. An hour later it was all in the can and back to the hotel for pasta and a well-earned bottle of local wine.

We were just relaxing in the small, typically Italian garden of the hotel restaurant, overlooking the harbour, sipping our third glass of *vino* and realising what a wonderful world we were in, when the news came over the radio of the massacre in Tiananmen Square. We were all numbed by the reports and the mood changed, leaving a somewhat deflated atmosphere. It's at times like this that the often self-important feeling you can have working in the film industry is driven home, and that, actually, what you are doing is all pretty superfluous when there are far more important things going on out there in the real world.

It's strange how you remember where you were when certain events occurred. The most famous example of this is of course Kennedy's assassination. I was too young to remember where I was when that happened, but Tiananmen Square I will always remember, along with Diana's car crash and 9/11.

The following four days, or should I say nights, were long and testing. There was initially one reshoot of the net-dragging sequence to pick up a few insert shots and then three nights in the harbour to complete the bomb-planting, net-capturing, Bobby-cutting-free sequence. It also didn't help that over two of the nights the visibility in the harbour had become considerably reduced to the point where none of the material would cut properly with any of the earlier shots. This would have to be rectified later with pickups in a pool with a mock up hull of the *Never Say Never*.

We also had prop trouble – though not like on *Leviathan* where we nearly ended up on the rocks. It was more like the magnetic bomb just wasn't magnetic and failed to stick to the underside of the *Never Say Never*. In the end we had to fix a clip to one side and try to wedge it between the prop shaft and the hull to make it stay in position – it's always the simple things that work the best.

The final day's filming for this part of the shoot involved the flying missiles and the dreaded artificial legs. It was quite a sad day as it was also the last on the *Never Say Never*. The remarkable thing was that all the time we had been on the boat we had been treated as the clients by the crew, which from their point of view, of course, we were. Even when we had headed down to the boat from the hotel in the evenings to watch laser discs on the TV in the sumptuous leather-furnished lounge, they always plied us with drink as if it was going out of fashion. We were quite glad then that we were back in the UK and long gone when a bar bill for several thousand pounds was presented to the production!

But for the last day we just savoured the early morning cruise up to a sheltered bay near Capri. Once there, it was into the water to knock off the missile shots. At least this time there were more than two of us, so we had missile wranglers who would eagerly fin off after the streaking projectile to recover it. It then became a game to see how far I could throw it to give us a breather before it was faithfully retrieved.

And then it came to the legs.

The shot called for 'a large number' of legs to come rushing to the surface. Since they were buoyant, they had to be physically held down in order to keep them underwater before they were released. Mike obviously had the camera, so he couldn't carry any. I had a couple, as I had to supervise from a safety point of view, and then there was Paola and Massimo with about four legs each. It was bad enough trying to struggle down with just two of the damn things, and I fought valiantly to try to keep them under control. I had just reached the seabed with both of them held securely under my arms when I was greeted by an incessant, garbled giggling sound. I turned to see Mike holding the camera to one side with a mask half-full of water and this shrieking coming from his mouthpiece. I thought he'd burst a lung or something, but when he saw me starting to move towards him, he shook his head and pointed towards the surface. I looked up, and there were Paola and Massimo, four legs each, trying to get down.

The buoyancy of the legs presented a major problem, and they were struggling and kicking like crazy just to leave the surface. Then, as they tried to make it deeper, it became a pantomime, with the buoyancy causing the legs to frantically try and head for the surface, more often than not kicking them in the face in their desperate bid for freedom.

As I watched, more howls came from Mike, which started me off, and I just couldn't stop. One leg would try to break free and Paola would hold it down. Then immediately another would almost make it, and so on. What made matters worse was that they clearly didn't think the whole thing was at all amusing as they valiantly struggled to get down. Mike and I howled even more as some of the legs almost managed to break free, only to be grabbed at the last second and held onto.

You know when you start laughing uncontrollably and then think you have it under control, but then realise you haven't a hope – well it was just like that, but try it thirty feet underwater!

The problem when you laugh underwater is that your

face creases up. When this happens a gap develops between your face and your mask and water pours into your mask. When you're creased up with laughter, air seems to enter your lungs from anywhere it can, and soon I was gasping for breath, as air, water and anything else in my mask found its way down my windpipe. Like I said at the start of the chapter, this must be the closest I had ever come to drowning in virtually any diving situation. Mike took one look at me convulsing and cracked up again. We couldn't film for about ten minutes as we were both paralysed on the seabed. I don't think Paola and Massimo ever quite saw the funny side of it, as they finally landed next to us, out of breath, bubbles pouring from their mouthpieces, and with their equipment in complete disarray.

We finally calmed down, took a deep breath, and it was back to business.

Our two leg-wranglers positioned the legs to Mike's direction. Everything was ready. 'Action!' was called. The legs were released, shooting up to the surface...

...and the camera jammed halfway through the shot.

Unfortunately, it was one of those occasions where time was short as we had to make the flight back to the UK the following day, so it wasn't possible to reshoot due to the restrictions of flying after diving. I think it eventually worked out that they had enough underwater footage to cut with shots of the legs breaking the surface from above, so there was no great loss to the film overall.

It's a problem to fly soon after diving because when you go up in an aircraft you are moving to an area of lower pressure, as the atmospheric pressure becomes less the higher you go. Obviously all commercial airliners are pressurised, but the cabin pressure is usually kept to around that of ten thousand feet. This means that, after a dive, any nitrogen that has dissolved into the body during the dive may be released too quickly if you ascend to a pressure equivalent to ten thousand feet. You therefore have to check decompression tables, or your dive computer, to see how long it will take for the nitrogen to reach a level where it is safe for you to fly. If in doubt, you should leave at least twenty-four hours before flying after diving.

On that final evening on board the *Never Say Never*, as we were whisked back to Amalfi, we could look back, exhausted, but satisfied, on a job well done. It somehow put it all into perspective, though, when we asked the crew what their next charter was. 'Oh,' replied Mike Rodilico, the captain. 'An American couple are hiring it for two weeks.'

'That's nice,' I replied, easily. 'What'll that cost them?' I was thinking it had to be at least a few hundred dollars a night.

'Well, the boat's thirty-six thousand bucks a week, then there's the fuel, food, drinks, harbour fees. Oh yeah, and a ten per cent tip for the crew.'

Right!

The final leg of the shoot would take place in a swimming pool near Rome. Middle of the summer, middle of Italy - think it would be warm? Think again!

We flew out in late July and were staying in a small hotel in the heart of Rome. If you've never been to Italy, let alone Rome, you won't have experienced the atmosphere and way of life that infuses the place. It's one of those cities you feel you've been to many times before because of the culture of movies and the reputation that precedes it, and you're not disappointed. It seems to be a far more laid-back, carefree way of life - apart from the driving that is, which is straight out of *The Italian Job*. But just sitting in a street café, watching people happily walking arm in arm or zipping around on scooters, you just have to think that they've got something right.

Then, of course, with Rome there is the architecture. Having lived in London for around twenty years and also having spent time in Edinburgh, I know there are some great buildings in the UK, but whether it's just that one becomes blasé after a while, or that it isn't actually that spectacular, there just seems to be a flamboyance to Italian design and the history that goes with it, but then you only have to look at their cars to realise where that comes from – or is it the other way round?

Our first day was spent at Cinecittà Studios, which was the production base for the film. Little known outside of the industry, Cinecittà is a massive studio complex in the south-eastern quarter of Rome, and you will no doubt have heard of many of the films that have been made there, including *Leviathan, Daylight, Cliffhanger, Ben Hur, Cleopatra,* and many others.

As with any studio, it's fascinating walking around the backlot and recognising dilapidated props from past films lying abandoned by the side of the road or stacked in a corner. There was also a large model of the *Never Say Never*, which would eventually be sunk for the film.

Having had a good look around the studio, we headed for our location, which wasn't a tank in the studio as we had at first thought, but a swimming pool at a private residence a few miles out of town. When we arrived, the equipment truck was already there, and we started to unload the gear and take a look at our new production base.

The pool was set on a hillside in a large rectangular garden overlooking a typically picturesque Italian valley, but there would be little time for sightseeing. On our arrival, there wasn't any water in the pool and they had just started filling it. I didn't think anything of this until I jumped in to help Mike do some camera tests.

It was freezing.

Cold mountain tap water was coming straight from the mains to fill the pool. I had only brought a thin wetsuit, thinking that as we were in a pool the whole time it would be nice and warm. After getting over the initial shock I realised it would soon warm up with the baking sun blazing down all day. My relief was short-lived, as later in the day a scaffolding construction appeared over the pool, which was then covered in black plastic. It made sense – the shots we were to film would be cut into the night shoot under the *Never Say Never* in Amalfi harbour, so in order to be able to shoot during the day, it had to be dark.

We ended up in the pool for about a week. The main shots were the pickups of the female agent diver placing the bomb on the prop shaft of the *Never Say Never*. To this end, a small mock-up of the underside of the hull was floating in the middle of the pool. It was way too small for a true-to-life scale of the real boat, but in the murk of the night shots, it would pass very effectively. There were also a couple of additional inserts of Paola stuck in the net. These were needed to cover a number of editing issues with the material in the rapidly changing visibility we had encountered in the harbour.

By the end of the shoot we were exhausted, but it had been a fascinating and exciting three weeks, albeit rather spread out. However, there was one final experience waiting for us, which occurred at the airport on the way home.

For logistical reasons, Mike and I were flying back with all the kit, and the others were travelling separately. We arrived at check-in with a 'fixer' from the studio to help us get the equipment through customs.

With the full 35mm camera and housing, lights and all the dive gear, it was quite a pile, and at the sight of it the check-in girl threw her arms in the air and launched into a tirade of 100mph Italian at the guy who had come to help us. The exchange ended with a stubborn expression on the girl's face and one that we were sure translated into a zillion lira in excess baggage. However, the fixer seemed unfazed by the outburst, merely looking at her rather coolly and picking up a phone on the desk. He spoke briefly to someone at the other end then passed the phone to the girl. She was still staring with a triumphant expression when she clearly heard something that made her go slightly pale. She clutched the phone tighter, her head lowered, now very quiet. She nodded quickly a few times, then put the phone down and her whole demeanour changed. We were checked in with no further delay and the bags and the mountain of equipment miraculously disappeared.

About five minutes later the chief of police for the airport turned up, shook our hands with a big smile and led us personally to our gate. When we finally reached it, he enthusiastically thanked us for using his airport, and if there was ever anything we needed in the future, we just had to let him know.

Someone, somewhere was very well connected.

9

Helicopters and Hedonism

Towards the end of 1989 the call came again to join Sebastian Rich and Lawrence McGinty on a couple of ITN projects. Fortunately for Lawrence this time we weren't going to subject him to quite so much torture as he'd had to endure on the Scapa shoot.

The first report was to investigate a wild dolphin called Freddie that had taken up residence off the Northumberland coast and was fast becoming a regular tourist attraction. There was concern as to how damaging human interaction might become if the numbers involved grew too high. There had already been incidents where people had nearly been injured by Freddie's boisterous play, or possibly even mating behaviour – after all, someone in a black wetsuit did look remarkably like a dolphin in the murky British waters.

Dolphins sometimes become separated from their family groups and end up as solitary animals having to fend for themselves. These loners often stay in fairly fixed locations and there have been a number of cases around the UK over the years where this has occurred.

While only here in a safety capacity for ITN, I had previously shot video of Freddie for a Channel 4 children's programme, so I was well prepared for what was to come. Diving with a dolphin in the wild is a completely different experience to diving with a captive one, such as those at *Flamingo Land*, and, in many ways, far more rewarding. Here you have a totally wild animal with no constraints choosing to come up to you and spend time with you. But it has to be remembered that the animal is wild and there is no guarantee how he or she will react to you entering their environment. The experience was, at times, highly unnerving, as the visibility could be as little as ten feet. Since Freddie was a large animal and moved quickly through the water, you were forever glancing around in case he suddenly shot out of the gloom unexpectedly. There was actually very little danger of him bumping into you, unless he wanted to, as his sonar was so highly developed. He could see far better in the murk with his eyes closed than I could with mine open, but there was still the feeling that I was in his world and if he took a dislike to me I would certainly be the one who came off worse.

As well as filming off the Northumberland coast, we also shot at *Flamingo Land* to hear Peter Bloom's views on dolphins in the wild interacting with humans and any potential dangers Freddie might encounter. It provided the perfect opportunity to throw Lawrence back in the water, this time in a fetching black wetsuit, but in the safe confines of the dolphin pool and, much to his relief, with no bubble helmet.

The second report was to investigate a particularly virulent strain of a virus (phocine distemper) that had been decimating the seal population around the UK coast and Northern Europe over the previous few months. It was similar to dog distemper and at the time there was no known treatment.

For this we returned to the Orkneys and were shown around Scapa Flow in a high-speed RIB by Ray Gravener of the British Divers Marine Life Rescue (BDMLR) organisation. Ray was one of those quiet yet completely determined individuals who was totally dedicated to the plight of marine mammals anywhere in the world. It was through Ray that Lawrence, Seb and I were to embark several years later, on the craziest, most bizarre adventure yet, but I'm getting ahead of myself here.

The week was given an extra burst of excitement, but also sadness, with the news that a whale had been washed ashore on one of the outer islands. We immediately headed off in the RIB in the hope that we might be able to help the stricken animal. Once on shore, we were given a lift in a Land Rover by some locals to a point on a road they thought was closest to the stranding.

However, once we arrived, no one seemed to be quite sure just where the animal was. It took a further hour of trudging along the coast and back again before we found the location.

And when we did, sadly it wasn't a pretty sight.

The whale was a sperm whale and it was lying in the tidal zone - very much dead. It was clear we were far too late to do anything to help. The bloated white carcass swayed gently in the incoming swell on the shingle beach, and as we drew closer the smell was overpowering.

The animal had probably died many days earlier of natural causes and had then been washed up on the beach in a recent storm that had hit the islands. It was likely its death had nothing to do with any virus. However, it was still poignant, seeing the enormous body of this magnificent creature now lifeless and at the mercy of the waves lapping at the shore. It made you realise just how senseless the continued killing of these amazing creatures really is, and that the decimation of their numbers could inevitably lead to the demise of the species forever. There was little we could do for this individual, but Ray was keen to retrieve one of its teeth to carry out some tests, which would give some indication of its age and possibly the cause of death.

The following days were spent filming seals when and where we could find them, and, when Ray could get hold of any, checking to see if the virus had spread this far north. The results were fairly optimistic, as none of the individuals found showed any signs of the virus, but overall it had been a bad year for seals, with over eighteen thousand of their number dying throughout Europe.

Fortunately, shortly afterwards, the virus disappeared and stayed away until a short blip in 2002–2003, when it alarmingly reappeared. It just goes to show how vulnerable animals are to unknown strains of a virus – and that goes for humans too.

Following the trip to Scotland, it was back to La-La land with work on a couple of pop videos and a number of commercials. But then came the opportunity to work on something that was fairly low key but also looked like it could be a lot of fun, and would hopefully come without much of the stress and pressure often experienced on many of the other jobs.

It may sound as though many of the projects appear to be just glorified holidays, but while they are certainly enjoyable, they are also hard work. On holiday, if you don't want to do something you don't have to. If you don't feel like getting wet one day, you stay by the pool. When you're filming, you have no such luxury - quite the opposite. There is normally never enough time to get done what you have to do, and this inevitably means working long hours, often in extreme cold or heat, with very little break. However, in June 1990 I was asked to go and help film a travel video in Jamaica − it was just what the doctor ordered.

Some months previously, amongst my trainee divers had been Martyn Cox and Alan Benns. Alan was a former lighting man turned cameraman, and Martyn was a freelance producer/director who specialised in corporate and travel videos. His background had been in the music industry, as head of video production for EMI, and whenever I mentioned a particular artist he would spout out just about every last-known fact about them - how this person was really nice and had bought him lunch when he'd given them their platinum album, or that person was a real jerk, etc. Martyn and I went on to become great friends, and we have worked together on a number of projects over the years, of which this was to be the first.

It turned out to be an interesting job and was about as close to a holiday as I was going to get, with some work thrown in to justify my presence, so I could hardly turn it down.

The video was designed to be shown to travel agents to educate them on the attractions of Jamaica as a holiday destination, and to provide them with facts and figures about the country. As one aspect of tourism was snorkelling and diving, I was there to add a bit of production value with underwater shots at the various locations. Also, since Jamaica was known as the 'water island', with numerous rivers, waterfalls and pools, there would be plenty of other opportunities to shoot in-water footage without actually diving, and so justify the expense of taking me along.

The crew in question consisted of Martyn and me, Alan on the surface camera and Paul Kennedy on sound. Paul was a highly proficient sound recordist who was in constant demand for many mainstream TV productions.

On arrival in Ocho Rios we were taken by minibus to our first port of call, the Grand Lido hotel in Negril at the north-western end of the island. It was one of those all-inclusive resorts where literally everything was included in the price. Each room had direct dial phone, satellite TV, stereo, mini-bar, views overlooking the sea, and all within a minute's walk of one of the many bars, which had their own hot tubs from which you could order food and drink any time of the day or night. It was a place we were reluctant to leave. Unfortunately, we had a hectic schedule, which meant a whistle-stop tour covering half of Jamaica in less than two weeks.

We were allowed the first night off though, but even this was spent networking with one of the local reps for SuperClubs, the organisation we were making the video for. We were taken across the road from the Grand Lido, past some ganja-smoking locals, who were quite keen to sell us their wares, to the now infamous Hedonism II resort, where quite literally anything goes - the first of which was usually your clothes, followed quickly by your modesty! The resort has since featured in a number of reality TV series, specifically for the debauched behaviour that goes on there. On our visit it was 'toga night', and despite the jet-lag we were quite happy to swig back a few beers while watching the guests cavort around in togas or substantially less. Unfortunately, we had to curtail our trip to the dark side before midnight, as we had to be up at the crack of dawn the following morning.

The first couple of days were spent doing fairly mundane shots around the resort, but at least I had the opportunity to accompany one of the dive boats out into the bay to shoot the tourists going diving. This was the first time I had dived in the Caribbean, and while it's probably one of the most famous diving regions in the world, I wasn't overly impressed with the reefs and fish life. They certainly didn't match up to the Red Sea or the Indian Ocean in terms of sheer numbers and spectacular colours. However, the water was clear and warm and there was the added interest of a crashed Cessna aircraft, which I was reliably informed had been on drug smuggling duty when it met its demise.

On the face of it, shooting a group of tourists going diving might seem fairly straightforward. Unfortunately, things are never quite as they seem. You need to spend the whole dive thinking about the shots you need and making sure you have enough to tell the story the editor and/or director might want to tell. This is one of the difficulties of not being able to shoot to order. On a job like this you don't have the luxury of staging what you need, as there isn't the time or budget to have personnel and equipment allocated specifically to you, and it certainly wouldn't be fair to take up people's holiday dives by asking them to do what you want. You just have to try to work around them. This means covering them jumping into the water, the descent to the bottom, the fact that the dive is led by a responsible dive guide, what they see on the dive - the types of fish, the terrain, and so on - all the time making sure there are enough shots to string the whole thing together as a mini, coherent dive – i.e. coverage. Quite often sequences like this won't be heavily scripted, as they aren't the main focus of the video, so any footage will inevitably be cut down to save running time, but you can never be sure of exactly what is required, so you need to cover yourself for any eventuality.

After a successful couple of dives filming the tourists, I met up with Martyn, Alan and Paul to report on how things had gone and work out a plan for the next few days. We were all still pretty exhausted from the previous day's travelling, and so there was no better way to unwind and relax than a cool beer at Rick's bar, further down the coast from the Grand Lido. We had been told Rick's was the place to be at sunset, when everyone congregated to watch the sun go down and the cliff divers hurl themselves from ludicrous heights into the choppy sea below. It was a sort of ritual, and since we were there to capture local rituals, we lugged the camera over, knocked off a few shots, then joined in the local beer-at-sunset ritual with added enthusiasm.

All too quickly it was time to leave the luxury of the Grand Lido and head east along the coast to cover the other slightly less exotic resorts on our shooting list.

One great thing about Jamaica, from a film buff's point of view, is the opportunity to see locations from well-known films. These included *Cocktail*, with Tom Cruise, and the Bond films *Dr No* and *Live and Let Die*, both of which had filmed extensively on the island. Couple that with Ian Fleming's house *Goldeneye*, where he had written the Bond novels, and the island is quite a haven for Bond fans. Two key locations used in *Dr No* were waterfalls that ran dramatically down from the mountains into the sea. One of them, Laughing Waters, created the backdrop to one of the most memorable scenes in film history, when Ursula Andress walked out of the sea onto the beach in *that* bikini. A second one, Dunns River Falls, cascades down several hundred feet of palm-lined rocks, creating a series of rock pools and ledges, before crossing the beach and spilling into the sea. It is so spectacular that it has become one of the major tourist attractions in Jamaica. All day long you can see tourists and their guides walking up the falls, through the pools, in what is quite frankly an idyllic location. Needless to say, I was drafted in to walk up with the underwater camera and get those not-possible-with-dry-camera shots in the water with the tourists in single file walking up the falls. It was highly refreshing moving through the cool water, which had started life high in the mountains in the centre of the island, and a welcome relief from the heat of the day.

This done, we headed east and to another of Jamaica's celebrity landmarks. Jamaica was for many years home to Noel Coward at his house *Firefly*, where he wrote 'A Room with a View'. It is perched high on a hilltop with the most incredible views you are ever likely to see. From the front room, a large rectangular window looks out

across a now concreted over swimming pool, across a
sloping lawn, which drops steeply away to the coast
hundreds of feet below, and then on along the coastline
for as far as the eye can see – truly spectacular. Coward
loved the view so much that his grave now lies at the
bottom of the garden, in perhaps the place where he was
happiest.

Heading further east, we came to the most surreal
encounter of the trip. Just off the town of Port Antonio is
a small island called Navy Island. It used to be owned by
Errol Flynn, and the tales of debauchery and hedonism
that emerged from there would put even the modern-day
resort to shame. At the time of the shoot, the island was
in the hands of the somewhat eccentric Harry Eiler, a
likeable but slightly manic American, who had turned the
place into a secluded and exclusive resort, known as the
Admiralty Club, while paying homage to its illustrious
past with photographs and memorabilia from more
flamboyant times.

Harry, however, was not your average resort owner.
This was made clear when we were invited into his living
room, where he promptly flung open his video cabinet
revealing the complete collection of *Fawlty Towers*,
accompanied by the line, 'I don't just watch 'em, I live
'em!' There was really no answer to that, and the more
time we spent on Harry's island, the more we believed
him.

It all started before we had even met Harry.

When arriving at the jetty in Port Antonio, we climbed
onto what appeared to be a small floating shed, complete
with tin roof, which we took to be an extension of the jetty
that the boats moored up to and was put there to provide

shelter from the scorching sun. When we had climbed on with all our gear, we asked the rather spaced-out-looking Jamaican sitting in the shed when the next boat would be in. He simply flashed a huge grin of dazzling teeth, turned an ignition and the whole shed started to vibrate. Through the bottom of the floor I saw the top of an outboard engine sticking out. With a laid-back 'You're in it, man!' he pushed the throttle forward and the shed took off at an alarming rate across the bay, creating a bow wave like I've never seen before. To complete the picture, our driver went by the name of Bongo, and it didn't take us long to discover that Bongo was partial to the occasional whiff of ganja. In fact, it was during one of Bongo's frequent lapses in concentration that we saw the true Basil in Harry.

We had just completed a long day shooting all around the island and were heading into town to sample the local culinary delicacies. Harry had told us to be at the jetty at 6pm as Bongo would be there to escort us to the mainland. Unfortunately, Bongo wasn't there, so we headed up to the bar to ask Harry if he could contact him. Harry wasn't too happy at this and immediately grabbed a pair of binoculars and a VHF radio from the side of the bar. You got the distinct feeling this wasn't the first time this had happened. He scanned the binos back and forth with no success, then lifted the VHF.

This was followed by the immortal line, 'Bongo! Come in, Bongo!'

Well, Bongo didn't come in, and you could see Harry becoming more and more flustered as time passed. The calls to Bongo on the radio became ever more frantic and Harry was clearly embarrassed about letting his 'film' guests down. It was no big deal for us, but Harry's cabaret was proving to be far more entertaining than anything we could have encountered ashore. However, we weren't prepared for what came next.

'I know!' yelled a now seething Harry. We followed him to a large cupboard at the side of the bar, where he proceeded to carry out Plan B in the contact Bongo handbook. He flung open the cupboard to reveal the largest electrical power switch you have ever seen. The name, Frankenstein sprang to mind.

'This should do it!' yelled Harry, with a slightly crazed expression. As he pulled the switch, the whole island fell into darkness. The main generator had been cut off. This was followed by a rapid yanking up and down of the switch in a vain attempt to alert Bongo to his misdeeds. God knows what the guests thought in the rooms around the island as their lights flashed on and off in a kind of drunken Morse code, all of which had absolutely no effect on a no doubt ganja'd-out Bongo in some local bar.

With Harry becoming ever more exasperated by the minute, we thought it better to call it a day and said we were quite happy to eat on the island. But I'm still not sure if any low-flying aircraft were diverted by the repeated dots and dashes Harry was sending up into the night sky. I guess we should just be thankful we made it through the night without any close encounters.

After recovering from Harry's exploits and finishing off the filming on the island, which had involved some snorkelling shots on the fringing reef, we headed back along the coast towards Negril. We had wanted to explore the Kingston area, which was the capital after all, but there just wasn't time in the schedule and there were still some other specific locations we had to cover for the video.

The first of these was river rafting on the Rio Grande. Now this wasn't quite your average rough ride down the Colorado in inflatables, more a gentle cruise on bamboo rafts that forever bottomed out on the wide but shallow river that meandered through the jungle. As there was clearly the potential for in-water footage, I was again commandeered to get wet and shoot some half in, half out of the water shots of the rafts going past. At one point it was even possible to get a shot of sunlight streaking through the bamboo poles of the raft from underneath. It had taken quite a while to find some water deep enough, and since there was no scuba gear available, it was hold your breath time, but the shot looked great, and it's those little things that, although they may only be on screen for a couple of seconds, can lift the production value of a programme.

Another area that can greatly enhance the production value is aerial footage. Martyn had specifically allowed enough flexibility in the budget to charter a helicopter for a day, which was hoped would result in some spectacular shots of the lush jungle and numerous rivers and waterfalls, not forgetting the spectacular coastline where most of the resorts we had filmed were located.

The helicopter we chartered was a Bell Jet Ranger from Heliair in Ocho Rios, and the pilot looked like the guy out of *Magnum*, right down to the Ray-Bans. He had even been trained by the US Air Force and certainly knew how to handle a chopper.

It was great being able to see all the locations from the air and put them into perspective, and our pilot's flying skills allowed Alan to virtually just point the camera while the helicopter's movement was used to make the shot. We flew up Dunn's River Falls, circled Noel Coward's *Firefly*, with an even better view, and raced along the surf-line of the coast *à la Magnum*, all the way to Navy Island. Nowadays, of course, all this would be done by a drone - but where's the fun in that?

Before we had left, Harry had implored us to land for lunch when we came back in the helicopter, but by the time we reached the island we were at the limit of the fuel range, so if we wanted to make it back to base there was no way we could put down and take-off again. So, despite a desperate Harry running around the island waving a flag at us like a demented landing controller, all we could do was wave back and head home for more fuel. I hope he wasn't too disappointed, as we had all come to warm to his, shall we say, somewhat unusual antics and persona.

On the way back, we were flying over some fairly dense foliage a few hundred yards from the sea, when the pilot pointed out a torn strip in the trees, like a gigantic scar. A small Cessna lay crumpled at the end of it. Another of the ganja boys who hadn't made it home.

The flight back involved no filming and we just enjoyed the thrill of skimming above the crashing surf-line. But the trip was really made when we realised our pilot fully appreciated us Brits. It was the day of one of England's games in the 1990 World Cup, and he tuned in the chopper's radio to our headsets so we could listen to the game as we flew at treetop level over Jamaica's luscious countryside. All that was missing was a cool beer, but we made up for that later when we landed and heard the score.

We had now virtually finished all the locations on the shot list and were looking forward to heading back to the Grand Lido for a few days' relaxation. But there was one last place we had to visit before we could finally put our feet up.

As mentioned, there were numerous locations from the Bond films on the island. Aside from the *Dr No* waterfalls we had shot at, we had also filmed some of the restaurants and hotels that made up the hotel Bond stayed at in *Live and Let Die*, but there was one location, possibly one of the most famous from any Bond movie, that we still had to visit.

As we drove up to the gate, the memorable sign was still there.

TRESPASSERS WILL BE EATEN

The crocodile farm where Bond is stuck on an island and then escapes by jumping across the backs of the crocs is a real location and not just a set built for the film. At the time of filming it had been owned by Ross Kananga, who actually doubled for Roger Moore in the sequence. If you look in the special features section of the DVD/Blu-ray of *Live and Let Die*, all the attempts Kananga made in trying to run across the crocs are shown. There were five in all, and he was lucky not to lose a foot in a couple of them. In deference to Kananga's stunt and the efforts he made for the film, the main villain, played by Yaphet Kotto, was named after him.

Going to any film location can often be a let-down. When you see these places on the big screen they are shot and lit in such a way as to show them off in the best possible light, or in the mood required for the film. This is often using wide-angle lenses, filters, and other cinematic tricks of the trade. In reality, the locations are usually a lot smaller than they appear on film, and far less impressive. The croc farm was no exception.

For those familiar with the scene, the whole swamp area where the crocodiles swam had become pretty much overgrown, but mindful of the tourist dollar, the small island that Bond had been stranded on is still there, though the retractable bridge that left him to his fate has been replaced by a more permanent structure.

The crocs themselves now live in small pens on the way down to the farm. Also still there is the wooden building that was 'destroyed' in the film. The structure that doubled as a lab for processing drugs was built as a set, but Ross Kananga asked if the crew could leave it for him to use after they had finished filming, so the special effects guys had to be more than careful when 'burning' it to the ground. Still visible, but again partly overgrown, is the small jetty where Bond makes his escape and starts what is still arguably the greatest boat chase in film history - which was filmed in Louisiana.

As I wasn't really required for any of the surface filming, I just tagged along to shoot some home video of the guys filming the crocs. Since the context of the sequence was to show the tourist attraction in light of the film, we wanted a croc on 'James Bond Island'.

Now, the keepers obviously knew what they were doing and insisted that the crocs were fairly sleepy at this time of day, so we entered a pen rather nonchalantly to film them moving one of the prehistoric beasts. However, I didn't think it was altogether a good idea when one of the keepers grabbed a ten-foot animal by the tail and pulled him out of his pool so we could film him. Initially he seemed to be fairly nonplussed by the whole affair, and of course that's when our confidence grew – bad move. We all edged closer and closer, with the croc's beady eye watching us all the time. Just when Alan thought it was safe to push the camera lens right in towards those open jaws, those jaws came towards us.

You've never seen a camera crew move so fast.

The croc just sat there, probably grinning from ear to ear. We got the message, though, and retreated, like the cowards we were, back over the side of the pen and watched the keepers as they grabbed the croc, bundled it onto a makeshift wooden trolley and unceremoniously carted it down the dirt track for us to get the shot of the croc looking menacing on the island. Unfortunately, the croc clearly hadn't read the script and promptly went to sleep, but as far as I was concerned that was fine.

The final few days were spent winding down and chilling out at Grand Lido. The whole trip had been a great adventure, as these things usually are, proving that it certainly isn't always about the money. It's about having the opportunity to do things you would never normally be able to, or at least not without great expense, and as I drifted off in the hot tub, beer in hand, I wondered what the next call would bring on my return home.

10

Skulls and Danes

One of my favourite films is probably one of those ones you either love or hate. *The Big Blue* tells the true but highly dramatised story of the free diver Jacques Mayol.

Free diving is that they've-got-to-be-nuts pastime of descending underwater to see how far down you can go on one breath of air. This can either be carried out unaided, i.e. swimming under your own steam, or aided, using a weighted system on a line to get you down and a buoyancy pack to bring you back up. The extremes to which these divers go are pushing the edge of medical science and revealing that those who take part are physiologically different to you or me, being able to slow down their heart rate, like marine mammals, when they dive. The film, directed by Luc Besson of *Nikita, Leon* and *The Fifth Element* fame, aimed to show all this, as well as introducing a rivalry between Jacques and his good friend Enzo.

The film itself is a masterpiece of the audiovisual,

featuring extensive use of slow motion accompanied by an evocative score by Eric Serra, which complements the images perfectly. Sadly, Jacques Mayol took his own life in February 2002, and although the film was made many years earlier, it is a fitting tribute to his achievements, albeit one told with a broad canvas of poetic licence.

To bring the story to the screen, Besson had to find an actor who not only looked like Mayol but would also be able to pull off a significant number of the underwater sequences. Mayol himself performed some of the diving for the film, but to engage the audience in the story, it would be necessary for the chosen actor to perform as much of the underwater action as possible himself. The actor they eventually found was Jean-Marc Barr. His dedication was such that he learned how to free dive for the movie. It was therefore with great enthusiasm that I learned I was going to be working with Jean-Marc on a film called *Europa*, to be shot in Denmark.

Europa is a fairly dark and slightly obscure film by director Lars Von Trier, who would go on to win the *Palm d'Or* at the Cannes film festival in 2000 for *Dancer in the Dark*. The film is set at the end of the Second World War and featured Jean-Marc's character, Leo Kessler, an American with German heritage, returning to Germany to try to assist in its reconstruction. Throughout the film he is drawn into a world of deceit and manipulation in the arms of the beautiful Katharina, who is in league with Nazi sympathisers.

This might seem a world away from underwater film-making, but the reason I was there was to supervise a complex underwater sequence in a railway carriage that had supposedly crashed off a bridge into a river, trapping

Jean-Marc's character inside a washroom as the carriage sinks. In the film the character drowns - no Hollywood ending here - but the washroom door is knocked open and his body floats down the corridor, out of the now mangled carriage, and on down the river, all the way to the sea.

The majority of the sequence was shot at Danish Offshore Laboratories in a large indoor wave tank near Copenhagen that was normally used for testing scale models of ships, harbour structures and the like. It was around a hundred foot square and twelve feet deep. It also had all the necessary cranes and gantries to lower and raise the mock-up carriage at will – but no heating, so drysuits were the order of the day.

Normally, when using actors underwater, the problem is making sure they are happy in the water and able to do at least the minimum to achieve the shots the director wants. Here, the problem was the reverse. With Jean-Marc's experience on *The Big Blue*, the issue, if anything, was holding him back. He could hold his breath far longer than I could, and I was amazed to find that after only a few weeks' training with Mayol he had been able to comfortably free dive down to a hundred feet.

As might be expected, the underwater filming went without any real hitches, but there was one shot we needed of Jean-Marc's character lying in the weeds in the open sea – his final resting place. As this was one of those small insert shots that required a location all of its own, and would take quite a while to set up and shoot, the schedule didn't allow for the lead actor to be available.

This often happens on shoots where the star's time is too precious and they aren't readily identifiable in a scene anyway, such as a long shot of them walking along a cliff or driving a car. You'd be surprised at just how many times the star on screen is actually not the star on screen. So it fell to me to don the uniform costume and head out to sea with Mike Valentine directing and shooting, and Angus McFarlane as safety diver, to get the shot.

Having worked together so often, it was really a busman's holiday, and a couple of hours later, after lying in the weeds on the bottom of the freezing Baltic for an hour or so, the shot was in the can. But unfortunately, as on *Castaway*, it never made it into the final movie.

Following the exploits in Denmark, my diving trips took me to Belize, Malta yet again, and the Red Sea. Belize resulted in one of the most memorable dives of my life, but more of that later. As for the Red Sea, we were there in the week leading up to the first Gulf War, which meant that in Sharm El Sheikh we were one of only two dive boats doing the rounds for the whole week – plenty of American helicopters and the odd aircraft carrier, mind you, but other than that the diving was probably the most diver-free it could ever be. We were slightly caught out on the return trip though, as our British Airways TriStar was turned back over France, it being the first night of air strikes.

We were unceremoniously left stranded by BA for several days in Cairo, at our own expense, and with no one offering any advice or assistance. Several days later, after pressure from friends and family back home, BA relented and a volunteer crew came out to take us back – but it had been worth it for the diving, and we did get to see the pyramids!

In February of 1991 I had undertaken a rebreather course at Fort Bovisand, along with Sebastian Rich, and John Cocking, a photographer friend, with a view to using the equipment on a future filming project. The course was run by Stuart Clough and Rob Palmer, one of the world's most experienced cave divers. Sadly, Rob died in February 1999 doing what he loved best, exploring the depths of the oceans. He was someone whom I had come to regard as a good friend and a great expedition partner.

The course was interesting and exciting, and the chance to dive with rebreathers was something I had wanted to do for some time. It was also through this introduction to Rob and Stuart that I would eventually go on to make a documentary for the Discovery Channel about the development of a particular rebreather, which was Stuart's brainchild, and is discussed in the chapter entitled *In the Loop*.

For now, though, I spent time getting to grips with the differences between an aqualung, or open-circuit SCUBA, and the totally different mindset and concepts one has to grasp when using a rebreather, or closed-circuit SCUBA.

A rebreather is actually a very old idea. Some of the first diving equipment ever used by the legendary Hans Hass back in the forties was based on rebreather technology, even before Cousteau was developing the aqualung.

The principle is very simple. The gas breathed by the diver is recycled, or 'rebreathed', so it goes through the lungs several times. There are a number of reasons why this is beneficial to the diver. It increases the duration of the dive, minimises decompression time, and allows greater depths to be achieved. In order to understand why, a few basics of biology are required.

The gas we breathe every second of our lives, which keeps us alive, is air. This is made up of approximately 80% nitrogen and 20% oxygen. It's the oxygen that's the important bit, and without which we would die. The nitrogen is necessary, though, as a diluent for the oxygen, as too much of a good thing can be bad for you - even oxygen, with the gas becoming toxic to the body above certain levels.

When we breathe air in, only around 4% of it (all oxygen) is used by the body. The remaining 16% oxygen is exhaled, along with the rest of the gas, and is lost to the atmosphere. The balance is made up of 4% carbon dioxide, which is a by-product of respiration, or the conversion of oxygen and food into energy – the whole reason for the process in the first place.

In an aqualung, or 'open-circuit', air from the cylinder is fed to your mouth allowing you to breathe in. When you breathe out, the nitrogen, oxygen and carbon dioxide simply disappear into the water. The duration of your dive is totally dependent upon how long the air in your cylinder will last. If you could reuse the exhaled gas in some way, things would be very different. By creating an enclosed loop, the gas can be recycled, or rebreathed. As the nitrogen is only a diluent, this just cycles round and round. The 16% of exhaled oxygen is breathed again, and the 4% waste carbon dioxide is removed by an absorbent, leaving the 4% oxygen deficit to be made up by adding more from a small cylinder at the end of each breathing cycle.

In modern rebreathers, the gas monitoring and the

injection of additional oxygen is carried out under computer control. Here, the percentages of gases breathed can be constantly and automatically varied to provide the optimum mixture for the specific duration and depth of dive being undertaken - in real time. Things have certainly come a long way since the days of the early pioneers, where extra oxygen had to be manually injected into a breathing bag.

One of the big differences in diving with rebreathers compared to a normal aqualung is the total lack of bubbles released into the water. When Cousteau wrote his seminal book *The Silent World* he was not being entirely accurate, as there is a constant inhalation/exhalation noise from your regulator as bubbles are expelled around your face. This can be far louder than people realise. With a rebreather, all this is gone. No bubbles – no noise.

One of the major benefits of no bubbles is that you find marine life will come closer to you. Many fish are sensitive to vibration, and the normal open-circuit diver, giving off a trail of bubbles every few seconds, makes many of them shy away and keep their distance. This can apply to even the larger, potentially more aggressive fish. Divers using rebreathers have reported, for example, that many species of shark have come far closer to them than they ever did when they were diving with an aqualung. Most people would probably think the bubbles were a good deterrent then, and would rather the sharks stayed their distance, but if you're studying them for research, or trying to film them, having them twenty to thirty feet away, or even further, is not particularly helpful.

Sharks are probably one of the most misunderstood species on the planet, primarily due to a certain book and film. At the end of the day they are just going about their business like any other animal in the ecosystem and food chain. As the apex predator in their environment, removing sharks would create an ecological disaster. From a diver's point of view, most sharks are far more scared of you than you should ever be of them. More people are killed by elephants every year than by sharks, even taking into account the numbers that come into contact with them. If you ever get the chance to dive with sharks, please do so – you won't be disappointed. And if you do, by all means keep an eye on them, but for ninety per cent of the species this wariness should be of the same level accorded to a pit bull or Rottweiler in the street – keep an eye on it, but don't panic. They are just beautiful creatures, perfectly evolved over millions of years, and I have yet to meet a diver who hasn't wanted to get closer to them when they finally see them - which reminds me of a tale recounted by the comedians Hale and Pace during the making of a BSAC promotional video. They had just started to learn to dive and were on a dive boat in Australia, when someone shouted 'Shark!' and everyone jumped INTO the water!

Another big difference you have to get used to when diving with rebreathers is the way in which your buoyancy is affected - or rather, isn't.

On any dive, buoyancy changes as we go down and come back up. This is because the diving suit we wear compresses with the pressure when we descend, increasing our density and making us lose buoyancy and sink. When we ascend, it expands with the drop in pressure, with the reverse effect. So one of the major skills you have to learn as a diver is to control your buoyancy.

This is true whether you use an aqualung or a rebreather. The big difference comes when we look at what happens to our buoyancy when we breathe.

If we use an open-circuit aqualung, during the breathing cycle our buoyancy will change. This is due to the change in volume of air in our lungs, which has the effect of changing the overall density of our body. So when we breathe in, we rise up. When we breathe out, we sink. With a rebreather, however, the breathing process is contained in a loop, where the total volume of gas never changes, so there is no change in buoyancy throughout the breathing cycle.

When using an aqualung, an experienced diver will be able to minimise the change in buoyancy by controlling breathing and compensating with fin and body movements where necessary. The skills become so ingrained that when confronted with a rebreather, you find it rather strange, as you are used to using the slight up and down motion to control your movements through the water. For a cameraman this is incredibly annoying, as you often use this buoyancy change to help with movement within shots, particularly those where you have to move in the vertical axis. Here, you would normally simply breathe in or out to perform the move, saving physical movement by finning and the possibility of an unsteady shot, but with a rebreather the rules are rewritten.

The time spent on the course with Rob and Stuart at Bovisand provided an invaluable introduction to these and other principles of rebreather use. It would take many more dives, though, before even a modicum of instinct was instilled in the use of this new and fascinating equipment – but the possibilities were truly exciting.

During the course, Rob mentioned an expedition he was running to the blue holes in the Bahamas to search for the burial grounds of Lucayan Indians. He wondered if ITN might be interested in covering the trip. Seb was obviously immediately on board, but as there was no specific date or schedule set at that point, or even a definite confirmation of who would be involved, I would just have to sit tight for the time being.

So it was with more than a little disappointment that Sebastian rang up several weeks later with the news that there was only the budget to send him out on the shoot, but that he'd quite like to hire my video camera and housing – at least that was something. He signed off with the less than hopeful comment that he'd ring me if there was anything he could sort out.

Normally when you hear something like that it's forgotten the minute it's said and you know you'll never get the call. I therefore quickly erased any hopes for the expedition and concentrated on some forthcoming teaching sessions. I was therefore somewhat startled to return home late one afternoon from a class to find the following rather crackly message on my answer machine:

Hello, Mike, It's Sebastian... er... slightly bizarre phone call. I'm on a boat in the Bahamas at the moment. Um... listen, if you are interested and you can pay your fare, economy to Nassau, I'll pay for you to... er... come back, and we can nick a couple of days at the end of it to do some rather spectacular cave diving. The diving itself looks absolutely fantastic... um... so listen, let me repeat. If you buy yourself an economy class ticket to Nassau and then get an internal flight or a boat to Andros, I'll pick you up in Andros. I'll get all your return flights arranged through me. I'll try and use this ship-to-shore radio link again today to see if I can get hold of you. So it would mean coming out tomorrow and you'd probably get a couple of days diving. Anyway, it wouldn't be a bad idea to have your help. Next time, be in when you get a phone call like this! I'll try and ring you in a couple of hours. Okay, bye...

Right – it was Thursday, five thirty, late afternoon, and I had more training to do at the weekend, but you really can't turn down messages like that, can you?

The first task was to make some rather humble phone calls to the students I was supposed to be teaching that weekend. As it turned out, they were all very understanding. First problem out of the way. Next was slightly more tricky - to work out how to get to Nassau TOMORROW and on a shoestring.

A few phone calls later - this was before the internet - and I had some people getting back to me with options. It could be done, but I probably wouldn't be able to fly direct. That was fine, so long as the budget was within reach and I didn't have to go via Alaska.

While I was waiting for the calls, Seb rang from the boat. I said I wasn't sure on the flights yet and could I ring him back? After a frustrated groan, he gave me the number of a local supermarket, as there was no phone where he was staying. He'd be there between seven and eight, UK time. After a few more urgent calls to travel agents, I managed to find a flight to Miami via Minneapolis and then a local flight to Nassau. What I was going to do then was open to debate. Seb hadn't been able to confirm if anyone could meet me. His rather 'helpful' suggestion was that I should walk along the harbour at

Nassau and offer dollars to a local fishermen to take me to Andros!

I rang the local supermarket, which I would later learn was a ramshackle shed down a dusty side street, and gleefully explained that the flights had been booked and gave the time of my arrival in Nassau. What I didn't expect was a slight pause at the other end - nothing to do with the satellite delay - only to be told that plans had changed and with the timetable I had given him I'd only have one day's diving. Anyway, the flights were booked and paid for, and things could always change again. I hurriedly threw my dive gear into my well-used and abused dive bag, managed to remember a few T-shirts for good measure, and was out of the door heading for who knew what.

The slightly good news was that someone MIGHT be able to meet me at Nassau airport - a Sir Nick Nuttall. After that, it was still a step into the unknown.

Of course, no one had told me that Minneapolis at this time of year was doing its best impression of Alaska. Before I landed I hadn't given much thought as to where Minneapolis actually was. It certainly wasn't on a normal route to Miami. In fact, it was close to the Canadian border and suffering Arctic conditions. I must have looked a right plonker dressed in loud shorts and a T-shirt, changing terminals in the snow.

Once in Miami, it took half an hour to work out where I was going to stay for the night, then I managed to find a bus that took me to a local airport hotel – not quite a Holiday Inn, and the roaches in the bathroom reinforced the hotel's room rate. Glancing nervously at the floor and walls in search of further insect locals, I fell into a fitful sleep for a few hours. On waking, there was barely time to collect my thoughts before it was on to the tricky part of the journey.

The small twin-prop aircraft took off from the ridiculously large runway at Miami airport that was normally the domain of giant 747s, and headed south-east on the nearly two hundred mile flight to Nassau.

On arrival, the temperature really hit me, along with the humidity. I hadn't slept properly for the last forty-eight hours, and following the unexpected conditions in Minneapolis, I felt like a frozen dinner taken straight out the freezer and popped in the oven.

I still had to see if anybody was actually going to meet me.

As I waited for my bags to come through, I scanned the gaggle of eager relatives and cab drivers looking for an elegant Englishman worthy of the title, 'Sir' – but there was no one.

Finally the bags arrived and I headed for the exit, pushing my gear through the seemingly impenetrable throng of humanity, vainly wondering how on earth I was going to convince a fisherman to take me to an island that I didn't know where was, to a location I didn't know existed, with money that I wouldn't have until I got there. Suddenly, a large hand was thrust out in front of me. I looked up at its owner. It belonged to a T-shirt wearing, sandal-clad, baseball-hat-adorned, middle-aged white guy.

'Sir Nick Nuttall! You can call me Nick!'

I took his hand in a bemused, relieved grip and allowed Sir Nick to escort me through customs and out to a waiting jeep. Once the gear was loaded, we sped off at high speed. He mentioned he had a boat ready to take me the sixty odd miles across to our destination on Andros and that he would be joining us the following day. I was still in a daze as we swept through the exclusive marina development, with Sir Nick pointing out the local golf club, Sean Connery's villa, and numerous other highlights on the way to the jetty.

When we finally reached it, I was completely exhausted, but happy that I'd met my contact and would eventually reach my destination without resorting to hijack or kidnap. Also, the prospect of a gentle sixty-mile boat trip seemed like the perfect way to sleep off the ravages of the journey.

If only.

The vessel in question was a twenty-foot deep-sea fishing boat with the traditional flying bridge and local wise-cracking crew. It was owned by one of the richest men in the Bahamas, who also owned a shipping line. He also happened to like playing captain. This became evident soon after we had set sail and the wind and waves had grown to storm force proportions.

He proceeded over the next four to five hours to take the longest, lumpiest and most uncomfortable route possible to Andros. What made matters worse, and led to a complete breakdown in confidence, was that the guy who usually skippered the boat was constantly suggesting alterations to the course due to the weather - and small things like knowing where the rocks and reefs were - but our dogged skipper would have none of it. He just couldn't grasp the concept that local knowledge should sometimes overrule the law according to the satellite navigation system.

Far from having a peaceful, relaxing sleep as we sailed the romantic waters of the Caribbean, I spent the entire trip thrown from bunk to bunk, wondering if at any minute we were going to be run aground by the madman upstairs on the bridge.

Finally, though, Neptune looked kindly upon us and we arrived at a small, rickety jetty on Andros. I was shaken and stirred, and been through several spin washes, but was just grateful to see *terra firma* again. As we approached the jetty there was a lone figure standing at the end of it - Sebastian. At least there was one friendly face I knew I could rely on. But as the jetty grew closer and I made out Seb's features more clearly, I had a slightly uneasy feeling.

We moored up and Seb put on his best enthusiastic grin and hauled me off the boat. Slinging my dive bag over his shoulder, he said, 'Mike, great to see you! You want the good news... or the bad?'

I'd been right. What had happened? Though I couldn't really imagine there was anything worse to go through in that particular twenty-four hour period.

'Go on then, the bad.'

'I've lost your camera.'

I looked up and almost smiled. Was that all? But I wasn't going to let him off that easily. 'Okay, what happened?'

As it transpired, he had been diving with the camera in one of the caves and had forgotten to secure it to himself with a lanyard. He had let go for a few seconds, distracted by something in the cave. The positive buoyancy of the housing, something that will normally save the camera by bringing it to the surface if you let go, now worked against him, causing it to float up into a fissure in the rock above.

The team spent around half an hour searching for it, even managing to find scrape marks where it had bumped its way along the cave roof, but they never found the camera.

'Okay then, the good news.'

'We've got another four days!' Apparently, a second camera was being brought out by a colleague from the UK. They also needed more time on the expedition.

At the end of the day, I didn't really worry too much about the camera – it was insured, though I must admit when it came to talk to the loss adjuster I was amazed at how calm he appeared to be when I told him that a four thousands pounds' worth piece of kit was sitting at the top of a cave somewhere in the Bahamas. The company paid up without argument, restoring at least some faith in the insurance business.

With the camera issues out of the way, and a relaxed chat over a few beers with Rob Palmer, who had been in the water when I arrived, I literally fell into bed and slept soundly for the first time in several days. There was the prospect of some of the best cave diving in the world to wake up to the next morning.

On waking, things seemed a whole lot brighter. Gone were the memories of the voyage from hell. Even the hazy dullness, so stark in contrast to the usual vivid colours when the sun is out, was gone, to be replaced with glaring brightness and the sounds and smells of a Caribbean island. The humidity was already starting to build and it was going to be hot. I could now start to get to grips with what the expedition was all about. Over an early breakfast, Rob explained the background.

Five hundred years ago, the Bahamas was one of the many places discovered by Columbus. Unfortunately for the local Lucayan Indians, the Europeans brought disease and slavery to the region rather than any form of progress and harmony. As a result, many of the Indians committed suicide or died tragically young from diseases brought to the islands.

Around four years previously, Rob had been diving in one of the caves on Andros, or blue holes, as they are called in the Bahamas, and had discovered some bones of what he thought was a Lucayan Indian, leading to the possibility that the cave could have been an ancient burial ground. As the team and resources to investigate further hadn't been available at the time, the current expedition had been designed to explore more fully and reveal the true secrets of the cave system.

Everywhere you go in the world, there seems to be a 'Blue' something or other just around the corner. There is the famous Great Blue Hole in Belize, explored by Cousteau, and more of that later. There is a Blue Lagoon and a Blue Grotto in Malta. There is even a 'blue hole' in the UK, though, grey, green, or downright dark would probably be more appropriate. However, in the Bahamas, on Andros, there are many blue holes, and where most others are merely named phenomena of the sea or ocean, here they are actual holes, formed at a fault line in the Earth's crust where seismic activity has split the levels of land by about twenty to thirty feet, creating access to the limestone caves beneath. Over time, these holes have filled with water and become a cave diver's paradise. It was into one of these that it was thought the unfortunate Lucayans had been buried.

While Rob and his team were off scouting potential new dive sites, I set off with Sir Nick, who had now joined us, to do a checkout dive and make sure my weights were adjusted correctly for the suit I was wearing. The local salinity conditions would also have to be taken into account, which would vary considerably while in the caves as there were pronounced haloclines. These are changes in water density, which occur when fresh and salt water meet. The two layers each have different densities and therefore affect the buoyancy of the diver as you move from one to the other. They also create a lack of focus in the mixing layer, similar to the effect of adding tonic to gin.

It was a great relief to get back into the water after the heat of the day, and it also washed away any remaining cobwebs left over from the trip. Underwater, though, the visibility was disappointing - only twenty feet or so - but there were a fair number of fish around, including a couple of barracuda, and Sir Nick absolutely loved it. His infectious enthusiasm was a perfect advert for anyone wishing to take up the sport and it must have been the first time I've seen a fifty-something-year-old behaving like an adolescent schoolboy.

With all the gear checked out, it was back to base camp, to meet and greet Henry Cole, Seb's 'courier' with the camera. He'd had a slightly easier trip with a direct flight from London and was as enthusiastic as I was at the prospect of the expedition. Although Henry hadn't dived before, Sebastian had regaled him of the joys of the sport on many occasions, and we had the chance to throw him in the water with some kit later in the week, which instantly created another convert.

At this point I had been diving for quite a number of years, and I'd experienced most conditions a diver is likely to come across. However, it is a foolish person who does not recognise something new and react accordingly when he encounters it.

Cave diving is a very serious sport. As far as insurance companies are concerned, they come no more dangerous. Even parachuting is considered mild compared to cave diving, so it isn't something to be undertaken lightly, however experienced you are. It is always a shame to see so-called 'advanced' divers entering into new territory, such as cave diving, or the use of new equipment, such as rebreathers, and thinking they know it all, because that is when fatalities happen. It is such a waste of life, not only for those that lose theirs but also for families and friends who will no doubt be scarred forever by the tragic loss.

So it was with particular interest that I listened to Rob's comprehensive briefing for the diving that lay ahead.

I had been on some cave dives before in the Mediterranean, even swimming through short passages, but these usually entailed being able to see light at the end of the proverbial tunnel. Here, we would be descending some way before swimming out laterally into the caves to explore them. This time there would be no quick route to the surface.

The first rule of cave diving is redundancy - you double up on everything. This means two cylinders and two regulators, in case your primary system fails, which is hopefully something that will never happen, but when your life depends on it, you can't take any chances. There is even a school of thought that suggests this is what you should do on every scuba dive, cave or not... and there are those that go a stage further into controversial territory by advocating that double redundancy diving should normally be undertaken with the diver solo, i.e. with no buddy. It is claimed by some that this is the safest way to dive. While not wanting to get into the pros and cons of this highly contentious issue, there are times when that sort of diving is acceptable if carried out by experienced, well-equipped divers who know exactly what they're getting themselves into.

Second rule of cave diving – stay attached to a line at all times. When you're in a confined cave, which may very well start off by having good visibility, it is very easy to kick up silt and sediment so you can quickly become completely disoriented and possibly lose your way back – never finding your way out.

Third rule of cave diving is the rule of thirds. One-third of your gas supply to swim in – one-third to swim out – the remaining third for emergencies.

After checking over all our gear, we piled into a small convoy of jeeps and Land Rovers and set off for the first dive site. About twenty minutes later the vehicles pulled up at the side of the dusty track. All I could see on either side was arid scrubland, but everyone climbed out and started unloading the equipment.

With a couple of cylinders on my back and more gear over my shoulder than is healthy, I trekked off following the others. About five hundred yards through the thorny bushes, and after I'd lost about three pints of sweat, the undergrowth parted to reveal a small clearing, beyond which was a twenty-foot wall. I still couldn't see any water. Guessing my predicament, Rob nodded towards the rock wall. I dropped the gear, almost floated into the air with the relief, and stepped carefully over the boulder-strewn ground towards the wall. As I approached, the ground dropped away, revealing a dark green-blue pool that disappeared into blackness. A mixed feeling of foreboding and excitement swept over me.

Stepping back from the chasm, you could see the effect of the earthquake hundreds of years previously. The wall extended in both directions, a clear fault line in the ground. Amazing forces had been at work here. After another quick glance into the murky water I'd soon be entering, and whose secrets were yet to be revealed, it was back to the jeeps to gather the rest of the gear.

Rob and his team were diving on rebreathers, but although Seb and I had gone through the course at Bovisand, we really hadn't had the experience to use them in the depths of the caves we were about to explore. We had to be content with a standard aqualung, albeit with the redundancy required for the cave work – a twin set with twin regulators, which seemed all the more bulky and heavy as I approached the ten-foot jump into the water.

Rob and his buddy Peter Ready had already made the jump, and the ripples were still making their way across the confined surface. I gave Seb a final briefing and we jumped. The drop seemed like forever and the impact with the water was harsh, but with everything held firmly in place we survived and started the final in-water checks before the descent. It was round about now that I realised the only way out of here was up a ten-foot climbing ladder that was hanging from the edge of the rock face. It was going to take a whole lot longer to get out than it had to get in.

With the checks completed, it was time to start the descent. On looking down, my foreboding grew. All I could see was darkness. Where was all this wonderful visibility we'd been promised? I gave Seb the OK and we swam after Rob and Peter, who were now several feet down the shot-line that had been set up a few days before.

As we descended, the visibility closed in to about a foot. I held firmly onto the line, even though I was securely attached with a metal karabiner, and headed on down, checking Seb was close behind. I could just make out his helmet lights through the murk.

As we descended, a remarkable thing happened. At about sixty feet, everything started to become hazy and out of focus. We had reached the halocline. While I knew this was what was going on, I wasn't prepared for the effect it would have on the visibility as we passed below the mixing layer. Suddenly all the detritus and suspended particles in the upper freshwater layer were held back, unable to pass into the denser salt water layer below. It was as though a transparency light had been turned on. The visibility jumped from a murky couple of feet to around a hundred feet.

It was like entering a huge cathedral. The walls of the cave stretched off into the distance, all in perfect clarity, lit by the lights that Rob and Peter had placed below. The water was so clear you couldn't tell it was there at all, and with no clear surface above, the only way to tell you were underwater was by the bubbles streaming from the regulator, though even these weren't present with the other guys who were on rebreathers. They looked like spacemen in zero G on an exploration of some mysterious alien planet.

Once I'd got over the shock of the visibility, I unclipped from the safety line. This may sound rash, but we needed to do this to film, and with the visibility so spectacular and the open nature of the cavern, it was quite safe to do so.

Once clear of the restraints of the line we could move freely throughout the cave and get a clearer idea of just where we were. The first unusual thing was the complete lack of water movement above. On a normal dive you nearly always have a shimmering of light reflecting and bouncing off the surface, and a sense of water movement around you. This can be so, even on a shallow night dive, but down here, where the only light came from the torches on our helmets and the filming lights, we were in our own enclosed bubble, cut off from the rest of the world.

The cavern itself was about fifty feet across and over a hundred and twenty feet deep at its deepest point. The walls were steep-sided, if not sheer, and at one end there was what looked like a large scree slope made up of shingle and small boulders that stretched down directly below the entrance tunnel above. It was in this area that Rob and Peter were concentrating their search. It would have been great to be able to spend the whole dive just marvelling at this amazing environment, but as usual, there was work to be done.

As Seb was filming and I was here to provide lighting and safety, I tracked his movement across the cave towards where the others were searching on the scree slope. Holding the light high up to illuminate the background, it worked quite well, with Rob and Peter's helmet lights shining on the area of interest in time with their head movements and my light putting the scene into perspective. As they worked through the scree, disturbing the silt, the light beams became focused, like spotlights in fog, highlighting the eerie scene a hundred feet down in the cave.

After a short while, Rob raised his hand, and we all drew closer. He slowly removed some small pieces of shingle to reveal a human skull lying on the slope. Carefully, he eased it out of its resting place, and as the lights hit it, reflecting off the hollow sockets, a shiver ran up my spine at the sight of this old Indian skull staring back with sightless eyes. It was also incredibly evocative, as I realised we were making one of the most extraordinary finds in the Americas since Columbus had stumbled on these beautiful islands all those years ago.

As Rob put the skull gently to one side, Peter was unearthing another only a few feet away. It quickly became apparent that this must have been an Indian burial ground that had lain undiscovered for over five hundred years.

It was all too easy to become so engrossed in what was being revealed in front of our eyes that we forgot where we were, and unless we wanted to rest in peace alongside the present inhabitants of the cave, we had to return to the surface every now and then. Before long, a near automatic check on my air supply showed that this visit was coming to an end. It was time to head back. I let Seb finish the shot he was taking, as he manoeuvred round the surreal scene at the bottom of the cave, then tapped him on the shoulder.

There is always the desire to stay for just one more, particularly for a cameraman shooting such remarkable footage, but I think the dive deep in the cave had also been on Seb's mind, as there was no complaint when I motioned upward. I tapped Rob on the shoulder to let him know we were leaving - he and Peter would be able to stay quite a while longer with the rebreathers. With a distracted wave of acknowledgement, he returned to the history unfolding in front of him and we headed back to reality.

The first priority was to find the line again. Fortunately, Rob's years of experience had meant he had put in a virtually foolproof escape route should things go wrong. This consisted of a grid of lines across the cavern, which, when you came into contact with them, would point the way to the surface. As the visibility was so good at this depth, we hardly needed them, but I think we both headed for the nearest one just in case some tidal wave of zero viz suddenly descended on us. It was also critical we found the shot-line, as there was an oxygen cylinder hanging at around eighteen feet for us to decompress on.

As we ascended, it was time to clip on again and enter the murk of the halocline. It was like flying a plane up into black clouds, and the suddenness of the change was startling. It was so abrupt that you could literally stick your arm up into the top layer and see your hand disappear.

After six minutes on oxygen, we emerged thankfully into the light of the surface and to a barrage of eager eyes staring down. The whole experience had been incredible and one that was quite humbling, realising we had been diving somewhere very few people have ever been and touching a part of history that is perhaps best forgotten but important to be remembered.

The following day we repeated the dive. This time some of the skulls were brought to the surface for further analysis, an event deemed so important that even Colin Hayes, the British high commissioner joined the group to witness the proceedings.

In all, Rob reckoned there were around nine fully intact skeletons in the burial ground, and no doubt others would be discovered as time went on.

On the final day of the expedition, the archaeology was put to one side and the sheer excitement of diving in the blue holes was brought home. We travelled to a site called Stargate. Again I was confronted with the rather bizarre situation of driving to a location, this time with the sea a hundred yards to the right of the road, then turning left, away from a perfectly good dive site, to trek through dense undergrowth to a hole in the ground. But again, the effort was worth it. Stargate turned out to be one of the most spectacular dives I have ever done.

The entry was similar to before, a long drop down, a long climb up, but this time the visibility was impressive from the start. There was still a halocline, but it was less pronounced this time, and once you passed through the mixing layer the view was mind-blowing. The cave was deep and narrow, stretching to the distance in either direction as far as you could see, and for underwater that was a long way. The water was gin clear.

We descended to around a hundred and twenty feet and still the bottom was way below us. As Rob told me later, the caves went for more than five hundred feet in each direction and were linear in shape. This spectacular underwater canyon eventually opened out into cathedral-like caverns at both ends. Rob had been further into the caves with underwater scooters and had seen caverns with massive stalactites and stalagmites of unimaginable beauty.

Unfortunately that would have to be something for the

future, as our time here was strictly limited by the gear we were using. After what had been a remarkable dive, we surfaced with elation etched on our faces at the end of an amazing few days. It was hard to believe that that was all it had been.

The whole trip was rounded off with a couple of days R & R in the States at the Hilton on Miami Beach, which brings me to a tale, nothing to do with diving, but one that makes you take a step back and gaze in stupefaction at the world we live in.

While in Miami we hired a small minibus and driver to take us round for the day. Our driver was one of those guys who didn't stop talking the whole time, but amongst his running commentary he told us about a story that was all over the local news.

A car thief had recently stolen a car, which had then been stopped by the police. When they had requested he open the trunk, they had found several severed heads and no bodies.

The guy was duly arrested.

It transpired he had stolen the local coroner's car and the heads were from autopsies that had been carried out previously. The car thief was then proceeding to sue the coroner's office for causing him so much trauma that he could no longer carry out his profession – that of a car thief!

Forget – *OITM*. How about *OIA – Only in America!*

While I would not normally go into detail about an individual dive unrelated to filming, there is probably one dive in every diver's career that stands out above all others, and when it comes along, you treasure it like a golden nugget.

While I get a kick out of diving wherever it may be, truth be told, a lot of dives can end up being rather similar, and the exception is greatly appreciated, particularly when it comes along completely out of the blue.

With all this talk of blue holes, probably the most famous one of all is in Belize. Located pretty much bang in the middle of the wiggle of land linking North and South America, Belize boasts the second longest barrier reef in the world, after Australia. Towards the northern end of the reef is a perfect 'blue hole'. This one, though, isn't a small crack in the ground, but a perfectly round 'hole' in the coral several hundred yards across. From the air it looks spectacular and was made famous in the seventies when Cousteau explored it in one of his minisubs.

It was because of this and other exotic stories of Central America that I had taken a group of sports divers out there in late 1990.

We were staying on South Water Caye, actually on the barrier reef. As well as being a wonderful, laid-back resort, they also ran a conservation programme, where they nurtured and protected baby turtles that had been born on the Caye and released them when it was safe to do so.

Along with a wide selection of dives up and down the reef, the Great Blue Hole was one of the projected dives on the wish list. However, we were told it would take too long to get there by boat from the resort. At first we were put out that one of the great attractions of diving in Belize would have to be missed, but then we were told of a far more interesting site called... wait for it - the Black Hole.

It hardly conjured up images of crystal-clear diving, but the locals said it was a dive very few people knew about and insisted we wouldn't be disappointed. I was sceptical, but having trusted local knowledge in the past, which had usually proven to be reliable, I was prepared to go along with them, despite thinking it might be a ruse to prevent us from having to travel all the way to the Great Blue Hole – how wrong I would be proved to be.

The Black Hole was an innocuous dive site, around thirty minutes fast boat ride from South Water Caye. When we arrived, we moored up and looked around. The site looked just like any other part of the reef, and we all started to get a bad feeling about this.

We were told to jump in and head for the small crack in the reef about twenty feet below. It looked murky, but we headed on down anyway. As we reached the reef the visibility was around fifteen feet – not a great sign. Suddenly we were surrounded by a shoal of batfish, which moved as one and swirled around us. One of the dive guides was aware of our scepticism and led us on through the shoal and down into what looked like a large black slit in the sea floor. It was about twenty feet across and ten feet wide. We followed him through with dubious glances at each other.

But as we headed on down we were met by an amazing sight.

Suddenly the visibility cleared - that halocline again, keeping the material in suspension in the less dense freshwater above. Below, the visibility was over a hundred feet. The cave opened out into a huge bell-shaped chamber about the size of St Paul's Cathedral, and we were descending from the top. Below us, in the centre of the cavern, was what appeared to be a white pyramid of sand, which had fallen in over the years from the gap above. Our dive guide told us later that divers had been down over two hundred feet to try to find the base of the pyramid. They had never reached it.

The top of the pyramid was at around a hundred feet, but in a strange world where distance was hard to judge, it again looked like you were in outer space, and it was very easy to sink far deeper than you expected. The dive was punctuated by the regular beeping of dive alarms on computers as people descended deeper than their intended depth.

However, what made the dive special was the fact that sharks slept on ledges on the bell-shaped sides of the cave. As we swam around the edge we could see a number of them just lying there, resting calmly on the numerous ledges, like some bizarre shark dormitory.

Then, when we looked back towards the centre, the sun had come out. Its piercing rays penetrated the murk above to shine down like a spaceship transporter beam, illuminating the pyramid of sand below.

We were then treated to a spectacular show, as a series of whitetip sharks entered the cave and swam around the beam of light. It was truly amazing, and one of those wondrous sights of nature that few are lucky enough to witness. The electrical currents generated by the mixing of fresh and salt water in the halocline stimulated the sharks' sensory system, so much so that they came from miles around to enjoy the effect.

It was one of those dives you hear about and hope you will experience every now and then, and it's for that reason you keep diving, as you never know what the next trip will bring.

Looking back, it's strange to think that two of my most memorable dives have been in caves, when I have done so little cave diving. It just goes to show that of the many facets of diving on offer, for those prepared to travel and make that extra effort, the rewards can be spectacular.

The whole experience on Andros had given me a taste for more expedition work, where the camaraderie and adventure to be had from a group of like-minded people really has to be experienced to be understood.

As it turned out, I wouldn't have long to wait.

11

Battle Ensign

In the winter of 1941, the battleships HMS *Repulse* and HMS *Prince of Wales* were sent to Malaya as part of Task Force Z to deter a Japanese assault on Singapore. At the time, it was thought by all concerned, including Churchill, that the battleships were invulnerable to any form of attack, including from the air, and particularly from the Japanese, who were thought to have inferior machinery and lacked the will to take on the might of the British Empire.

On the 10th December, three days after Pearl Harbor, everything changed. Following a devastating assault from the Japanese air force, operating from aircraft carriers, both ships were lost at a cost of nearly twelve hundred lives. It was widely considered to be Churchill's greatest mistake, and it forever changed the balance of military power, from sea to air, at a stroke.

For many years these magnificent ships lay peacefully at the bottom of the South China Sea, a testament to man's ability to build and destroy great machines at great cost. However, they inevitably drew the attention of divers, some in search of exploration and adventure, others with less admirable intentions, determined to salvage and plunder, despite the ships' listings as official war graves.

In July 1992, a joint forces expedition, named *Operation Battle Ensign*, set out to commemorate the 50th anniversary of the tragedy and investigate what, if any, damage had been done by unscrupulous divers. The team would lay wreaths as a mark of remembrance and hoist battle ensign flags on the now peaceful decks as an enduring mark of honour and respect. The expedition had always planned to take along a documentary crew, but as is often the case, it was a circuitous route from idea to final funding.

A trap many expeditions fall into is to think that TV companies will trip over themselves to fund an expedition in exchange for the coverage. In reality, this is highly unlikely, unless you have a prize like the *Titanic* at the end of it.

In the case of *Battle Ensign*, this problem was already taken care of as the forces team was totally self-funded by its members. They simply had to find a documentary crew that could supply the funds to cover all aspects of the filming.

After the success of the blue holes expedition, Sebastian Rich and Henry Cole had put together an outfit called Adventure Television. The idea was to come up with adventurous projects to film around the world, with a strong emphasis on underwater. *Battle Ensign* fitted the bill to a tee, but the funding still had to be found.

In the rounds to obtain finance, the project went through various phases, from being a programme under the *40 Minutes* banner to a piece for ITN news and documentaries. The funds were eventually secured through a producer who was putting together a magazine-style adventure series for the BBC. The understanding was that the full cost of filming would be covered by the BBC, but any payment, or salary, for those doing the filming would be based on the number of minutes of final footage used. No definite duration of footage was given, but around twelve minutes was pretty much guaranteed. This would result in a few thousand pounds to split between the crew. In hindsight, this wasn't a good idea. Always avoid deals where the words 'pretty much guaranteed' appear.

The problem with expedition documentaries is that you can never be sure what is actually going to happen. The very nature of most expeditions is that of the unknown – you are going to try to find something, or to search for things that have never been seen or filmed before. So you never know, going in, whether it will achieve its goals and be regarded as a success.

Battle Ensign was no exception.

Going in, of course, you never really think of all the potential problems, other than from a logistical point of view. It is merely the excitement and adventure side that makes you say 'yes.'

As far as the forces were concerned, the film crew would not be part of the actual expedition and would simply film what the forces guys got up to, but as things progressed, it became more of a joint expedition, with the two teams merging to cope with the conditions that arose during the three weeks of the project.

In fact, it turned out to be an expedition fraught with problems and setbacks but ultimately one made out of respect and reverence for those that had died fifty years earlier.

With a budget in place to at least get us there, it was time to make sure we had the right team and equipment to be able to execute what would potentially be an advanced underwater filming operation.

The first problem was depth. The wrecks lay in around a hundred and eighty feet of water, sixty miles out in the South China Sea, off the Kuantan region of Malaysia. It was therefore essential that we had competent divers and specialised equipment if we were to get any usable footage from the dives.

The obvious team was the one that had shot in the caves of the Bahamas. Any advanced diving expedition ideally needs people who know each other well and can react to problems almost before they've arisen, as well as being able to adapt to an ever-changing situation. This is even more so when filming, because not only do you have to remain safe under what can be fairly adverse conditions, but you also have to bring back the footage that will tell the story and justify you being there in the first place.

On this trip, Henry Cole would act as overall producer, while Sebastian would shoot Betacam on the surface and direct the project. He would also use the Betacam underwater in a specially designed housing, which took two people to lift. My role was as overall dive supervisor, but also to shoot second unit underwater with a small semi-pro Hi8 camera. Since the idea was to use the

Carmellan rebreathers we had used on the course at Bovisand, Rob Palmer would come along as supervisor for the rebreather dives and technician to ensure the prototype units remained functioning throughout the expedition. He would also arrange the supply and transport of the helium and oxygen required to run the rebreathers, which would be delivered to our boat before departure.

The use of the rebreathers was deemed crucial to give us more time on the wrecks with reduced decompression penalties to allow us to shoot as much footage as possible on the limited number of dives we would be able to carry out. They would also allow us longer duration repetitive dives, which would increase the shooting time per day.

With all the personnel and equipment in place, we headed east for Singapore, where we would pick up the boat for the trip out to the wrecks. It was perhaps fitting that Singapore was the same port the two battleships had left from on their fateful voyage. But whereas their departure had been under the most tense and dangerous of circumstances, ours was in an atmosphere of excitement and anticipation at the prospect of a three-week adventure on the South China Sea.

As we flew high above the clouds on the overnight BA flight from London, we looked down on numerous dramatic lightning storms. The flashes streaked across the Earth in an awesome show of nature's true power. But somehow we felt distant, safe from the drama playing out thousands of feet below. If only we'd known the storms we were to encounter in a few days' time - ones that would have nothing to do with the weather.

After the usual slog of negotiating customs with a ton of

equipment, we made it to a jetty in the heart and heat of Singapore's expansive dock facility, where our boat, the 120-foot, *Sinikurt,* was moored up. We were pretty exhausted from the trip, but any thought of gently relaxing on a mega gin palace, *à la Never Say Never*, was quickly discarded.

Although she was normally used as a pleasure cruiser with all mod cons, including a sauna, which we hardly needed given the extremes of the temperatures we were to endure, at first sight the *Sinikurt* didn't exactly look like the sort of vessel you would want to travel sixty miles out into the South China Sea on.

She was fairly long and narrow, which didn't suggest great stability in the open sea. There was a large open foredeck with a raised mid and aft deck with a small bridge towards the rear of this raised section. When we first saw her she was lying quietly against the dock as the forces guys loaded the mass of equipment required for the trip.

One reassuring item was the large recompression chamber strapped securely to the foredeck. This essential piece of equipment could save lives when we were pushing the diving limits far away from any assistance. At the moment, though, it just seemed to make the whole vessel look slightly top heavy.

A recompression chamber is necessary to treat divers who have suffered from the bends, or decompression illness, which also includes a particular type of burst lung known as an air embolism. Both problems are serious and occur because gas of one type or another has expanded somewhere in the body where it shouldn't, i.e. the bloodstream or the body tissues. If this isn't rapidly treated by putting the body back under pressure in a chamber, the bubbles can expand and cause pains in the joints, brain haemorrhages, neural disturbances, even heart attacks.

As I cast my eye over the ship, I noticed a small tender lying alongside. It looked like one of those small inflatables used to carry yachtsmen from their moorings to the shore, and its dinky little outboard motor was one of those that clearly should never leave a harbour.

To my concern, I learned this was our pickup boat.

I could just imagine the scene, stuck in the middle of the South China Sea with a pitiful outboard chugging away, unable to keep up with the currents that were sweeping us off towards Australia.

With a shrug and a slight feeling of unease, I carried my gear onto the deck and was introduced to the local crew before being shown down to the cabins below.

Below decks the uneasiness grew, as the boat seemed to be swaying alarmingly even though we were still securely tied up to the jetty. Interesting times lay ahead.

I emerged, with growing misgivings about our ride, to meet the forces team with whom we would be spending the next three weeks.

The team leader was Captain Murray Whiteside, an army helicopter pilot, and as close to a modern-day Biggles as you could possibly get, but in the nicest possible way. Murray has since gone on to greater things, including working with special forces and with Apache attack helicopters.

Murray's number two was Captain David Wilson, another army captain, who was responsible for the diving logistics of the forces team.

To ensure treatment for any diving incidents during the expedition, as well as running the recompression chamber, a fully qualified doctor/surgeon, Jamie Buchanon, was on board. As numerous, repetitive dives to over 150 feet would have to be made, it seemed likely there would be the occasional issue, and when you're dealing with the highly variable and inexact science of nitrogen absorption and release, you need to be prepared for all eventualities, especially when you are so far from shore.

Our skipper was Andy Buchanon, father of Jamie, and a former Royal Navy submarine commander, with that typical British air of understatement and confidence so prevalent in our forces.

One of the key members of the team was John Stuart, the youngest on board, and at the time a serving diver on the present-day HMS *Repulse*, a nuclear submarine. It would be John's duty to place the ensign on the wreck when we finally found her. There were also a number of other divers from various forces who played key roles in the success of the expedition.

The army team had been in Singapore for around a week before we arrived and had been testing out a small two-man minisub called 'Dad'. The idea was to recce and explore the wrecks using the sub and also to use it as a lighting platform for the TV lights. This would allow us more freedom from cumbersome lighting equipment and also allow the use of large, high-powered lights for which the sub could carry the power source.

This was all a great idea on paper, and it would have been a key component of the expedition; that was until everyone saw the sub in Singapore. The contraption in question was small, yellow and the spitting image of the one from the Beetles' film. It looked like a toy, and after the tests it was put through in Singapore harbour, it may as well have been. It had apparently recently had a refit, but there seemed to be major problems with the seals and graining on the glass viewing ports. If these failed, it was sayonara for anyone inside. An engineer advising on the project said that anyone who went in the sub to any great depth was inviting a quick death.

This was quite a blow to the expedition as the sub had been planned as an integral part of the project. But as with all expeditions, when problems arise, you just have to work around them, and plans were changed to accommodate the loss. In some ways it made things easier. For one thing, there would be more room on the deck, which was already cramped due to the presence of the recompression chamber. Secondly, there was now only one type of diving to think about and everyone quickly focused on bringing the plans back on track and moving forward.

In hindsight, the sub would probably have had major problems on the wrecks even if it had worked properly, as the currents we were to encounter were extremely fierce. Trying to pick up the sub, sixty miles out to sea, if she got swept away, could have been particularly hazardous. But these were all things we were yet to learn, and despite the positive attitude on the surface, everyone was feeling somewhat deflated at the loss. Apart from anything else, the sub would have provided fantastic visuals for the documentary – something that would come back to haunt us later.

The first few hours on board the *Sinikurt* were spent

getting to know everyone and finding our space on board. On any boat, space is at a premium, but when you cram nine divers, a film crew, boat crew, recompression chamber, helium and oxygen cylinders, and all the associated paraphernalia into one small area, you're talking cramped.

From our point of view, the important thing was to keep all our rather delicate film gear away from anything wet, and to establish a dry base of operations in a large bunk room in the forward section below decks. All the dive gear would then live topside along with the camera housing and rebreathers. Once the territories had been established and everyone realised there was actually room for all of us to function, we could relax and start to get used to our new home.

Something that at the outset had been considered to be particularly important was a shark cage, to be used for the inevitably lengthy decompression stops. The South China Sea is renowned for numerous large and potentially dangerous sharks. Miles out to sea, the wrecks would attract them like a magnet as they cruised the water looking for easy prey, which the fish populations built up around the wrecks would provide in abundance. The last thing we needed, while having to remain stationary in the water for maybe over an hour at a time, were circling fins looking for a tasty morsel.

As no shark cage had been found by the time we arrived in Singapore, one had to be cobbled together at a local welding shop. It consisted of a large, four-sided, plus top and bottom, barred structure that could be tied together to form a box shape and was big enough to hold a number of divers. It wasn't an official shark cage, but it was made of metal, had a set of bars all round, and would keep out any overly inquisitive animals.

As it had been constructed at short notice, the grimy metal had to be steam-cleaned before we could use it safely with the pure oxygen we would be breathing during the decompression stops. The oxygen was necessary to help remove the potentially dangerous concentrations of nitrogen that would build up within the body during the dives, but if the pure oxygen breathed out by those decompressing in the cage came into contact with oil and grease on the cage sides, there was the potential for an explosion.

By the time the cage was finally clean, the helium and oxygen bottles had arrived and been stored safely below. It was time to set sail for our appointment with history.

With the last rope flung onto the boat, we gently slipped the mooring and headed out through the massive natural harbour and bay that surrounds Singapore.

It was quite strange to see small sampans weaving their way past modern hydrofoils and massive cargo ships. It was almost as though this was where all the ships had come for a holiday. On the route out past the impressive futuristic skyline, I counted well over two hundred at anchor, either waiting for charter, for permission to load or unload, or else standing by for repairs. A truly amazing display of merchant naval tonnage.

Soon though, we were past the last of them and heading north along the Malaysian coast.

It was time to go to work.

While Seb and Henry shot interviews with Murray and Andy, Rob and I prepped the dive gear and started to work out the complex rebreather systems, making sure the right gases were in the right places and all the cylinders were accessible and clearly labelled with the correct markings. It wouldn't do to start filling the small, spherical rebreather cylinders with the wrong gas by mistake. Also, with the rebreathers being under computer control, it was possible to connect them to a laptop and monitor their performance. This provided valuable feedback on how the equipment was functioning and also how the humans were doing, as it showed readouts of breathing rate and gas consumption from the dives - all-important information for assessing just how everyone was performing.

After several hours steaming, we eventually reached our stop for the first night, close to the island of Tioman just off the east coast of Malaysia. With final checks on the gear complete and after a pep talk from Murray on the schedule for the next few days, we could put our feet up for what would turn out to be the last respite for quite a while.

The following day dawned calm and bright and we were eager to get in the water to check out the gear. The worst part was kitting up. With temperatures in the high 80's°F/20's°C and a high humidity factor, we were completely drenched in sweat before we entered the water.

Because the wrecks were at significant depth and we would have to be carrying out long decompression stops, we were wearing thick wetsuits to counteract the cold. The extra thick neoprene, however, didn't help things when standing around on the boat with full rebreather kit on. Finally, though, it was time to jump in, and the relief on entering the cool water was overwhelming.

After checking buoyancy, there was a quick once-over of the rebreather display and then it was off - or was it? I did a double-check of the display, hesitated, then called Rob over. I thought I must be wrong, but the helium readout wasn't where it should have been. Rob came over, looked at the display, then glanced at me.

'Just checking,' he said nonchalantly as he rapidly turned on my helium cylinder.

I gave him a curious look and then we were off. This could have been quite serious. If the helium hadn't been turned on there would have been no diluent for the oxygen and I would have been breathing pure oxygen for the whole dive. As these initial shakedown dives were shallow, there would probably have been no real problem, but if this happened later, on the deeper dives, the consequences would be far more serious, possibly leading to oxygen poisoning.

Most people would think it would be hard to be poisoned by oxygen, as we obviously need it to survive. But when you go underwater, the increased pressure raises what is known as the partial pressure of oxygen. If this reaches a certain level it can become toxic to the diver, resulting in convulsions, blackout and, in severe cases, death. This is normally not possible with a standard aqualung, where you are simply breathing air. However, with a rebreather, where the gas mixture is controlled electronically, it is possible for too high a concentration of oxygen to be given to the diver if things go wrong – like the diluent isn't turned on. At least our checks had shown up the error before the descent, and the rest of the dive went off without any hitches. We all just prayed that was our one glitch for the mission - but then that's what they did on Apollo 13.

These early dives were all shallow and basic in nature, really just a time to get things sorted out and procedures engrained. When we were at depth, and filming, everything would have to be on autopilot if we were going to bring back the footage we needed.

Following the dive, we checked out the rebreather's performance on the laptop. Rob was concerned about the reliability of one of the oxygen sensors on his unit and he had also had some problems with the display. There would be a long night ahead with a soldering iron.

The sensors are the key to the whole control system of a rebreather. There are three of them, and they are responsible for measuring the pressure of oxygen in the gas in the breathing loop. This is the one single most important factor needed to be known by the on-board computer, as from this data it can then calculate, based on your depth and real-time dive profile, how much extra gas to add to the system to keep you safe. So if the oxygen sensors are wrong, this could be fairly serious. The reason there are three sensors is so the computer can take the majority reading, so if one isn't working properly the other two can override the errant figure.

The next couple of days involved more work-up dives, increasing the depths each time to allow our bodies to acclimatise to the pressures we would encounter on the wrecks. We also started taking in the camera kit to give it a full shakedown and get used to manhandling the large housing.

A Betacam camera is a large and heavy piece of kit when it's sitting on your shoulder. When you take it underwater its size and weight is massively increased.

While the weight is countered by the density of the water, making it effectively weightless, it does require a large housing, which takes two people to lift. Couple this with the sheer bulk of the thing and you have something incredibly unwieldy both in and out of the water.

The only way to get the housing off the boat was to lower it down the ten-foot drop from the deck to the water by rope. The hard bit, of course, was hauling it back up again. Once in the water it required two people to effectively swim any distance with it, particularly if there were any currents. At this time we weren't sure what to expect once we were on-site over the wrecks, but on the first test dive we encountered a two-knot current in around forty feet of water, which made the housing incredibly difficult to handle. This would not be good news out on the wrecks at the greater depths of a hundred and fifty feet, where there would also be the prospect of long decompression stops, though with the planned use of the shark cage for these it would at least be somewhere to rest the housing until it was time to ascend to the surface. But the cage would only be at the shallowest stop. Any stops carried out at greater depth would be shorter, but would also require holding onto the housing in any current.

The secondary housing, which I was operating, was an altogether different affair. Using a semi-pro Hi8 camera, the housing could be easily lifted and handled with one hand, if necessary, and so provide the ability to get shots with an ease and balance that could not be achieved with the Betacam, though there would of course be a reduction in picture quality, but probably not as much as you might expect.

Nowadays, with the advent of 4K GoPros, you have a camera and housing the size of a small pile of sugar cubes that easily produces images that far exceed the quality of Betacam - the advance in technology is truly incredible.

The test dives proved successful, and once the camera was in the water it worked perfectly. Not a drop of water inside.

It meant that, technically, the underwater camera crew were ready to go.

The remaining checkout dives were used for testing delayed SMB deployment and general kit configuration.

An SMB, or surface marker buoy, is a small inflatable buoy towed behind the diver throughout certain types of dive. It's a complete pain in the backside but a vital safety procedure, as it allows those on the surface to keep track of the position of the divers. Out in open water this is fairly critical, particularly if there are currents and you become detached from the wreck. If you aren't seen in these circumstances, you might not be seen again. A 'delayed' SMB is one that you release part way through a dive. As to whether you use a buoy at all depends upon the type of dive you are doing. In our case, if all went to plan, we wouldn't need a buoy. This was because the aim of the dives was to explore the wrecks, which occupy a finite area. Since we would be reaching the wrecks down a fixed line, staying on the wreck throughout the dive, then ascending up another fixed line to decompress in the shark cage, we would return to the surface at a specific point and would therefore have no need for a buoy. However, you always plan for the unexpected, and should any of the divers deviate from the plan, it was vital they deploy a delayed SMB so the pickup boat on the surface could track their position as they drifted in any current. This could potentially take them several miles while they completed the ascent, along with any decompression stops. When they finally surfaced they could be picked up and ferried back to the *Sinikurt*.

The checkout dives were finally complete and we fell into our bunks that night well pleased with progress and ready for the job ahead. Rob was still slightly concerned with the rebreathers and so stayed up late into the night with the rigs in pieces, trying to ensure all was ready for the coming days.

The following morning dawned bright, but with a light chop on the water as we headed further up the Malaysian coast. Everything was on track and looking good. But none of us were really prepared for what happened next.

It came right out of the blue in the form of a Malaysian Navy gunboat.

The South China Sea is notorious for smugglers and pirates, and the navy was presumably doing its thing by patrolling the waters where they operated. I must admit, any pirate boarding the *Sinikurt* during those weeks would have got the shock of his life, with the army, navy and a sprinkling of special forces guys on aboard. But before we knew it we were staring down the barrel of a naval canon and being told to heave to.

Reassuringly, Andy, our esteemed skipper, seemed pretty unconcerned by the whole affair and merely checked his instruments while keeping an eye on the gunboat. He glanced across at them, then said easily, 'Now, let's not get worried. We're on their patch, we're the only show in town and they've no doubt nothing better to do.'

He walked out on deck, Panama hat in place, and looked over at the 'enemy' captain, who indicated for him to come aboard. Andy stepped smoothly over the guardrails between the two ships and beckoned Sebastian, with camera, to follow him. 'Can he come with me?' Andy asked a bemused crewman, who probably didn't speak a word of English. 'He's from the BBC.' A line that either gets you out of trouble… or deeper into it.

Fortunately, we weren't shot on sight and Seb was allowed across to take some shots from the bow. Murray had now joined Andy, and rather worryingly he had all our passports with him. Meantime, our crew were preoccupied with the state of the *Sinikurt*. As the deck of the gunboat was several feet higher than we were, and the swell was rocking her to and fro, the edge of the gunboat was crashing alarmingly against the side of the *Sinikurt*.

Suddenly there was a loud crack and a piece of decking came away. This looked like it could develop into a major diplomatic incident as the forces guys tried to hold the vessels apart. Things weren't made any easier by the fumes from the gunboat's engine pouring into the gap between the two boats where everyone was doggedly trying to prevent a further collision.

After about twenty minutes of wrangling with the Malaysian skipper, he finally realised we weren't actually smuggling anything or a threat to anyone and let us go. It had all been fairly dramatic at the time, but not quite the way you wanted a three-week expedition to begin.

The rest of the day was rather tame by comparison, but we soaked up the afternoon sun with the spectacular backdrop of the Malaysian coastline and islands slipping by behind us.

Come the evening we were making final preparations for the trip offshore and attending the now regular briefing from Murray. I was starting to get used to this military thing - but I would have drawn the line at saluting.

The next day would be a test of Andy's navigation. He had the challenging task of locating the wreck sixty miles out in the middle of nowhere. But considering he had managed to navigate submarines across the oceans of the world and bring them back in one piece, I don't think anyone was seriously worried he would have a problem.

It would also be the first time I had been on such a small boat so far from land. Not that I was unduly concerned, but at the back of your mind there's always that 'man against the elements' thing, where you know you're going somewhere and you don't have complete control of your destiny. We also knew it would be a tense few hours as we tried to locate the wrecks.

And with those thoughts, we headed east, away from the coast and into the night.

We woke early the next day to the constant throb, throb of the engines and the sight of water all around. Land was nowhere to be seen. The wind had picked up and whitecaps were skimming off the tops of the waves, but the sun was shining and there was a positive atmosphere from all on board now that things were finally underway.

Suddenly, a shout from the bow sent us hurrying forward to watch one of nature's great spectacles – dolphins riding the bow wave. Their sleek torpedo-like bodies hardly seemed to be exerting themselves as they shot in and out of the pressure wave at the front of the boat. Every now and then they would break the surface in a dazzling splash of spray to whoops and cheers from all watching. It only added to the exuberance of the team as we headed further out to sea.

An hour or so later, things were very different.

Still positive, but with an edge of tension, it was now time for Andy to earn his keep.

We had to find the wrecks.

There were no visible landmarks to take bearings from, so the whole thing would have to be done using electronics. Murray stood on the foredeck checking the portable GPS and reading off the co-ordinates. The wreck's latitude and longitude were well known, so what Andy had to do was drive down one imaginary line on the ocean, as accurately as he could, in the hope that when he met the other imaginary line, they intersected where the wreck of the *Repulse* lay, a hundred and eighty feet below.

All held their breath as we closed in on the critical spot on the Earth's surface at the intersection of two imaginary lines. Our eyes and cameras were glued to the depth sounder. The waiting was unbearable, but as I looked at the completely unflappable Andy, he seemed totally calm and relaxed, as though he was out for a Sunday afternoon drive, actually relishing the challenge.

And then, without any real warning, a large target slowly appeared on the sounder.

There was only one thing it could be.

The smooth shape of the hull could clearly be seen standing proud of the seabed. With a shout of 'Now!' from Andy, a large shot weight was thrown over the side and sent spinning into the depths.

This was the first of a number of errors.

The shot consisted basically of a large block of metal on the end of a line. The idea was to provide a fixed downline to the wreck so the divers could swim down and fix a main mooring line for the *Sinikurt*. The last thing we wanted was to be constantly steaming round in circles over the dive site for three weeks.

What no one had anticipated was the fierceness of the currents over the wrecks, coupled with the fact that the wrecks were virtually upside down. In the case of the *Repulse*, she was lying about two-thirds over, and the *Prince of Wales* was completely upside down. The smooth hull of a large ship doesn't provide a good anchor point for a large block of metal. The ideal answer is a large anchor or grappling hook that can grab onto any small protrusion and at least provide an initial anchor point until divers can go down and make a secure fastening to the hull. So, as might have been expected in hindsight, the shot weight merely bounced across the hull without holding on, and before long we were back to square one – unattached from the wreck.

Despite the fact that Andy had steamed straight over her on a single bearing almost straight out from Malaysia - a remarkable feat - it now took several long hours to relocate her. When she was finally found, it was decided to drop the shot upstream this time, so that the strong current would drift the shot over the wreck, giving it more of a chance of catching onto something secure.

The shot went over with a splash, the line streaming out behind. Finally, the buoy followed it into the water. We drifted back in the current and watched as the buoy moved through the water following our movement, then suddenly it stopped and held fast on the wreck below.

There was an immediate cheer, until everyone saw just how fast the current was moving. The small buoy was pulled dramatically sideways, so much so that it almost disappeared beneath the surface.

The next task was to take down a full-size ship's mooring rope and secure it to the wreck so the *Sinikurt* could moor up. This supposedly simple task was to prove far tougher than anyone could have imagined.

The main problem was the extreme current, which was running at between three and four knots. That may not sound much in relation to what happens above water, but when you consider that a diver can just about swim against a one knot current, you're looking at a situation where you have to be tied onto something just to stay in one place and not be swept away. Also, since the existing downline was fairly precarious, it couldn't be pulled on, to any great degree, to provide assistance in getting down, in case it came adrift and the whole process of snagging the wreck had to start again. It took two days of hard diving to finally fix what was thought to be a secure mooring point.

Once this was in place, it gave a chance for the camera team to get in the water. I went in with Murray, Seb and Rob to film the attachment point and make sure it was secure.

Although we had originally planned to use the rebreathers for all our dives, they were proving to be too temperamental; they were prototypes after all. So we ended up wearing twin twelve-litre cylinders, breathing a 25% mixture of nitrox.

Nitrox is an enhanced oxygen mixture of air - i.e. more than 21% of the gas breathed is oxygen. This is used to help prevent the problem of nitrogen absorption into the body, which on returning to the surface can lead to decompression illness or the bends, caused by nitrogen coming out of the body too quickly and forming bubbles, which in turn cause damage. The raised levels of oxygen dilute the amount of nitrogen in the gas breathed. This results in less nitrogen to cause problems on the way up. Different concentrations of nitrogen and oxygen can be used, depending upon the depth and duration of the dive. You might think the best option would be to just breathe pure oxygen and so eliminate all nitrogen problems, but this could then lead to the previously mentioned problems of oxygen toxicity. It's a fine balance that has to be achieved to be able to choose the right mixture for a particular dive. The 25% mix that we were using would just take the edge off the possibility of decompression illness, while giving a greater duration at the planned hundred and thirty foot depth. It would also help in allowing more leeway for subsequent dives, which are accumulative with regard to the amount of nitrogen that stays in the body within a given period of time.

As I jumped off the side and hit the water, I immediately had to grab hold of the line that had been laid from the ladder forward to the downline at the bow. The current was so fierce there was no way I could have swum against it. I was quite glad that Seb had agreed for me to just take the Hi8 camera, so we could get used to the conditions without the Betacam. I think about a minute into the dive we all realised that there was no way the Betacam would make it down to the wrecks - it was just too big and bulky given the extreme conditions. It looked like the Hi8 was promoted to first unit.

The water was moving fast along the side of the hull and I slowly pulled myself forward until I reached the line at the bow. Once there, I checked the group was behind, then headed on down.

It was good to get away from the surface, where the water movement had swept me back against the hull. Once free of this constraint, you are in the diver's world, and experience and training takes over, making you feel at one with your environment.

Except here.

As I started descending, the current was so fierce it was necessary for me to physically attach myself to the downline with a karabiner attached to my BC. As I looked back I was met with the sight of a string of divers spread out on the line, all with bubbles streaming away horizontally, like a row of aquatic steam engines.

Heading deeper, the amazing hundred-foot visibility soon revealed the full scale of the wreck below. It was truly awe-inspiring. This was no small tramp steamer we were diving - she had once been part of the might of the British Navy and certainly looked it. Although it would have been far more impressive if she had been sitting upright, guns pointing skyward, the sheer size of the nearly eight hundred foot long hull lying there, a broken mass on the sea floor, almost took your breath away.

She wasn't entirely upside down, and as we approached I could see she was lying half on her side, the superstructure away from me. The downline had been attached to a piece of twisted metal on the uppermost, port side of the ship.

By the time I finally touched down on the hull, I had used far more of my gas supply than expected. I think we were all taken aback by the ferocity of the current, which was definitely something that would have to be factored in to any future dives. The decision to leave the Betacam on the boat had been a wise one.

Once at the wreck, I quickly grabbed hold of the superstructure and pulled myself into the lee of the current, where the water swept over the wreck above - a quiet backwater. I could now finally get my breath back.

To one side, Murray, Rob and Seb were clustered around the jagged strut the main mooring line had been attached to. There was much gesticulating and I could see their concern. The strut in question was simply a long, thin, twisted piece of superstructure that had somehow been pulled away from the main wreck and was sticking out to one side. I started shooting the set-up so we could discuss it back on the surface. I had barely completed this when I checked my computer and realised our allocated bottom time was already up and it was time to head back. Bottom time is the calculated amount of time the dive can take, from leaving the surface to leaving the maximum depth, based on depth and duration and the amount of decompression stops planned.

We spent the entire twenty-minute decompression stop hanging on the line for dear life. At this stage we were using the mooring line as the up/downline, and so the delayed SMBs weren't in use. The shark cage was also not in the water yet and the dives so far had shown that it probably wasn't necessary, as the few sharks that had been spotted had stayed well clear of the divers and never ventured far from the wreck. It was therefore suggested we could use the cage for decompression stops with pure oxygen piped down from the *Sinikurt*. This would be put in place once the boat was securely moored up and the main dive schedule was underway.

When we finally made it back on deck we were all pretty shattered, and as there were more dives planned for the next day, it was necessary to sit and breathe pure oxygen for about twenty minutes. This would ensure any excess nitrogen was diluted and released from the body as quickly and safely as possible. It is quite amazing the effect this can have, and before long we were feeling fit as fiddles and ready for anything else the day could throw at us. It's also a great cure for hangovers.

The immediate task was to play back the video from the dive and check the mooring line. We all crowded round the monitor and Andy cast a critical eye over the footage. 'Hmmm,' was his initial reply. 'That's going to break you know.'

The rope had been securely attached to the wreck, but looking closely you could see that the metal was highly corroded and not very strong. The rope also seemed to be chaffing over a particularly sharp piece of metal.

Things did not look good.

It was now a race against time to put another team of divers into the water to move the line to a more secure position. With a frantic rush to action, the team scrambled to throw their gear on. They were almost fully kitted when the shout came from the bow.

'We're adrift!'

We rushed forward to see the inevitable. The mooring rope snaked out across the surface, clearly no longer attaching us to anything. We were back to where we started, having to drop a shot again to put a light line down first, which would then be followed by the divers with the main line.

After several failed attempts to snag the wreck with a shot, it was time for serious decisions. We only had a finite period of time on the dive sites, and so far no real diving had been done on even the first of the two wrecks. It was decided that a more secure grappling hook would be needed if we were to have any chance of securing the *Sinikurt* in a reasonable period of time. For this we would have to make the long trip back to Tioman to find some iron that could be welded together to make up a grapple – more wasted time, but it would at least provide an opportunity to top up the boat's supplies and give everyone a much-needed break after the efforts of the previous days in far from ideal conditions.

It turned out to be quite an opportune moment to be heading for land, as the weather was starting to deteriorate. In fact, we caught the tail end of a typhoon system, one that, we were to learn later, had had tragic consequences. Further to the north in Hong Kong, where the true force of the storm had hit, a commercial dive support vessel had been capsized. At the time there had been divers in saturation in the on-board recompression chamber. They had all been killed.

As we raced for the comparative shelter of Tioman, we didn't know how lucky we were.

The next couple of days provided some much-needed rest and recuperation and allowed a more effective grappling hook to be cobbled together. We also took the opportunity to knock off some shots of the team decompressing, and descending and ascending a shot-line, just in case they couldn't be filmed later in the heat of the real dives at depth. While this couldn't legitimately be cut into dives on the wrecks, it would provide cover footage, over which a voice-over could describe the types of things that had to be carried out on the deep dives. At the end of the day, it comes back to that unknown factor of documentary making, and with the way things had gone so far, we needed to make sure we had as much footage as possible to be able to tell the story of the expedition one way or another.

With this complete, it was time for a final meal on *terra firma* at a real restaurant in a real hotel before heading back out to sea. Unfortunately, high spirits overcame the better of everyone and Andy was thrown into the restaurant swimming pool, fully clothed, sitting in a chair, sipping a brandy! Needless to say we beat a hasty retreat to the boat and were not asked to return to the establishment.

The next day things had to turn serious. There weren't many days of the expedition left and we hadn't even put one flag or wreath on either of the ships. Everything was starting to become slightly desperate, and it was with an air of determination and tension that we headed back out to sea.

As we arrived over the *Repulse*, the weather was blowing hard, but even with the chop on the water we could make out a faint slick of oil that had leaked up from the wreck and still marked its position after fifty long years.

With our return, back came the optimism, and it was with renewed vigour that the grappling hook was thrown in and allowed to drift back over the wreck. There were a tense few minutes as we waited to see if it had caught securely, but once we felt we had a hold, the dive teams went in to tie on the larger mooring line. But the currents were still running fast, and after a couple of failed attempts, everyone realised we were fighting a losing battle and it was finally time for Plan B.

Plan B would mean the one thing Andy had wanted to avoid from the start, but it was the only option left: to leave the downline attached to a large buoy and ferry the divers out to it in the inflatable. This would also mean the *Sinikurt* would have to constantly steam round, day and night, to maintain position. It wasn't ideal, but with time running out, it was all we could do.

We were also now unable to put the shark cage in the water, so we had no safe haven to rest in during the decompression stops, and no possibility of oxygen being piped down to us for the final stop. This required a rethink of diving procedures and a use of the most risky option - coming off the wreck at the end of the dive and drifting with the current, using a delayed SMB, and decompressing on the move. We would have to carry our own oxygen with us and hope the boat was above us when we surfaced.

Since the small, underpowered inflatable wasn't considered reliable enough to track the decompressing divers, the *Sinikurt* would have to follow the SMB. We could therefore only have one team in the water at a time. The whole operation had now become a race against time to get the flags onto the wrecks, the footage in the can, and the wreaths laid before we had to head back to shore for good.

As if things couldn't get any worse, Sebastian chose this moment to fall headfirst into the forward hold. No one quite knew how it happened, as he was found unconscious by one of the crew. The first I knew about it was a group of people rushing past the cabin window. When I arrived at the hold, Jamie was leaning over a rather groggy heap in the corner. Although he couldn't remember much, Sebastian thought he had gone to look for a piece of camera equipment, when the boat must have lurched in the growing swell and tipped him in. He had been unconscious for about fifteen to twenty minutes, which can be potentially fairly serious.

Despite the fact that Seb had responded positively to all the usual tests you carry out in these situations, Jamie, as crew surgeon, had been left with little choice other than to recommend he undergo a full check-up at a hospital in case his condition suddenly deteriorated. This meant heading back towards Malaysia, and it was now a major hindrance to the success of the expedition.

A rather exasperated Murray made several frantic ship-to-shore phone calls to see if he could arrange to have Sebastian medevacked by helicopter to the mainland to save vital time. In the end this turned out not to be possible, and after a difficult decision, Jamie decided that since Seb hadn't had any further undue effects from his experience, he would be okay to stay on board, but not to enter the water. It therefore fell to Rob and me to shoot the crucial footage of the battle ensign flags being raised on the wrecks.

The first dive would be the most critical. It was made up of two teams: John Stuart and Steve, one of the army divers, who would carry the flag down to the *Repulse* and do the honours on the wreck; Kevin Luckham and I would be the film team. Kevin was a forces diver who ran the joint services diving operation at Fort Bovisand in

Plymouth and was the sort of guy you could count on in an emergency. Laid-back and self-assured, he inspired confidence underwater, which was exactly what I needed on this dive.

At the end of the day, the reason we had come five thousand miles and spent all this time at sea was for the footage I would potentially shoot over the next hour or so. It had to work. So being able to hand over the running of the dive to Kevin meant that I could concentrate fully on the shots, without having to worry too much about depth, duration and decompression.

To get above the wreck site, however, was the first obstacle to overcome.

The procedure was for the *Sinikurt*, with the inflatable alongside, to position herself up-current of the wreck, then drift back, ready to follow our delayed SMB when it appeared on the surface at the end of the dive.

Once she was in position, we would climb, fully kitted, down the steep set of steps into the inflatable. This took a while, as the gear was heavy and bulky, me having twin twelve-litre cylinders containing a 25% mix of nitrox, plus a third, a smaller cylinder of pure oxygen for decompression stops, strapped between the two. There were also six of us in the boat, the last two being the boat-handler, Chris, and Sebastian, who would shoot the trip out with a Hi8 camera.

By the time we were all in the boat and ready to push off from the *Sinikurt* we had drifted some considerable distance downstream from the buoy marking the line down to the *Repulse*.

The next few minutes turned out to be tense and more than a little worrying, and that was before we hit the water. The reason: the long foreseen problems with the cover boat. A small inflatable with a five-horsepower engine in the swells and currents of the South China Sea does not make for easy diving. With the engine flat out it took twenty minutes just to make it back to the buoy. All the time, water was sloshing into the overladen boat.

By the time we reached the buoy, things were getting fraught, and we still had the tricky part ahead of us. We had to enter the water and grab hold of the buoy without being swept away. If we were, we'd be gone in an instant and the boat would have to give chase to pick us up, then make the whole laborious journey back to the buoy again.

As the water was running so fast, we wouldn't be able to hang on at the surface for any length of time, so Kevin and I, who were going first, would have to head down as soon as we hit the water. If John and Steve had any problems, we would be in trouble, as we wouldn't know how long they were going to be, while all the time our valuable bottom time would be ticking away. It was even conceivable we would have to start our ascent before the guys had started their descent – something none of us wanted to consider.

As we chugged slowly towards the buoy, Seb decided this was a good time to interview me on camera about the prospective dive – not quite what I needed as I considered the challenges ahead, but it was why we were here after all, so you just have to smile and try to think of something intelligent to say. I had barely mumbled a few probably totally incoherent words when we bumped against the side of the buoy. Chris immediately shouted, 'Grab it!' and Steve leaned over the side, desperately trying to hold on as the inadequate engine vainly attempted to hold station.

There was no way Steve could have kept hold of the buoy without some assistance from the engine, as the current was running faster than I'd ever seen it. I was now on the wrong side of the boat to enter the water and so crawled clumsily over to Steve's side. Once there, I grabbed hold of the buoy line from inside the boat and flopped unceremoniously over the side.

It was like falling into a river. My legs were immediately torn from under me and it was all I could do to stop from being swept away. There was no way I could remove my mouthpiece to ask for the camera to be handed in, but I think they got the message. Holding on desperately with one hand, I grabbed the housing Steve offered me with the other, flicking the lanyard round my wrist. I would need both hands for getting down. As soon as I had the camera, there was no time for thank yous, and I started to pull down and away from the waves that were bashing me against the underside of the inflatable.

Once I was about ten feet below the surface, the wave action became less pronounced and it was merely the constant tugging from the current that was now the problem. That was, until I caught my breath and glanced down at the line stretching into the deep blue below.

My heart sank.

Instead of a clean, near vertical drop leading straight down to the wreck, the line seemed to disappear almost horizontally into the distance.

When they had reattached the line to the wreck, they had been so concerned about it breaking free again that they had laid out a few hundred feet to reduce the strain on the attachment point. The upshot of this was a mammoth swim at an angle of less than forty-five degrees to reach the bottom - all into a four-knot current while pulling the camera. I set off on what was to be the most exhausting few minutes I have ever spent underwater, all the while knowing that the whole reason for us being here was for the footage that had to be shot when we got to the bottom.

To ensure I wasn't swept away, I clipped myself to the line and started down. Immediately it became clear I would have to let go of the camera and trust the lanyard to keep it from disappearing then haul myself down one pull at a time.

I managed to get to about twenty feet before even bothering to see if Kevin was following. Looking back, I could see my bubbles streaming out horizontally, and there, somewhere through the curtain of air, I could make out Kevin making his way slowly down the line towards me. We nodded at each other and I turned and headed deeper.

At this point there was no sign of John and Steve. I was to learn later that after we had rolled in and disappeared there was a major crisis in the inflatable - it was half-full of water. While Seb and Mark tried to bail it out, Steve had flopped in but not been able to catch the buoy, so the boat had had to circle round and drag him back - all five horses working overtime.

Fortunately I was unaware of all this as I headed for the wreck.

At about forty feet I started to make out the massive bulk of *Repulse*'s upside-down hull, and from this position, further along the wreck than the previous dive, it somehow looked even more impressive. The line had been tied close to a forward gun turret, which was currently hidden by the mass of the hull. Closer still and I could make out massive trawl nets that had caught on her over the years. As mentioned before, nets can be a diver's worst nightmare, but with the visibility as good as it was and the nets being heavy trawl, there was little chance of becoming entangled in them, but they were still an ever-present reminder of the potential dangers of diving on wrecks.

Another glance back at Kevin showed he was right behind me. I swivelled on the line and managed to get some shots of him pulling himself down, then it was onward and downward.

About ten minutes later I arrived on the wreck, completely exhausted, and made my way into the lee where I could take stock and get my breath back. I realised there had been moments on the descent where if something had gone wrong, or my nitrox supply had hesitated, even for a second, I would probably not have made it back.

I am normally very easy-going on my gas consumption and I can usually make a ten-litre cylinder last for a good hour on an average dive, depending on depth, but on this one I had already used up a full twelve-litre cylinder just getting to the bottom of the shot-line. It was all I could do to change over regulators to the second cylinder before the gas ran out on the first. A couple of minutes later I had managed to get my breath back and looked up the line. Kevin, who had now joined me, glanced back too.

There was no one there.

This was worrying, but there was nothing we could do about it. We would just have to wait until our bottom time ran out, then head back up, pictures or no pictures. It at least gave me a chance to look around at my surroundings.

The downline had been attached to a jagged piece of metal on the port side of the hull, probably torn off in the death throes of the ship on that tragic day fifty years earlier. Below the metal, the once proud ship disappeared into the gloom. The seabed was around a hundred and eighty feet down, but despite the excitement of potential exploration, we couldn't go any deeper and reduce our bottom time further.

Suddenly the sun seemed to go in, and I glanced up as the massive shadows of a dozen huge stingrays soared overhead like a squadron of deep-sea bombers. On some of the other dives dolphins had been reported and even a couple of sharks had been seen, but these rays and the accompanying shoal of fish gliding overhead started to make the dive a memorable experience for all the right reasons.

A second later and Kevin tapped me on the shoulder, pointing up the line. To my relief I could see John and Steve about thirty feet away. I indicated for them to unfurl the flag and swim down past me to reveal it in all its glory. After a couple of seconds of confusion, they cottoned on and soon had the flag flying in the current. It was quite a poignant moment and drove home the true significance as to why we were here – to honour the hundreds that had died on that tragic day and were still lying in the metal tomb of the hull of the ship beneath me,. But there was little time to dwell on the enormity of the events as John and Steve were approaching fast.

One of the joys of video is that you don't need to worry

about running out of film. Knowing the importance of the footage I was shooting, I just hit record and concentrated on framing the images that would tell the story.

As John finned past me with the flag streaming out behind, a shoal of fish swam behind him in the distance – the 'money shot', as they say in the trade. It really couldn't have been staged any better. He then moved down to a point about fifteen feet below, where, along with Steve, they found some metal to attach the flag to. I continued to film as they released a small buoy on a two-foot line that would hold the flag upright and proud of the deck. Then, as if on a windy day, the ever-present current did the rest, unfurling the ensign as though in the breeze created by a ship ploughing through the ocean waves – a wonderful sight.

I had been shooting for about five minutes when I received another reassuring tap on my shoulder from Kevin. It was time to return to the surface.

The key shots were in the bag, but there was no time to relax. We now had to concentrate on what was effectively the most dangerous part of the dive, the ascent. On any dive the ascent is considered to be the most risky stage, due to the possibility of decompression illness. This is increased when decompression stops are involved and extreme exertion has taken place. On top of that, we had the additional hazard of possibly surfacing in the middle of the South China Sea with no boat to pick us up.

To hopefully avoid this, Kevin unfurled the delayed SMB for release before we left the wreck. This should give those on lookout duty on the *Sinikurt* time to get a fix on our position before we were whisked off in the current once we let go. First, though, we had to release the SMB, ensuring it shot straight to the surface without any jams or entanglement, which could drag us up with it. To this end we carried a backup in case the first one had to be cut free.

Once unwound in the water, Kevin inflated the elongated buoy from one of his secondary mouthpieces. You only needed to partially fill it at this depth, as the expanding gas, with the reduction in pressure on the ascent, would do the rest. Once he was sure we were both firmly secured to the wreck, he released it. The buoy shot upwards, pulling the thin nylon line behind it, unravelling at the speed of a deep-sea fishing reel with a Marlin on the end. Within seconds it had reached the surface.

It was time for us to leave the wreck.

Hoping, more than you know, that the *Sinikurt* had seen the buoy hit the surface, we launched ourselves off into the roaring current, and a few seconds later everything was quiet and orderly. Once you are in a current, going with it, the speeding water vanishes, as you are going at the same pace. It's only when you pass things in the water, or glance below at the scurrying seabed, that you realise you're travelling at a fair old lick.

Once clear of the wreck, it was time to check each other over and start the laborious task of decompression. Fortunately we only had about fifteen minutes on this dive, as we had been breathing 25% nitrox. We were also breathing oxygen for the decompression stop.

Before we knew it, we broke the surface to the welcoming warmth of the sun and the reassurance of the *Sinikurt* bobbing not a hundred yards away. We breathed a sigh of relief and waited for the inflatable to chug over to haul us on board. The only thing still of concern was how did the footage look?

After sorting out our gear, we piled into the monitor room and played back the video. I knew it had looked great through the viewfinder, but until it is shown on the screen and met with approval by everyone else, you can never be too sure. Fortunately, it was as I had remembered and I needn't have worried. Everyone was happy. From our point of view, we could have gone home there and then as we had the key shots covering the placing of the flag.

As there had been so much grief over fixing a line to the *Repulse*, it was thought best to conclude our dives here as quickly as possible and see if there was time to dive on the *Prince of Wales*. So over the next couple of days I made one more dive on the *Repulse* to make sure we had additional material of the flag and the wreck for options in the edit suite. This time things weren't so dramatic, and we had the benefit of not having to worry about the second team being in the water to place the flag as it was already there. This gave Kevin and me a chance to explore further along the wreck.

In many ways this was the more enjoyable dive, as the pressure was off and we could start to get a true sense of the scale of one of the most impressive battleships ever built. It was a shame that it was effectively upside down, as the really interesting superstructure was largely hidden from view, but there were sections where you could peer into the mysterious interior and imagine events of fifty years earlier.

Part of the condition to receive permission from the Admiralty to dive on the wrecks had been the understanding that no one would venture inside or bring anything up. This was strictly adhered to, and in any case, the memories and footage were testament enough to an experience none of us will ever forget.

There was now only one day left to put the flag on the *Prince of Wales* and Rob filmed the action. Unfortunately, the visibility wasn't so good during the dive, but they did manage to catch a glimpse of some dolphins, whose constant whistling and clicking could be heard throughout.

With the expedition deemed a success, all that was left was for a poignant ceremony on board the *Sinikurt* in memory of the brave sailors who had died. With a short prayer, and to the strains of *For those in Peril on the Sea*, the expedition was concluded.

I am normally fairly good on ships and have never been seasick, though I came close once as a kid on a car ferry crossing the Bay of Biscay where people were literally being thrown across the deck, but I have never lost my lunch, so to speak. However, after three weeks of being tossed around on the South China Sea, it was starting to take its toll, to the degree that I was never fully operating at a hundred per cent while on board. Couple that with the heavy diving and filming, and I came back at the end of it rather shattered. Needless to say, on our return to Singapore we were in need of some serious R & R.

The army guys had a few more days left on the boat before the flight back, but Sebastian had other ideas. In his travels for ITN he had stayed at some of the more impressive hotels around the world, and for this trip it was decided to transfer from our one-star boat to the five-star Singapore Oriental.

This of course left the forces guys rather green with

envy and slightly incredulous as we headed off to one of Asia's most exclusive and spectacular hotels dressed in ragged T-shirts, cut-off shorts and worn-out sneakers in a pickup truck loaned by the *Sinikurt's* owner.

As there wasn't enough room for all of us in the cab, Henry, Rob and I lay on the gear in the open back, making sure it didn't bounce out as we hurtled through downtown Singapore.

When we pulled up at the entrance to the exclusive hotel, we were met with jaw-dropping stares at our attire from the porters who had to deal with all our equipment. However, after calming things down with some small pieces of paper from a local bank, the gear was stored in a downstairs locker room and we were escorted through into the Bond-style interior. It was quite the most spectacular hotel I had ever been in, with glass-sided scenic elevators whisking us up the inside of the huge atrium to the luxurious rooms overlooking Singapore harbour.

The first toe in the first bath for over three weeks was an experience of extreme pleasure, and the moment was made even more sublime at the thought of Murray and the gang sharing showers in the depths of the *Sinikurt*. It's a cruel world!

After a couple of days of unabashed luxury it was time for the flight home - a chance to catch up on sleep and look back on a memorable few weeks.

However, things were not destined to work out quite that easily. We made it to the airport several hours before check-in to make sure we could get all the gear through and ensure we had good seats for the thirteen-hour flight.

Once on the plane though, Henry, Rob and I found we

had been put on a row next to a toilet, with seats that didn't recline. A thirteen-hour flight with no reclining seats – come on! When I put this to the stewardess, her reply was, 'Well you won't enjoy the flight, if that's your attitude, will you?'

Really - the world's favourite airline?

Back in the UK there were two more things waiting for us that were completely unexpected. The first, which was the most crucial, was the amount of footage the production company would use for the segment in the programme, as this related to how much we would get paid.

We knew this was highly variable, and although some aspects of the expedition, like the submarine, hadn't materialised, we also knew we had shot plenty of high drama footage, with the Malaysian gunboat, the breaking free from the wreck, Sebastian falling down the hold, etc. Not to mention we had the footage of the ensigns being placed on the wrecks, which after all were the key sequences and the aim of the expedition. We were therefore fairly confident there was enough material to make an interesting half-hour documentary, let alone a short segment of a magazine-style programme.

So how much was used – NOTHING!

To say we were not amused was an understatement, and the unfortunate lesson of not being able to trust anyone in this business, unless it was in writing, in triplicate, was driven home. In all, we had worked at the limit for three weeks, doing some of the most extreme diving for no reward.

You win some, you lose some.

A slight compensation was the second unexpected

272

event on our return. The project would go on to win the Duke of Edinburgh Award for expeditions for that year, so there was a trip to Buckingham Palace to receive it from the Duke of Edinburgh.

At least there was some recognition for all the trials and tribulations.

12

In the Loop

Throughout my life I have always looked beyond whatever I have been doing to the next level, to see how I can use the skills I've learned and experiences I have had to try something new and more challenging.

One of the areas I had been trying to pursue since leaving university was working as a stuntman, and although all the physical skill qualifications were achieved, the required Equity card that would allow me to become a member of the Stunt Register in the UK proved to be somewhat more elusive. In the long run it hardly hindered my underwater adventures, but it would have been fun to be involved in some of the other exploits this side of the industry gets up to.

A second area I was trying to develop, was creating ideas for documentaries and other TV programmes, but when you consider how much material and how many ideas are being submitted, you have to be incredibly lucky.

Most people could probably come up with a perfectly acceptable idea for a TV programme if asked to. What really matters is being in the right place at the right time to see it through to production.

After much persistence, numerous rejections and much hair pulling, in February of 1995 the stars seemed to align.

Most of the ideas, for obvious reasons, centred around diving and the underwater world. There is such a wealth of visually interesting, historically fascinating and technically impressive material here that you could probably make underwater programmes *ad infinitum* and never repeat yourself.

Amongst the ideas I had been considering was the story of the development of the rebreather. Enough has been said about rebreathers to give an idea of how significant a leap in technology they would be for underwater exploration, but, suffice to say, they would make a whole new range of depths accessible to the diver, for longer periods of time, and all with reduced decompression requirements.

As has also been mentioned, rebreathers have been around for a long time, but what had been lacking were the complex computer control systems to monitor and regulate the mixture of gases. There had been numerous attempts at this, mainly on the military side, with varying degrees of success, but the holy grail was a foolproof, user-friendly system that wouldn't break the bank if you wanted to buy one. A number of people had been working towards this goal for some time, and curiously, those making the greatest advances were enthusiastic amateurs rather than major diving equipment suppliers and manufacturers.

One of these individuals was the aforementioned Stuart Clough, whose units Rob Palmer had been helping to develop, and the ones we had taken to the South China Sea on the *Repulse/Prince of Wales* expedition. As was evident at the time, they still had a long way to go, but this was now two years on and a lot could happen in two years in the world of electronics development.

I had kept in touch with Stuart over this period and he seemed like the ideal guy to base the story around. His story was quite amazing, having the excitement and high-tech appeal of technology and diving at the extreme, together with the emotional story of one man's struggle intellectually, financially and personally to develop his life-long dream. To cap it all, when I heard he had started developing the original systems in his back garage and was shortly going to be taking the units for trials at NASA, it had the added David and Goliath drama and the appeal of the little guy battling overwhelming odds.

It was the perfect documentary idea.

Once the idea was there, I had to rope someone in to help with the logistics. This would be my first attempt at writing and directing a programme, and I would also be shooting all the underwater material, but all the logistical aspects and procedural ins and outs were new to me and I needed someone I could trust to take care of that side of things and allow me to get on with the creative side. Whoever the poor soul ended up being, they had to be enthusiastic and willing to work for very little.

Martyn Cox immediately sprang to mind.

Martyn was always enthusiastic about shoots, and he understood the problems of getting programmes off the ground. As I had helped him out on the Jamaica shoot, I felt sure he would be receptive to the idea. He would also bring a certain level-headedness to a project that for me would be a bit of a wing and a prayer, though I wasn't admitting that to anyone.

Thankfully my judgement was well placed and Martyn was soon on board. With both of us now committed to trying to move the project forward, it was time to pitch the idea to various TV channels and commissioning editors.

This can be the most soul-destroying part of any venture, as the inevitable rejection slips come pouring in, and you have to be pretty thick-skinned to keep going. Belief in the idea is paramount, and with enough perseverance, never taking 'no' for an answer, and a bit of making your own luck, there is every possibility you will succeed. As mentioned, there is a lot of right-desk-on-the-right-day going on, and for us, the right desk turned out to be Chris Haws, commissioning editor for Discovery UK.

Chris had been developing a series called *The Professionals*, which would follow teams of people as they carried out potentially dangerous activities in pursuit of their day's work. It included window cleaners on high-rise buildings, pyrotechnic experts who put on firework displays, the development of the McLaren F1 road car, and so on. Although the rebreather story was somewhat different to the above, it did fit the general brief, and it would make a great complementary addition to the series.

The other important criteria we met was being prepared to work for very little. The series was aimed at giving new documentary-makers a break into the business, so the programmes would have low budgets, which under normal circumstances would never meet the full production costs of a fifty-minute programme – but it was the opportunity that was the payment. Just like with *Castaway*, I would almost have done it for nothing.

After a couple of meetings with Chris, where Martyn and I outlined the project and showed him some of our previous work, we were commissioned to make the programme.

It really had all been down to walking into the right office on the right day, when they were looking for that type of programme to fill their requirements.

As the budget was going to be so low, it would mean having to take on many of the major roles myself, doubling as writer, director, underwater cameraman and overseeing the production and editing stages. Other decisions, such as music, voice-over artist, type of graphics, all had to be considered, both in relation to the scope of the project and the limited budget. But everything comes back to the story - that is the starting point for any project, be it a feature film, documentary or news piece. What is the story? Once you have that clear in your mind, you can break everything else down into small, manageable chunks.

The basic script shows what sequences you need. They in turn dictate the locations, interviews, graphics, archive footage, music, etc. Next is to design a schedule that can realistically include all these components. Finally you can work out a budget that has to include the crew, equipment, editing, music, travel, food, legal fees, tape duplication, voice-over, paper clips and on and on. Hopefully, at the end of the day, it all adds up to a figure that is within the budget you have been given and you can go and make your programme. Inevitably there will be an excess of expenditure, which has to be curbed, but usually this can be made to fit. If not, you just have to reduce the amount of equipment, see which locations you can do without, and, if all else fails, plead with the crew to reduce their rates or work overtime for an all-in deal.

With this last concept in mind, I roped in as many of my contacts as I could, and it was really only down to their generosity in reducing their rates to help us out that the programme ever got made. The list includes: Chris King, Steve Padwick and Paul Stapley on camera, Barry Read on lighting, Phil Barthropp on sound as well as a sprinter on camera, and Mike Ray as editor, sound recordist, graphics creator and provider of music, and of course, not forgetting Martyn Cox, who was involved as producer throughout the project. I also threw in some of my existing rebreather/diving footage as archive for free.

Throughout the pre-production process, Martyn's experience in pop video production and corporate and travel videos was invaluable. I'm sure he became more than a little exasperated with my first-time director insistence on doing things my way, but he did manage to get me to listen occasionally when he knew I was about to do something I probably shouldn't, and the whole experience became one of discussion and resolution when problems occurred. Some things, of course, were completely out of our control, such as sudden changes in budget, but more on that later.

The first day of shooting was as simple as it could possibly be, but for me, it was completely nerve-wracking. I would have to make decisions on the content of what we were about to shoot, the camera positions, and the type and number of shots needed, in order for the whole thing to work in the edit. And all this for a simple master interview with Stuart Clough at his home near Cambridge. Fortunately I had managed to convince Paul Stapley, a cameraman friend, to come along, and he was continually on hand to offer much-needed advice and make the whole exercise a pleasurable learning experience as well as shooting the material we needed.

On this first day, we would also be shooting Stuart in his garage talking through some of the earlier stages of the rebreather development, but the main interview was the critical thing. Since much of what would be included in the documentary would be the lead up to where Stuart currently was in the development process, a good deal of what he would say would be used as voice-over for archive footage. In essence, it was the back-story in his words.

With a successful first day out of the way, it was a massive relief and the next job was to start what is one of the most tedious, but essential, parts of any interview shoot – the transcription of what has been said.

Transcribing is basically the writing down of every single thing, said or otherwise, in the interview. This must be precise and accurate, and include every cough, stutter and error made by the speaker, as the reading back of the transcript will be used to determine which sections will make it into the final programme. If a sentence is full of false starts, 'ums' and 'errs', it wouldn't be usable. These are things you need to know when reading through the transcription. Of course, as we were trying to keep costs down, it fell to me to slog through it all. At the end of the day it was no bad thing as it gave a feel for aspects of a production you can only learn and appreciate by actually doing them yourself.

Something that is critical for any programme is a strong and interesting opening, otherwise people will just turn off. The way we decided to go was to compare the dangerous aspects of breathing underwater to that of astronauts in space. Images of divers and astronauts are always visually strong and tend to grab people's attention. If we could hook them with this, we could then move on to explaining the concept of having to breathe to stay alive, and that certain people relied on life-support equipment in order to carry out their everyday jobs. This in turn would lead into the mechanics of breathing and the necessity of oxygen to stay alive.

Since too much theory too early on could be potentially off-putting, we had to try to make it interesting. It was decided to use an athlete, both above and below water, to show the breathing process needed in someone taking exertion to the extreme. For our star I was fortunate to have to look no further than Phil Barthropp. Phil was obviously qualified from a diving point of view, but he was also an international hurdler in his own right and had run for England on many occasions.

The sequence started at night at a running track in Battersea in South London. Phil ran a hundred metres straight towards the camera, breathing heavily. We would then mix to a sequence of shots of Phil in the same running kit, but underwater. He would act as though he was breathing heavily with no discernible air supply, to make the point that air is required underwater.

This was filmed in a small blacked-out swimming pool, which was lit to show Phil against a black background and would therefore mix with the material shot at night at the running track. When finally cut together in slow motion, it proved to be an eye-catching, if not slightly surreal opening, which hopefully made people want to watch more of the programme to at least find out what it was all about.

With the opening complete, it was on to the most exciting part of the shoot, and the one that, in all honesty, was what had made me want to make the programme in the first place.

In Stuart's pursuit of his rebreather gas control system, he had looked at all potential applications for the equipment, both from the point of view of sales and also sponsors, to help move past the advanced prototype stage. This included organisations such as Disney, for use in their exhibits at Epcot and other theme parks, and what must be seen as the ultimate technical backer, the space programme and NASA.

You might ask what NASA would want with an underwater breathing system, but its uses could effectively be twofold.

Ultimately, Stuart would like to see his gas control equipment at the heart of the life-support systems on any potential missions to Mars, but for now it could be a useful tool to be used by the support divers at the Neutral Buoyancy Simulators (NBS) at the Houston and Marshall Space Flight Centres.

The NBS at Marshall was a massive water tank, seventy-five feet across and forty feet deep, built above ground and housed in its own support building. It held 1.3 million gallons of water, all heated to 90°F/32°C.

Some years after making the documentary, the Marshall facility closed down, making the larger rectangular tank at Houston the sole facility of its kind at NASA's disposal.

The NBS is required because all hands-on training for space missions takes place underwater. This is the only realistic way zero G can be simulated on Earth when you require large complex backdrops, such as the shuttle's cargo bay and mock-up satellites.

A more accurate experience of zero G is possible on board the aptly named Vomit Comet, a specially adapted aircraft that carries out a series of parabolic curves, putting its occupants into effective weightlessness when it dives towards the Earth. The dramatic results of this can be seen in the zero G sequences in *Apollo 13* with Tom Hanks, and *The Mummy* with Tom Cruise - both of which used this sort of aircraft for filming. However, the plane is in no way large enough, or able to provide the duration – only about thirty seconds at a time – required for lengthy and complex space mission simulations.

The reason NASA was considering the use of Stuart's rebreathers for the safety divers, and ultimately the 'suited subjects', as the astronauts in the tank were known, was because every underwater operation was monitored by an array of video cameras mounted both on the walls of the tank and also operated by free-swimming divers. These cameras recorded the close-up detail of the astronaut's actions for later analysis. This allowed them to check and recheck every procedure to ensure they had covered every possible contingency before the astronauts had to perform the tasks in orbit. The problem with using conventional SCUBA was that the exhaust bubbles from all the divers could obscure the cameras, and also the dive teams had to frequently change over because they were running low on gas and the decompression requirement was such that they needed a break. Since the trials could often go on for hours at a time, this was highly inefficient, particularly as the astronauts had an umbilical to provide the gas supply and could stay down far longer. The umbilical reduced the zero G simulation, so would be another area where replacement by a rebreather would be highly desirable.

We were hopefully going to be able to see how Stuart was getting on persuading NASA to buy his kit. It was certainly a long way from a garage in Cambridge and made a great arc for the story.

The NASA sequence was clearly a key element of the whole programme, and we were keen to make sure this aspect of the story was shown in full. There were times though where the whole trip looked highly precarious.

Everything, of course, had to go through Stuart. It was his story after all and his contacts, and we didn't want to jeopardise in any way his chances of sponsorship and commitment from the potential clients he was dealing with just because we wanted to make a TV programme. Not everyone is happy with a camera stuck in their face, even though there is the attendant publicity. The first to fall by the wayside was Disney, as they placed too many restrictions on what and how we could film. This wasn't too much of a blow though, as we were really focused on NASA.

The early signs were encouraging. In fact, NASA are normally extremely keen for any publicity, as the more their operations are seen in the public eye, the more acceptance there is for them and the more funding they will eventually receive from Congress. As the saying goes, 'No bucks – no Buck Rogers!' So as long as they weren't presented in a negative light, it looked like there would be every possibility for us to film there.

After some initial groundwork by Stuart, he passed me over to Steve Roy at the Marshall Space Flight Center to go through the procedure. Steve couldn't have been more helpful, though there were a number of things to be sorted out and okayed, particularly if they were going to let me dive and shoot in the NBS, which after all was the main purpose of the trip.

The first thing was that they wouldn't accept any of my professional diving and instructor qualifications, other than to note that I could at least dive. I would have to go through an assessment process when I reached the tank and also undergo a rigorous US Navy pilot's medical before they would even entertain me entering the water. Quite why they needed me to be fit for aerial combat I have no idea. I wasn't exactly going up in the shuttle!

The medical included everything from having your teeth checked to a full-blown AIDS test. Waiting for the results of the latter was rather nerve-wracking, even though I had no reason to think there would be a problem. Fortunately I passed with no issues, and the first hurdle was out of the way.

The other concerns related to general vetting for their databases and going over a breakdown of what exactly we wanted to film.

With this sorted, the next stop was the US Embassy in London to secure an American work visa.

Despite the official nature of our film and the acceptance from NASA, there was no guarantee of us receiving a visa. We had heard numerous horror stories of permits being denied for the simplest of reasons, so again it was a tense time while we waited for the US officials to decide our fate. When it finally came through, it started to look as though it was all going to happen.

For budgetary reasons, it wasn't possible to take a full crew to the States. At the end of the day, the most important aspect of the trip was to see the rebreathers in action, working with the camera teams and astronauts underwater, so the surface shots weren't hugely critical, though obviously the more we could shoot the better. So it was only Martyn and I, with a semi-pro Hi8 camera and Amphibico housing that made the trip. We also took dive gear for use in the tank and a small steadicam for the Hi8, which would allow greater freedom of movement when shooting above the water and hopefully produce professional-looking tracking shots around the facility with the use of minimum equipment and personnel.

One other thing we were waiting on was a possible injection of funds from West Country TV, who had said they might contribute around ten per cent of the budget in order to be able to show the programme first on terrestrial television. Their interest lay in the fact that Stuart was testing the rebreathers with Oceanic, a US diving equipment manufacturer whose UK HQ was based near Honiton in Devon. The aim was that eventually Oceanic would manufacture the rebreather, now known as the Phibian, and would also train divers in its use at a purpose-built, thirty-foot-deep tank at their facility.

If we received this extra funding there would be the option of hiring a Betacam cameraman out in the States to shoot some background shots and interviews around the NBS and the Marshall Space Flight Center. This would help considerably, but we would have to wait for a definite, final response.

One thing that did help with the budget was NASA's notorious generosity with archive footage. You might have thought that to get hold of space footage for commercial use in a TV programme would be prohibitively expensive, but on the contrary. In keeping with their promotional policy, NASA were only too happy to let us have any footage we wanted for free, which would of course add hugely to the production value of the programme. Things were starting to look up.

So in August of that year Martyn and I set off for Miami. A quick change of aircraft and a short hour's flight later found us in Huntsville, Alabama, the home of the Marshall Space Flight Center.

On arrival you certainly knew you were in Spaceville, USA. The whole airport terminal was full of giant space posters and models of rockets and shuttles suspended from the ceiling, making the place look like a giant toy shop, and a foretaste of the real thing to come.

Huntsville itself had built up around the space programme and virtually all employment in the area came from NASA and the related industries that supported it.

We were staying at the same motel on the outskirts of town as Stuart and one of his colleagues, Dudley Crosson, and we had arranged to meet them there shortly after our arrival. Dudley was helping Stuart develop the interaction control systems for the rebreathers. He also worked extensively for NASA in the field of 'human factors', or the way in which humans interact with technology.

We had barely dropped our bags down at reception

when Stuart and Dudley walked in, looking slightly the worse for wear. This was in stark contrast to our unrestrained enthusiasm and excitement.

Our bubble was about to be well and truly burst.

There had obviously been quite a few long and sleepless nights during the previous week, as both Stuart and Dudley looked completely drained. Dudley was a slightly built, bald-headed guy in his mid thirties, quietly spoken and clearly brilliant in his field, but his first words weren't that brilliant to us.

'Hi, guys, nice to meet you. Problem is, they may not let you in. They're pretty touchy at the moment and things are fairly fraught over there.'

'Stunned' was probably not quite the word for it. There are moments in life where one is left completely speechless and this was one of them. It is probably difficult to grasp the enormity of what Dudley had just said, but leaving aside the disappointment of possibly not being able to dive with the astronauts, we had committed a significant portion of the budget to coming over here and shooting the scenes at NASA. Probably one of the reasons we sold the idea to Discovery in the first place was the prospect of all that high-impact NASA footage.

In short, if we couldn't get to dive in the NBS, we were screwed - creatively, visually and financially.

At the time we were also fairly exhausted from the flight and the adrenaline was still running from the pent-up excitement. I believe a few expletives were muttered before Stuart stepped in to say that nothing was definite.

If I had been alert enough to put things into perspective I probably wouldn't have worried so much. After all, we had the invite from Steve Roy, and I had my US Navy pilot's medical, but people could always change their minds, and there would be nothing we could do about it if they did.

Fortunately, Stuart defused the situation by suggesting we all go up there the following day, meet up with Steve and see where the land lay.

While we were mulling over this new situation, the receptionist handed us a fax that had arrived while we were in transit.

More bad news?

It turned out to be from Discovery, confirming the extra money from West Country TV. We could go ahead and hire a cameraman. We had to laugh – we might not have anything to film.

The next day we woke rested, refreshed, and better prepared to face the problems and challenges before us. If nothing else, we were going to look round one of NASA's premiere space facilities. The trip would have been worth it for that alone.

We followed Stuart and Dudley north from Huntsville and had our first peek into the world of all things space, in the form of the Huntsville Space Park, where, amongst other space memorabilia, there was the only full-size mock up of the space shuttle, boosters, fuel tank and all. It dominated the landscape at the side of the freeway, and as we approached, the hairs on the back of my neck started to stand on end. As a kid, when everyone else had wanted to drive fire engines, aside from my desire to go underwater, I had always wanted to go into space – this was about as close as I was ever going to get.

Alongside the park was one of America's space camps. Here, kids in American schools from the 4th to the 12th

Grade could take part in what can only be described as kid heaven.

Courses are run in all aspects of space exploration, from an introduction, which includes space sciences, astronaut training, propulsion exercises and a NASA tour, all the way up to US Space Academy levels, which, over five days, includes everything from intense astronaut and mission training academies, and a simulated mission to the space station, through to engineering, technology and aerospace studies.

The aim of the whole exercise is unashamedly clear – to get kids hooked on space at an early age and to encourage them to become the astronauts and technicians of tomorrow - or, no doubt, should they stray into the political arena, to ensure funding remains on track for NASA in the future.

Before we knew it, we were following Stuart off the main highway, through a belt of pine trees and up to a security gate. We had arrived at the Redstone Arsenal, where the Marshall Space Flight Center was located.

The Redstone Arsenal was a massive area of over a thousand acres, with one of the longest runways in the world. Here, America tested many of its rockets and missiles against potential enemy hardware, such as tanks and aircraft, which were flown in on massive transports onto the huge runway.

Nearby were vast facilities belonging to Boeing, and of course the Space Flight Center itself.

It was here that NASA's main rocket propulsion systems were designed. These ranged from the original Redstone rocket, developed by Werner Von Braun after the Second World War, and in which America took its first tentative steps into space, all the way through to the giant Saturn V, built to take man to the Moon, as well as the engines for the space shuttle. The Center was also responsible for the design and construction of the lunar rovers, and at the time we were there, many of the components of the soon-to-be-launched International Space Station were being assembled before shipping to Cape Canaveral for launch into orbit.

It was into this legacy of America's space history that we were travelling and it was truly impressive. As we pulled up to the main building, I had to pinch myself that we were actually there, and it was a wrench to start acting like a professional director of a TV programme and not some starry-eyed teenager who had just been given the keys to the kingdom.

The potentially disastrous meeting with Steve Roy went off without a hitch, and he couldn't have been more helpful and encouraging. So, after big sighs of relief and receiving our NASA passes, it was time to head down to the NBS and a procedural briefing from its staff.

The trip through Marshall was an eye-opener at every corner. The first thing I noticed were the large boulevards between the main buildings, all with names like Mercury Road and Gemini Avenue, which reminded me of Pinewood Studios, which has the equally impressive 007 Drive and Goldfinger Avenue. Also, throughout the complex, massive silver tubes ran along the side of, and over, the roads and disappeared into most of the buildings.

What were they? I wondered. Some form of sophisticated exhaust system for the rocket engine tests? Some new form of material design in the advanced test stage?

No, it was a steam heating system.

One of the world's most sophisticated technical facilities ran on steam!

Once we had got over that shock we turned right into Mercury Road and past Marshall's own Rocket Park. Here was a collection of just some of the rockets that had been developed at the Center over the years, and an impressive array it was too, all with their sleek silver nose cones pointing skywards, as though they would give anything to be free of their earthly tethers and fly as they had originally been designed to.

All too quickly we were past them and pulling up at a large grey shed with massive twin sliding doors. It must have been all of a hundred feet high, and the doors resembled a smaller version of the huge Vehicle Assembly Building at Cape Canaveral.

Behind the currently open doors was an enormous circular grey structure, over sixty feet high, with what looked like three rows of portholes around the side at different heights. This was the Neutral Buoyancy Simulator.

We went inside with permanent cricks in our necks from staring up at the massive tank in which I'd soon be diving.

The interior of the building housed your usual range of offices and technical rooms, like any conventional facility, the difference here being that everything was designed to fit around the massive circular tank in the centre.

Our first duty was to meet Dave Romero from Oceaneering, who operated the tank and was responsible for the tests and trials that went on inside. Dave was a very cool, laid-back American with a slow drawl that made you wonder if he was ever going to get to the end of a sentence, but with a lot going on upstairs. Again, he couldn't have been more accommodating, and our earlier concerns quickly vanished as we started to feel welcome at the facility.

Next it was on to see the resident doctor to have my medical inspected and be asked some rather pertinent questions. Then it was time to meet up with the dive team and go through the protocol for general safety procedures that had to be strictly adhered to while in the tank.

One thing I found slightly odd was that after checking over my qualifications and making sure I had the requisite form signed by the doc, the head of diving said that I would be unable to use a buoyancy compensator (BC) in the tank. To me this was the craziest thing I had ever heard. No diver should go into the water without a BC. It controls your buoyancy and makes things easier and safer in an emergency. The logic explained to me seemed rather bizarre.

The first part of the explanation was reasonable enough – since the water in the NBS was so warm, you didn't need a wetsuit; this would mean if you weighted yourself correctly at the beginning of the dive you wouldn't need to change your buoyancy throughout the depth range of the tank, therefore no need for a BC.

This is true up to a point. There is some buoyancy change during a dive from the reduction of gas in your cylinder, but this is minimised if using steel tanks. However, the second reason for disallowing BCs seemed completely off the wall. It was explained that the safety divers had to be able to bring up the astronauts immediately if there was a problem with their suits, i.e. they started leaking. So, if your BC failed, you wouldn't be able to rely on it to bring the astronaut back to the surface.

While this is true, the chances of your BC failing are pretty remote, and surely, having the ability to use the buoyancy in the jacket to help bring an astronaut up would facilitate getting him/her to the surface even quicker. Also, as there were always many divers in the water, even if you let go of the subject there would always be others to immediately help out. I wasn't altogether too sure about this policy.

After much discussion and insistence on my part that I really needed a jacket to help stabilise me while filming, I was given a concession. However, I would have to have both my jacket and regulator checked out and certified by a local dive store. This would mean an extra trip into Hunstville, and the expense, but I guess we were playing in their sandpit so we'd have to stick to their rules.

The rigidity in the way they followed safety procedures was also made clear when we were shown their own weather station at the complex. Since Alabama was prone to massive thunderstorms, sometimes even hurricanes, there were frequent lightning strikes in the area. Their weather radar monitored these storms and strikes. If there was a strike within ten miles of the facility everyone was immediately brought out of the water and the NBS was shut down. If a lightning strike actually hit the building, the facility was shut down for several months so that every system could be checked and double-checked. After all, there are no second chances in space, as was so tragically demonstrated with the *Challenger* and *Columbia* shuttle disasters.

Once we had made our introductions and worked out who everyone was, we had to leave to sort out the dive gear certification. On our return, it was time for the first dive.

When you stepped out of the small lift at the top of the tank, it initially looked like a large circular swimming pool, but as you approached the edge, you realised the depth and sheer scale of the structure. The water was totally, and I mean totally, transparent. I have never seen water this clear, and there in the middle, forty feet down, was a full-size mock-up of the shuttle's cargo bay, complete with robot arm and mock-up entry/exit airlock for extra vehicular activities (EVA).

It was truly awesome.

With my newly certified BC and regulator, and the camera and housing checked out, it was time to enter the water. Those initial dives were a chance to make sure all the gear worked properly and to get an idea of what the tank was like from beneath the surface and to work out the potential shots I needed to get.

The trials Stuart was running with the rebreathers had a number of objectives: to acquaint the NASA dive teams with the equipment's capability; to cover the set-up, use and maintenance of the units; and to dive them with an astronaut in the water, so Oceaneering could assess the benefit of divers without bubbles.

It was effectively a glorified training course.

Once Stuart was in the water with his first batch of trainees, I accompanied them out into the middle of the tank.

I can safely say that the only other time I have felt I was

diving in outer space was in the gin-clear caves of the blue holes in the Bahamas, where the water was so clear, with zero water movement above, that you felt you weren't in water at all.

Here, there was a surface above, but it was completely flat, enabling you to see right up through to the skylight above, and there was so little particulate matter in the 1.3 million gallons, dare I say none, that you truly felt as though you were flying. And as the trainees were using rebreathers - no bubbles - it really did appear as though they were moving through a void and were truly weightless.

After the first dive, I checked the footage and was amazed at the quality. Hi8, although not a full professional format, was at that time acceptable for specialist filming. Even so, using a Sony three-chip camera and filter in the Amphibico housing in that clarity of water produced some amazing results. It was at this point we knew we had the footage to make a great section of the programme. We now just had to shoot the sequences and interviews to tell the story.

The next couple of days were spent on the more technical aspects of Stuart training the divers, and on interviewing the guys at the NBS to see how the rebreathers would help them in the trials they conducted there. They all seemed pretty impressed with the units, which meant that Stuart could well be on his way to a lucrative contract. We all went back to the motel that night in buoyant mood.

In the US there is a channel devoted to NASA material, which shows live, unedited missions as they happen. It just so happened that on the STS-69 shuttle mission that was up at the time, one of Dudley's best friends, Mike Gernhardt, was making his first ever spacewalk. We spent the rest of the evening glued to the TV watching one of exploration's greatest images – Man walking in space. It was all the more riveting as I had been swimming in the shuttle's cargo bay earlier that day.

The next few days brought more dives in the NBS, and it soon became almost routine to be diving at NASA, but so far all the dives had just been with the divers using the rebreathers - the really interesting visuals would be with an astronaut underwater.

As the normal trials conducted in the tank related to upcoming missions, unless one was going to happen, there wasn't much going on in the tank. If we had been there a few weeks later we would have seen a full-size mock-up of the Hubble Space Telescope in the water, ready for the major repair mission that was sent up in 1999.

Our next filming duty was to interview Dudley to discuss his involvement with Stuart. As we were looking for different locations to shoot the interviews in, and as Dudley dealt with human factors, i.e. interaction with hardware, where better than the suit room? This was a small storeroom cum office that housed all the spacesuits used in the tank. Most of them were fairly well used and abused but they were honest-to-god spacesuits. When Dudley first opened the door, the sight was slightly surreal. There was a row of spacesuits hanging up like a row of suits in a wardrobe. It was like opening the bat cave and seeing a row of batsuits to take your pick from. To complete the effect, there was a row of helmets on the shelf above.

Later in the day, Martyn and I followed up on our

request for library footage and were given directions to the archive building. They seemed pretty simple as we read them out, but it was all very well saying, go to the grey building on the left, turn left past four grey buildings and it's the grey building on your right behind the other grey building. After the umpteenth grey building had been passed, we got a bit confused. We finally ended up at a grey building with a door slightly ajar. It was as close to the directions as we could work out, so we pulled the door open and walked inside.

We were met by banks of supercomputers arranged in rows and about the height of an average man. Some had panels on them with numerous buttons and dials. We almost expected the word 'Hal' to shine in dull red tones from the displays, but there was no calming monotone voice, just an earnest hum in the background. This certainly didn't look like the library archive to me, but there was bound to be someone here who could direct us to the correct grey building.

We had made it halfway down one of the long aisles between the computers when a technician in a lab coat glanced up, and with an alarmed look on his face, he demanded to know who we were and what we were doing there. We were a bit put out at his slightly aggressive manner, and as he herded us back towards the door, we explained our dilemma. He still looked suspicious, but pointed out where we should be headed. As we left, we asked why there was such an urgency to remove us from the building. Once we had heard the explanation we could see that he had a point. The computers we had been casually strolling past were controlling the shuttle mission in orbit two hundred and fifty miles above our heads.

Good job I never pressed that red button – Mike Gernhardt could have had a very bad day!

Towards the end or our stay at Marshall, we had a rare day off, so we did the tourist thing and took the public tour of Marshall and spent time at the Space Park, where they had the full-size mock-up of the shuttle. They also had an unused Saturn V laid out on the ground, and when you stand next to the massive rocket motors, which laid on their side stand higher than your average house, you realise these guys weren't kidding around when they decided to go to the Moon.

Back at the Center there was also the chance to see some of the initial components of the International Space Station being assembled. This included Node 1, which formed the hub to which all the initial modules would be attached. The next time I saw this rather awkward, square-shaped structure was on Sky News as it was being manoeuvred into orbit out of the shuttle's cargo bay.

Speaking of which, we had one last task before we headed back to the UK and the other more mundane, but just as important, aspects of the documentary - a dive in the NBS with a suited subject.

Unfortunately it wasn't an astronaut on a vital training mission, merely one of the technicians doing laps of the cargo bay to test out a nitrox mix they were experimenting with, but it really didn't matter. It was the fact that we were swimming with a real space suit on a full-size mock-up of the shuttle that made the visuals so important. It also gave us the opportunity to see Stuart's rebreathers in action for their intended purpose – to relieve the cameras of the obstruction caused by the bubbles. Afterwards, we would be able to interview Dave

Romano on his views of the gear and hopefully have some positive news for Stuart.

Before I could jump in the water though, the technician had to be suited up. If you thought getting into your dive gear was a struggle – this was on a whole different level.

The planning and preparation just to put one guy in the water was impressive. Two technicians oversaw the dressing procedure, starting with an all-in-one undersuit. Next came life-support equipment that had to be plumbed into the suit. This was followed by the oversuit, which was in two halves - top and bottom - which were clamped together at the waist. Finally there were gloves and the helmet, which were connected to locking rings on the main suit. Once fully kitted, the numerous safety checks could begin. These covered life-support, leaks, comms, and the numerous procedures and technical aspects of the dive itself.

During the whole procedure the technician was attached to a swivelling lift that ultimately lowered him into the water. The suit's backpack, which was normally the astronaut's life-support system in space, was in this case merely a mock-up, as the suited subject was connected by an umbilical to the control centre, which monitored and fed the gas supply.

When all the checks were complete, the subject was swivelled round and lowered gently into the water. Once submerged, he was fairly helpless, so two support divers manhandled him down to a depth of around ten feet. Here they placed small amounts of lead into numerous strategically placed pockets all over the suit to try to ensure he was completely neutrally buoyant and as close to weightless as possible.

After around ten minutes, they gave him the OK and started the descent to the cargo bay. Since the suited subject wore no fins, he was basically helpless until he could grab hold of something and pull himself around with his hands. To this end, there were at least two divers in contact with him at all times he wasn't attached to something solid, and even then they were never far away.

Throughout the dive the technician was in comms talkback with dive control. This conversation could be heard over what has to be the clearest underwater PA system I have ever heard. I've worked with many a system in the past and most of them sound like a radio channel that is not quite tuned properly, but this was almost like a top-end hi-fi for clarity and definition. It allowed any divers in the water to be kept abreast of what was going on and to be instructed by mission control to do anything that was required for the trial. It was quite weird hearing someone talk to you as though you weren't actually underwater, and you kept looking behind yourself every now and then to see who was making the announcement.

The trials being conducted were pretty straightforward, but visually impressive nonetheless. The suited subject would simply do laps of the cargo bay breathing the new nitrox mix to see how he performed. All telemetry would be recorded in mission control, which showed images from all the cameras in the tank.

I was limited by how close I was allowed to go to the subject, but with the images so crystal clear in the water I just had to get in as close as I could – an action reined in every so often by the voice of God booming round the pool suggesting I ease off a little.

Having breathed my way through one tank of air, I

quickly changed cylinders and dropped back in to finish off the roll of tape. But all too soon that was finished as well. All I needed now were some close-up 35mm stills, but as I was about to climb back in, the trial was called to an end and I would just have to wait until the following day – but that was going to prove to be a problem. The following evening we were flying to Miami to catch the flight back to the UK. As flying and diving don't mix, I couldn't risk going under pressure, particularly with a transatlantic flight following so soon.

Stuart offered to put me on an oxygen-rich dive using nitrox and give me pure oxygen to breathe afterward, but I couldn't take the chance.

There are times when you just have to know when to say 'no'.

So it was with reluctance that the final day was free of diving, but we headed home knowing we had done all we could to enhance the status of the programme and the trip had provided more than we could ever have hoped for.

With the key material from NASA in the can and a veritable library of archive footage to use, the next location was Oceanic in Honiton. Here we would interview Kelvin Richards, the managing director, about the current sponsorship and development of the rebreather from a commercial and manufacturing point of view.

Oceanic were the manufacturers of reliable, solid dive gear and also innovators on many levels, including dive computers, drysuits, regulators and BCs, so it was no surprise to find they were interested in helping develop this new technology and be one of the first onto the market with what effectively had the potential to be the

Rolls-Royce of rebreathers.

When we started shooting the documentary, Stuart was at the advanced prototype stage with the units, but there were still technical and end-user problems to solve to make it commercially viable. It was all very well having this fantastic piece of kit, but you had to get the public to buy it in large numbers or else there was no point in the investment in the first place. Stuart's philosophy had always been science first, and from his point of view, as the inventor, that was fair enough, but you still needed money to develop your inventions and that financial backing had to be paid back with long-term sales.

One of the key things concerning Kelvin was the sheer size of the unit. In its current form it was proving to be a problem for smaller users. This was one aspect we would see, all too clearly, at the session we had come down to Oceanic to film.

A course had been arranged to give experienced divers the opportunity to learn about the concept of rebreathers and the specific advantages of Stuart's system over some of the others that were about to come on the market. There would be a theory session, followed by a hands-on preparation and maintenance session, then a chance to dive with the units in Oceanic's thirty-foot-deep tank, nicely heated to 85°F/29°C.

It would be interesting to hear their responses to the kit, as these were the potential clients of the future.

It turned out that most really liked it and they all seemed to quickly see its advantages, as well as some of its quirks, such as the lack of up/down movement during the breathing cycle and the relative quiet without bubbles streaming past your face every few seconds. One aspect the decidedly British divers picked up on was the temperature of the gas breathed, which is significantly warmer than usual since it has been through the body several times. This is a big plus when diving in UK waters as a large amount of body heat can be lost through the exhaled air, which is normally expelled into the water.

Overall, the impressions seemed to be favourable. One of the main stumbling blocks though was the likely cost - several thousand pounds. Also, the point was made that it would be difficult to take on an aircraft, due to its bulk and weight and the need to carry high-pressure cylinders. And finally, the size issue was graphically shown by one of the smaller, female divers, who could hardly keep it on her back as she struggled out of the water at the end of her session. All in all, though, a successful demonstration, but one that had highlighted the pros and cons all too clearly.

The next major test would be at DIVE '95, an international diving show at the NEC in Birmingham. This was an annual event where divers from all over the world came together to discuss all aspects of the sport, from basic training to advanced technical diving. There would also be a number of the new, competing rebreathers from different manufacturers on show for the first time.

The show would provide us with an opportunity to interview many of the people who had been instrumental in helping Stuart progress to where he was today.

I already knew a number of those we would be talking to, such as Rob Palmer, and Kevin Gurr, a highly experienced technical diver who was also working in the development and use of rebreathers with a company called Cis-Lunar.

There was also Christian Schultz from Dräger, one of the world's oldest diving equipment companies, and someone who Stuart had received technical help from at an early stage of development. Dräger were in the process of launching their own rebreather, albeit a semi-closed model called the *Atlantis*. It was clear there was a certain rivalry between the two camps, but certainly no hostility.

The difference between a semi-closed and fully closed rebreather, such as Stuart's, is that in a semi-closed system some gas is vented from the unit during the dive, and the gas breathed is a nitrox mixture, rather than being able to use helium. It therefore doesn't have the depth/duration performance of a fully closed system, but it's still a step up from a basic aqualung.

We also spoke to Chris Allen, at the time, chairman of the British Sub-Aqua Club, to hear his opinion on the future of diving and how the rebreather would play a part. There were also some interesting views on the use of rebreathers in the commercial field from Ralph Mavin of the Health and Safety Executive. The whole weekend proved to be highly productive, providing some important views and statements from key people in the diving world.

It was shortly after this shoot, just as we were heading for the home straight on the production phase of the programme, that we received some devastating news from Discovery.

The money that had been confirmed from West Country TV – wasn't confirmed any more.

No specific explanation was given, but whatever the reason it left us with an extreme dilemma. When we had been informed we had the money, we had spent a portion of the budget on the surface cameraman in the States. We now didn't have enough money to shoot what was ultimately, from a technical point of view, the most crucial part of the programme, Stuart re-enacting his test trials in the recompression chambers at Fort Bovisand. This would form the central section of the programme, linking the history of the development with where he was present day.

We were in big trouble.

The bottom line was that we couldn't finish the programme without the Bovisand sequence, and we couldn't film the Bovisand sequence without the extra cash. After a number of somewhat frank phone conversations, I think Discovery finally realised they weren't going to get a completed programme unless they found some extra finance.

The amount we eventually received allowed us to complete the filming, but it wasn't as much as had originally been promised, so some creative thought had to go into which other sections would have to be dropped. The piece that eventually had to go was an interview with Jack Kelly, a key figure in the finance of Stuart's development programme. Jack was an American entrepreneur who had bankrolled Stuart for a number of years. His background was as an architect, and he had been responsible for a number of the tallest buildings in America. He now spent his time, amongst other things, dallying in projects that took his fancy. Since he was a keen diver, Stuart's work was right up his street. Unfortunately, as he was based in Texas, even the travelling expenses would have been beyond us at this point. In fact, just to finish the sequences we couldn't do without, it was a case of more overtime for free. But once you get so far into a project, you have to do whatever you can to stop the whole thing unravelling when things start to go wrong.

The key sequence we still needed was at Bovisand in Plymouth. I looked forward to returning there after so many years. I knew Commander Alan Bax, who still ran the centre, as well as a number of the other divers who worked there.

The facility we would be filming at was the Diving Diseases Research Centre (DDRC) that, at the time, was based at Bovisand. DDRC was run by the inimitable Dr Maurice Cross, who had been there when I had originally worked as an instructor in my university days, and who had struck the fear of God into all young divers as he patrolled the eerie underground stone corridors in search of victims to stab a syringe into for blood samples for medical research. Now, though, Maurice had come above ground to run what was one of the most respected diving medical research centres in the world, and which has since taken up residence at Derriford Hospital on the outskirts of Plymouth.

Here, most of the diving injuries on the south coast were treated, as well as ongoing research into diving illnesses and treatment. This was the reason Stuart had gone to the DDRC in the first place. The chambers allowed him to test his equipment under pressure and in comparative safety.

Due to the lack of funds, Stuart had had to test everything on himself, and the staff had allowed him to try things that were perhaps less than conventional, always knowing he was in good hands should anything go wrong.

He was trying to create a whole diving system, from decompression tables and protocols to the software for the dive computers, and finally the hardware that operated it – a very ambitious task and one that had taken its toll over the years financially.

However, when we arrived to re-enact some of the trials, Maurice, as ever, was only too happy to have someone to stick his needles into. I think he also took a perverse pleasure in watching Stuart slog away on a treadmill and exercise bike in the chamber wearing full rebreather kit.

The re-enactment was a very powerful sequence, as you suddenly started to realise the sheer physical effort Stuart had put into his dream, and just how much he had sacrificed to achieve it.

With a final revealing and affectionate interview with Maurice, we had all the footage we needed to complete the programme. It was now just a case of putting it all together, or as it is commonly known, the post-production or editing stage of the process.

Editing is where a programme is won or lost. It's where you see if all those ideas you had actually work. Hopefully, if you have done your job right, they will, as you will have planned the edit as you were writing the script and shooting the footage.

You will often hear an editor complain that a sequence 'won't cut'. What he means is there isn't enough footage to be able to tell the story the sequence is trying to tell. That doesn't mean that the action hasn't been shot, but it does mean there are not the right camera angles to be able to smoothly and dramatically tell the story. You can't stick two shots together if they don't flow properly, or if the action between the shots is mistimed. You ensure this doesn't happen by having good 'coverage'. This means shooting the same thing from a number of different angles, which will also allow you to speed up or slow down the pace of a sequence by cutting in shorter or longer shots to condense or stretch the action on the screen. This can only be done if the continuity of the shots works. This means that if you have someone picking up a glass in a smooth movement, you could extend the shot by showing it from a couple of different angles, but in all the angles the fingers holding the glass must be in the same position, otherwise they will appear to jump suddenly in the picture when the sequence is played back. In other words, continuity has to be checked for every shot you want to join to another one.

The first place to start in an edit is with those tedious transcripts of the interviews. Now is the time you realise just how important they are. The easiest way to approach things is to write down every single shot, even if you did it several times, and write the time-code recorded on the tape next to each shot. Also, a description of how good an individual shot is will allow you to pick out the best take in a group of similar takes later on.

With this full list you can then do a 'paper' edit of the entire programme. This means watching all the shots, picking out the ones you want to cut together in sequence and then writing the time-codes of these shots down on paper. If you do this carefully you can have a fairly accurate cut of the whole programme before you even go into an edit suite, which may be costing you hundreds of pounds a day.

The physical act of editing has changed over the years.

In the old days everything was of course done on film, where the film itself was physically cut and spliced together with the next piece in line. Then, with videotape, editing would involve each shot being copied onto a new bit of tape in sequence, and the programme built up from there. The problem with that was that if you made a mistake it could be awfully time-consuming to put things right.

These days virtually all editing is carried out on a non-linear system on a computer. This means you can decide to work on any part of the programme at any time – nothing needs to be done in order. At the time of the shoot, we were using videotape. This had to be 'digitised' into a computer, and once on the hard disc, it exists, just like any other data, as a series of ones and zeros, so it can be manipulated just like any other data. In other words, you can cut and paste video and sound like words in a word processor. This totally frees the editor to try new and interesting ideas without wasting too much time. It also means that if the 'paper' edit was done correctly, all the time-code information from that edit can be typed into an edit decision list (EDL). If this time-code information includes data relating to the tape it came from, the computer can pick out all the shots from any number of tapes and put them in sequence onto what is known as a timeline, all automatically – instant programme.

Okay, it's not quite that simple, but that's the principle. Once all the data is on the timeline, you can then refine and pace the whole programme, adding transitions, graphics, music and voice-over.

Nowadays, of course, everything is digital from the get-go, with all data being recorded onto SD cards or such like, so the 'digitising' stage is bypassed and the whole transfer from camera to computer is faster and more efficient.

When it came time to choose someone to do the narration I went cap in hand to Lawrence McGinty to see if he would help us out. There were two reasons for this. First, being the science editor for ITN, Lawrence could easily get his head around all the scientific aspects of the programme and would add an air of legitimacy to things; and second, I felt that given our previous work together he might be amenable with regard to his rates so that they wouldn't be too hard on our rapidly diminishing budget!

After working through a number of versions, we showed the final low-res cut to Chris Haws at Discovery. Fortunately, he was extremely pleased. The transmission date was just over a week away and I started to relax.

A dangerous thing to do.

Just when you think it's all in the bag, something comes up and bites you – well two things actually.

The first was completely out of our control and it began with a phone call from a rather harassed Stuart, which started along the lines of: 'You can't show the programme!'

The reason for this cataclysmic statement was the result of legal wrangling behind the scenes that I had hardly been aware of. For various reasons, a disagreement between Stuart and Jack Kelly on one hand, and Oceanic on the other, had resulted, rather sadly, in a court battle that was due to take place any day in Los Angeles.

There was a feeling amongst the Stuart camp lawyers that if the programme was broadcast before any hearing it might influence certain parties, or show Stuart and Jack in a bad light. Now, at this point, neither Stuart nor any of his team had seen the completed edit, and for the life of me I couldn't think of anything that showed anyone in a bad light – but they were somewhat concerned.

Fortunately, after a couple of calming phone calls, explaining there were no sensitive components to the programme, that particular catastrophe was averted. At the end of the day, it was unlikely they could have stopped the programme being shown, but it put me in a particularly difficult position having got to know and like Stuart throughout the duration of the shoot on the one hand and my obligations to Discovery on the other.

The second bombshell hit a day or so later. The wonders of non-linear editing systems are only equalled by the potentially catastrophic problems they can cause when they want to. In this case, our electronic friend decided to lose all the video footage on the hard drives – which basically meant the entire programme was wiped clean – five days before transmission, and before we had finalised the high-res version of the programme.

Time to take a deep breath.

Fortunately, what had not been lost was the EDL, which meant the programme could be reconstituted from this magic list. What could not be reconstituted easily was every tweak, nuance and polish that Mike, the editor, and I had slaved over for hours on end to refine the final cut and make it as good as we could get it.

This meant we had a number of very late nights ahead of us. We managed to reassemble most of the pieces, but I will forever watch the programme knowing the numerous flaws and small errors that may not be noticeable to others but are glaringly obvious to me.

When the final transmission came though, it was quite something to sit watching a real-life presenter announcing your programme and seeing it go out – live! It was called *You Only Breathe Twice,* and it was transmitted in March 1996.

Even though you've seen the whole thing a thousand times before and are virtually sick of it, just to see the credits roll and know that it all came from an idea you had months previously made the whole adventure worthwhile.

In retrospect, it was an amazing learning experience, and considering the money we had available and the problems we had to overcome, particularly at the last minute, I think we managed a credible job and put the bucks on the screen, so to speak.

One of the best compliments I received came from a highly experienced technical diver I'd known for many years, who said that the explanation of how a rebreather worked was the best he'd ever seen.

Well, at least you can please some of the people some of the time!

13

Ad Break

Some of the most creative work in the industry can be seen in the area of advertising and commercials. These short-form pieces allow directors to truly stretch their creative muscles in search of different, innovative, and sometimes quite stunning pieces of work.

You may have seen one of the many TV shows dedicated to commercials over the years, and I'm sure we've all watched some of these with a sense of nostalgia for ads we may have seen growing up. It is quite remarkable how they can bring back feelings of childhood, or evoke a certain time, like almost nothing else.

And while on the surface these commercials may look fairly simple, a great deal of thought and talent has gone into making them. Some of our greatest visual directors have honed their skills in the world of advertising - Tony and Ridley Scott, Alan Parker, Zack Snyder, Michael Bay, Adrian Lyne, Guillermo del Torro, David Fincher, to name but a few. There is a certain discipline in being able to tell a story in thirty seconds or less, while at the same time being visually creative, which translates, in most cases, to efficient, competent moviemaking.

As has been described, my first foray into the industry was on the Mu-cron commercial with Tony Scott, and although it didn't register at the time, one story related by a crew member about another Scott-directed commercial summed up the lengths directors will go to to get the perfect shot.

It related to a Levi jeans ad, which was one of a series of commercials where the construction of the jeans was highlighted. This one concentrated on the stitching used when putting the jeans together. The comparison was made with the strength and integrity of fishing line used for Marlin fishing, and that the jeans were stitched together with material made of similar properties.

The story goes that Scott had a shot set up at some fabulous tropical location, the sun in just the right place, the perfect composition, and everyone ready, when a cruise liner steamed into frame and dropped anchor. Scott's response was to send one of the crew over to ask the captain to move his ship. Needless to say, the crew member returned with a somewhat negative and unrepeatable reply!

Given the thirst to create ever more attention-grabbing ads, it is no surprise that directors would look to the opportunities presented by shooting underwater. Here there is an immediate visual interest, as well as the possibility of having artists effectively weightless in this other-worldly environment. It is an area where a considerable amount of work has been done, some of it quite spectacular.

Probably one of the first and most memorable examples of this was a British Gas commercial shot by the innovative director Mike Portelly on a coral reef in the Red Sea. It featured a model, Lauren Heston, and a baby underwater.

The ad showed shots of the reef and the baby seemingly floating around happily a few feet beneath the surface. There was initially public concern at this, with the thought of the babies used in the shoot being forced underwater. In fact, the footage was presented in slow motion, so for any shots of the infants, they would only ever have been underwater for a few seconds at a time.

It is quite amazing how resilient and capable babies can be in the water, so much so that Lauren went on to start a school where parents could bring their infants along to introduce them to the water in the safe confines of a warm pool. If they can accept water at this age, it gives them confidence not to be frightened of it as they grow up, and it can also install an instinctive reaction as to what to do should they ever fall in.

One particularly memorable shoot I was involved in on the safety side of things was for Ricard, the liquorice-flavoured aperitif, and centred around a group of adventurous archaeologists searching for lost artefacts underwater.

The story involved a group of divers finding a Greek temple beneath the waves and a statue in a cave, which they subsequently raised using lifting bags. The statue was then hauled aboard their boat and all celebrated with a drink of Ricard to top off the success of the operation.

This could, of course, all be done in a studio tank with appropriate backdrops, but commercials are notorious for having large budgets, particularly as well-known companies are always trying to outdo each other.

So instead of a studio, we travelled back to my old hunting ground of Malta to film off the island of Gozo, and also Comino, where the underwater scenes for *Leviathan* had been shot.

As well as having to construct the whole temple as a set underwater, to create the look the director wanted of the statue being raised in a shaft of light shining down through the centre of a cave, a location on the west coast of Gozo known as the Blue Hole was used. This natural structure within the rock, around thirty-five feet in diameter, was covered with a scaffolding frame, followed by a large tarpaulin. A hole was cut in the centre of the tarpaulin for the light to shine through, and the divers then went through their paces in the water below. A lot of trouble you might think, but then the shots did look spectacular.

Of course, the finished product always looks slick and polished, but the viewer often has no idea of the work that went into creating it. In this case, we were working for about a week, made over fifty dives, and were in the water before sun up, out of the water after sundown, and only came out during the day to fill a cylinder or for a forty-five minute break for lunch.

Another inventive idea, which, like many, was inspired by those that had come before, was for a Cussons soap ad.

The concept was for a girl to be soaping herself down in a bath, and the roof of the bathroom appears to be a ceiling of water, which descends to completely cover her.

She then appears underwater, still happily washing herself.

The original idea came from the previously mentioned Luc Besson film *The Big Blue*. Here, the lead character Jacques Mayol is lying in bed having a nightmare. He sees the ceiling as a wall of water descending towards him, and it finally engulfs him.

While the idea might seem fairly straightforward, how do you go about making it happen? As is so often the case, it is largely camera trickery, and it is often the simplest of tricks that are the most effective.

In both cases the artist would be suspended upside down above a surface of water, and then slowly lowered down into it. If the camera is also upside down, or the resulting film is inverted, it will appear as though the surface of the water is descending to cover the artist, either in bed or in the bath.

While simple in concept, it was somewhat more complex to make happen.

In the case of the Cussons ad, it was carried out in a small open-air underwater studio in a private house near Winchester in the UK. The pool itself was about the size of a normal private swimming pool, but it had a deep end that was around twelve feet deep.

Constructed over the pool was the upside-down set of a bathroom, with a bath suspended from the 'floor', which was at the top. The whole assembly was mounted on a rig that could be lowered and raised by a mobile crane, allowing the set to sink into the surface of the pool, which, when played back with the film inverted, would look as though the surface of the water was descending onto the girl in the bath.

On the practical side, to allow model Mayumi Cabrera to be able to enter the bath and be safe throughout the action, the bath was mounted on a rotating floor, which could be swung into a vertical position so she could climb into it when on top of the gantry. Once seated in a specially moulded seat, she was then secured with a quick-release car seat belt. This was necessary in case the rig became stuck in the 'down' position when she was underwater. Just before shooting, the bath would be swung upside down and she would be suspended for the whole of the rest of the take. Once 'cut' was called, she would release the seat belt and swim out and up to safety on the surface. As backup, I would be close by with a secondary air source should there be any problems and she couldn't escape.

I had trained Mayumi for a previous job and knew she could carry out the task with ease, but I think even she showed a little trepidation when suspended twenty feet above ground and then swung upside down in the bath. She performed flawlessly though, and much of the success of the shoot must go down to her professionalism and courage.

Overall, the shoot went without a hitch, and the finished ad was highly memorable. Again, it just shows what a little imagination and a group of talented technicians can achieve - this time all in the pursuit of selling soap!

There was one commercial where I turned up for the shoot and thought the company must have got something very wrong.

It was actually a fairly straightforward job, with nothing

too over the top, and was shot in the Paddock Tank at Pinewood Studios - their equivalent of the infinite horizon tank in Malta. The tank is 228 feet wide, narrowing to a 106 feet, and 213 feet long. For most of its area it is 4 feet deep, with a central section that extends down to 7 feet.

The commercial was back in the days of the Blockbuster video store, when the only way you could watch a new movie was by running down to your local video shop and grabbing the latest VHS copy if they had any left. There was a phase they went through when they would produce arresting ads centred around the latest video release to build the hype for your next rental.

This time it was for the Denzel Washington, Gene Hackman film *Crimson Tide*. For those who haven't seen it, the film centres around the dilemma of whether you should fire a nuclear missile from a submarine if there is any doubt about the orders to do so - what do you do? A gripping and tense thriller.

The concept for the ad was to have a 'TV viewer' sitting watching the video of *Crimson Tide* on a TV on the deck of a nuclear submarine, and then for the sub to submerge beneath the waves.

Now, while it might be physically possible to do this for real, as has hopefully been seen from other chapters in the book, having control over the conditions when shooting in or on the water is essential to be able to shoot efficiently and to schedule.

To achieve the shots required, a mock-up of the conning tower and surrounding deck section of the sub had been built on a trolley platform that could move forward and sink into the deep section of the tank. This could be easily repeated and was all done in a safe, controlled environment.

From my point of view, I was only required as a safety diver in case there were problems in the tank or if they needed to access anything beneath the surface.

The reason why I thought they must have got something very wrong was that, on arrival, me and a colleague were taken to an area behind the tank by one of the assistants and told that was where we would be based and be able to change. All I could see was a Winnebago, no doubt for the main actor, and some scrubland. Now I know divers aren't exactly far up the pecking order on a crew, but to expect us to have to change out on scrubland in the wind and cold was pushing it a bit. I was about to protest when the assistant thrust a key into my hand and pointed at the Winnebago. 'You should find tea and coffee inside, the showers work, and oh, there's a selection of today's papers - will that be okay?'

It was very okay!

First and last time that ever happened.

The Paddock Tank at Pinewood Studios is smaller than the one in Malta, but the sequences that have been shot there would amaze anyone. The sheer creativity and ingenuity that goes into the sets and action that can take place in such a small area is simply mind-boggling.

Probably some of the most recognisable scenes come from the Bond films, which for the most part have nearly all been shot at Pinewood. The tank has seen everything from the burning speedboats in the chase in *From Russia with Love* to the large-scale model of the sinking villa in Venice in *Casino Royale*. Along the way there has been what was probably the most complex set ever to grace the tank - that of the caviar factory in *The World is Not Enough* where Bond is chased at night along elevated platforms over water by bad guys in a helicopter with massive rotating saw blades beneath.

However, the most impressive set I ever saw in the tank was from the Tim Burton film, *Dark Shadows*, where a whole seaside village, complete with working harbour and real fishing boats had been constructed.

The magic of the movies!

But not everything is quite so flashy.

As well as commercials providing a home for eagerly creative directors, another short-form format is the music video, or pop promo. Here, anything really does go, and quite often, the wackier the better.

On one job for the band James, all the facilities of the Paddock Tank were used to the full, but the action was as simple as you could possibly make it.

The concept was for the band to be playing their latest track as though they were in the middle of an ocean in a raging storm. Ignore the fact they were actually standing on the bottom, and you had quite a fun idea.

To create the storm, all the available toys were used - wind machines, wave machines, rain machines, tip tanks, and, to top it all, a helicopter circling above to provide additional wind, as well as an aerial camera platform. To provide other shots, the main camera was mounted on the end of a long arm that moved in and out of the band as they played their instruments in increasingly dramatic conditions. There were also a number of cameramen in drysuits, acting as roving cameras that could shoot from water level and give the director and editor a wide range of angles to choose from.

In the middle of all this the band played on, as they say. The end result was an innovative and creative video that was something that hadn't been seen before, and it was a fantastic example of what can be achieved a million miles from any sea or ocean with a few simple tricks of the trade.

14

Digital Diving

Fifty feet in front of me, behind a secure door, four small levers, each about the size of the average car gearstick, were pushed smoothly forward. At the same time, a muted roar encroached from outside the oval window to my right. About ten seconds later, with an increasingly violent vibration, I started moving forward, along with over five hundred other people, as the four Rolls-Royce Trent 900 engines screamed up to full power, delivering a thrust of more than 3,500 family cars to push the Malaysian Airlines Airbus A380 down the nearly two and a half miles of tarmac just outside of London.

Within a couple of minutes the vibration had eased and the massive machine had banked steeply round as it lifted up through the dense, overcast ceiling that had covered south-east England for much of the day.

With the aircraft stable, but still climbing and now free of the impenetrable clouds, the sun streamed down the cabin in intermittent shafts of light. Finally, the altitude levelled off, the noise quietened, and the engines settled back, resigned to their task of the 6,500 mile flight to Kuala Lumpur in Malaysia.

The take-off of an aircraft means different things to different people. For some, it is the thought of seeing a long-absent loved one; for others, the mundane start of a tedious business trip; for a few, it is a period of sheer terror, a moment in time they wished would be over and never had to happen; but for me it had always been the beginning of another adventure - the promise of a far-off land, usually involving the exploration of fascinating marine life and mysterious shipwrecks that only the underwater world can provide.

This time was no exception.

What lay ahead were eleven flights, five hotels, two liveaboards, forty dives, twenty wrecks… oh, and the most powerful storm to make landfall in living memory.

But all that was in the future. For now, I just had to go over everything in my mind and make sure I had planned for every eventuality in order to complete the assignment I had set myself.

The assignment in question was to enter the new era of digital publishing - a world of iPads, apps and worldwide digital distribution.

In parallel to the diving work I had done over the years, I had also been quietly trying to develop a fiction-writing career, to the point that I took quite a period of time out from film work to concentrate on this.

I had always loved creative writing, as far back as my school days, and had even completed a novel between finishing school and going to university. Nothing came of it, but a major publisher at the time said they would be happy to read anything else I came up with, so at least that was encouraging.

However, with all the involvement with movies, it was inevitable that I should be drawn to the screenplay as a format in which to tell stories - so it didn't take long to realise I should really be writing film scripts. I also had one of those lightbulb moments that if I wrote scripts with a lot of underwater sequences in them, that could lead on to more time spent doing the day job!

To be honest, I should have been slightly less naive. I was writing material that would require tens of millions of dollars to produce - with no experience.

Many years and eight full screenplays later, and somewhat wiser, a number of the projects have come close to production - one almost being optioned by a Hollywood production company, and one getting as far as lunch with Nigel Havers at Shepperton Studios to discuss the possibility of him playing the lead. While it's possible some may still make the final leap, as of writing, the most successful outcome was a short film entitled *InSane*, which was produced in 2009 and directed by Howard Greenhalgh, one of the UK's most creative and successful commercials/promo directors. It was a gritty, twisty, whodunnit serial killer story with a running time of around twenty minutes. It was generally perceived to have turned well, with twists that worked and a certain style and atmosphere. But above all, it was a wonderful feeling to be on set and realise that all the cast and crew were there because of words I had written.

Today, things have come full circle. With the advent of simple digital self-publishing, and the cost of publishing a book about large-scale action adventures similar to that of a book about cooking, I have returned to the novel format, turning the script that received the most attention, *Deep Steal*, into a novel - a revenge thriller set in the world of commercial diving. It is the first in a planned series of John McCready thrillers, which will see our hero criss-cross the globe, thwarting bad guys and righting wrongs - all with a strong underwater theme.

With writing being the way I saw my future developing, I still wanted something to keep the diving/filming muscles active, so in 2012 I started work on a series of interactive digital books that would transport readers to some of the best dive sites around the world, using maps, photos and video. The books would be accessed using the new wave of digital smartphones and tablets that are more and more becoming the way we experience our written, audio and visual media. The series is called *SCUBA DIVING - Underwater...* with the final part of the title being made up of the destination each book concentrates on.

The digital revolution has changed the way we conduct our lives. In some ways we are now never 'off the clock', so to speak, but in others, such as creatively, design-wise, and with the access to information, it has made many things so much more attainable.

This is no more so than in the publishing world.

Before digital publishing came along, spearheaded by Amazon, and more recently Apple Books, to get a book published was an endless series of rejection letters from publishers and agents. If you wanted to go it alone, you stepped into the oft-maligned world of vanity publishing, where you paid a considerable sum of money to a company who would provide you with hundreds or thousands of copies of a title but with no practical means of distributing them, resulting in piles of books rotting away in people's garages.

Now the distribution problem has been solved. Anyone can publish high-quality books and have an instant distribution channel worldwide, all for minimal cost.

The true power of this only really hit home after completing the first title in the diving series.

The book had been designed and the components assembled on a computer at home. Then, after setting up an account, at the simple click of a button, it was all uploaded to Apple - a couple of days later millions of people in over fifty countries around the world could purchase it at the click of a mouse.

Truly amazing.

It was another of those lightbulb moments when I fully realised the potential of this.

But before all that could happen I had to pick the destinations I would be featuring in the series and shoot the photos and video required to make up the bulk of the content.

Along with the technological advances in the publishing industry, so too there has also been a leap forward in photo/video/editing equipment. It is now possible to edit a feature film on a laptop and, as has already been described, hold in the palm of your hand a camera and housing whose picture quality far exceeds that of one that took two people to lift not that many years ago. Full-length cinema-quality feature films have even been shot on an iPhone.

So, for anyone out there who has an idea and wants to make a programme or film of some description, there really is no excuse. You don't even need to go to the mainstream TV companies to show off your finished masterpiece - just create your own channel online and broadcast to the world.

With all this amazing technology readily available, it was a relatively straightforward decision to decide to create all of the content for the books myself.

The next choice was what would be the best kit for the project.

With so much to choose from it's always worth taking time to select the most appropriate tools for the job, taking into account the end distribution platform and, most importantly, the budget - i.e. are you shooting for *Blue Planet 2* or YouTube? I used a number of systems for the series, but the one that turned out to be most suitable was a Sony RX100 camera in a Nauticam Housing and two Light and Motion Sola 2000 lights. A very portable system that can easily fit into carry-on luggage and is more than capable of handling both stills and video for a project of this sort.

One of the major issues with travelling the world, while diving and filming, is that of baggage and weight allowance.

Once your baggage reaches a certain size and weight, you have no option but to put the camera equipment in the hold of the aircraft. However, this could be taking a huge risk, and often going for a more modest, more compact set-up may be the wiser choice.

The potential problems are numerous. The obvious one is that baggage handlers don't treat your cases with kid gloves - they throw them around. If you plan for this by using a protective case, like a Pelican case, then you are virtually advertising the fact that there is camera gear inside shouting 'Steal me!'

Of course, as well as these issues, there is the possibility your baggage may just get lost amongst the millions that travel through the international airports of the world every day. With the tracking systems used by the airlines you may well get it back, but three weeks after you return home isn't going to help your chances of a successful shoot.

Where possible, I would always carry camera equipment in the cabin to minimise the risk.

With my thoughts turning to the current trip, there were many things racing through my mind.

On any project there are numerous variables that can come into play to affect the outcome. These include weather, bad visibility, engine breakdowns, camera malfunctions, and illness, but I did at least think there was nothing to worry about for the next couple of days – I just had to get there.

And 'there' was going to be spectacular. The twin destinations of Truk Lagoon and Palau in the western Pacific.

Twelve hours after lifting off from British soil, the plane touched down on tropical tarmac in Malaysia.

I spent a few hours browsing the shops and cafes of KL airport, and then the second flight of the four required to reach Truk took off. This leg would drop me in Manila in the Philippines, and a stopover for the night.

By the time the fourth in the series of flights, this one from Guam to Truk, sped in to land on the short sliver of tarmac on the island of Weno, in the lagoon at the far side of the world, I was well and truly exhausted, but the anticipation was also high.

I had visited Truk once before, back in 1990, but this time I would be better prepared to document the amazing sights I knew I was going to see.

Truk Lagoon, also known as Chuuk Lagoon, is located in Micronesia in the Pacific Ocean to the east of the Philippines. It is a lagoon that forms a natural harbour of over eight hundred square miles and is made up of over fifty islands. It was the perfect place for the Japanese to have a forward operating base for their ships and aircraft during World War II.

In February 1944, during *Operation Hailstone*, the US Air Force destroyed a large proportion of the Japanese fleet at Truk, ensuring the lagoon would become one of the world's great wreck-diving locations and making it such a Mecca for divers today.

With over sixty wrecks in the enclosed, sheltered waters, including war and cargo ships, aircraft, and even a submarine, it is unrivalled anywhere in the world, and it was for this reason I had to include it as one of the destinations in the series.

To be confronted by a human skull in any situation would give you pause for thought, but when you are underwater, deep inside a World War II shipwreck, and it is staring back at you, wedged between two metal structures, where the unfortunate sailor had been blown backwards by an exploding bomb, the pause is slightly longer. The wreck was the *Yamagiri Maru*, a 436 foot military cargo ship of six and a half thousand tons, and the brief pause was enough for the enormity of the events that had taken place around me back in 1944 to sink in.

It was the third day of shooting in Truk and things were

going well.

The aim of the series is to give an idea of what the dive sites are really like – the topography, water conditions, wildlife, etc., or, in the case of the wrecks, a sense of the scale, atmosphere and any special features that make the site unique. As well as photographs, a key component is video. Video can give a far greater feel for a location than photographs ever can, and each site would have a three- to four-minute video edited to music, which showed off what there was to see in a concise but comprehensive manner.

Quite often when you are filming in open water, you are challenged by the elements you encounter, which can complicate and often disrupt the filming process, but in Truk the diving conditions are as benign as they can be. With 82°F/28°C water temperature, virtually zero current, and visibility generally in the sixty-foot-plus range, it doesn't get any easier.

Where problems usually lie are in the penetration of the wrecks and some of the depths that can be reached on a number of the dives. It's all too easy to become lost in the work process and momentarily lose track of depth or where you are inside a wreck, which is why it's essential to have an experienced guide with you at all times if penetrating deep inside. As well as the safety issues, they can find the interesting features and navigate to locations as quickly as possible, allowing the maximum filming time that will ultimately provide more usable footage.

The other issue with wrecks is trying to make them look different. This is easy if you are dealing with planes and submarines, but trying to make very similar cargo ships have a character of their own requires research and a bit more thought in the style of the shots and the features you show.

The wrecks featured in the Truk Lagoon book include two aircraft (Betty Bomber, Emily Flying Boat); twelve cargo ships (*Fujikawa Maru, Heian Maru, Shinkoku Maru, Yamagiri Maru, Nippo Maru, Kiyosumi Maru, Unkai Maru, Hoki Maru, San Francisco Maru, Rio de Janeiro Maru, Kansho Maru, Sankisan Maru*); a submarine (I-169), and a tug boat (*Futagami Maru*).

As wrecks are large objects, it's obviously not possible to show the whole location in a three- to four-minute video, so the best way to distinguish them is by showing different aspects, such as guns, cargo or marine life, and also by the choice of shot. If each video has a certain style to it, that will distinguish it just as much as the content on screen. This, along with the choice of music, can transform a video, making it entirely distinctive.

It is often hard to make underwater videos exciting. Diving by its very nature is a slow-motion event. For divers, the mere fact they are watching underwater images is often enough, but for most people, the slowness of movement through the water can become a bit, to be frank, boring after a while.

This can be solved in a number of ways. The first is to cut the video fast, which can work, but it's likely to leave the audience with mere snippets of images, which often comes out as a montage that doesn't form a coherent whole – fine for a promo, but nothing of any substance. The second is to move the camera. Most shots should ideally have some sort of movement/action within them, or else you can create the movement with the camera. This can be vertically, panning from side to side (not too fast), or, most effectively, by moving forwards or backwards.

Hollywood directors pay tens of thousands of dollars to have equipment that allows the camera to move smoothly in any direction – from cranes and dollies to steadicam and sophisticated gimbals. As a diver you have all this built in, as you are weightless and can move in three dimensions.

Movement in the shot shouldn't only apply to wrecks, but to any subject you're filming. Even macro shots will have more interest if there's a very slight, slow movement around or towards the subject. But for wrecks there is the huge advantage of being able to be close to the structure, and with a wide-angle lens it makes the movement appear faster and more dramatic as the wreck shoots past close to camera, while disappearing into the distance ahead, ensuring exciting, dynamic footage.

With all this movement, the next problem is holding the camera steady. While there has been a trend in recent years of having jerky, unsteady shots in action films, this can often lead to disorientation and a sense of unease and being taken out of the images on screen.

The obvious solution is to hold the camera steady, something not always as simple as it might seem, particularly if you are moving through the water.

It's easier with a larger camera, as there is a greater mass to move, which dampens any wobble, but if you have a compact camera or GoPro, it's virtually impossible, and there will always be a slight wiggle in the shots, which can be distracting.

To help solve this you can use an image stabiliser, which many cameras have built in. In most cases this works by slightly cropping the image through software, thereby removing the movement. The downside of this is a slight reduction in quality. This is fine if shooting at 4K resolution and exporting the finished file in 1080p HD or lower, but a preferable system is optical, which physically stabilises the camera lens or sensor by moving it. If all else fails it is possible to steady the shots in post-production on a computer, where, again, some systems are better than others.

Following my previous visit to Truk, it was interesting to see how the wrecks had deteriorated. There were many instances where, before, I had been able to swim through rooms or corridors, and now the roofs or ceilings had collapsed. It's a sad inevitability that with time all the magnificent wrecks will end up as piles of steel plate on the floor of the lagoon.

It's also important to remember that wrecks provide perfect artificial reefs for marine life to build an ecosystem around. When diving at Truk, you know to the day when the wrecks were sunk, so it's fascinating to see the extensive coral growth on many of the structures and the attendant fish life that has grown up around it, and to realise the exact timeframe it has taken to achieve this. The marine life is also an important component of any photographs and video, as it provides a great visual balance to the hard, cold metal of the wrecks themselves.

As my time in Truk came to an end, it was great to have a couple of days off before reaching the second destination of Palau. All things given, the week had gone well and there was more than enough footage for the project. The problem would be deciding what to leave out in the editing process - but then that was always the right sort of problem to have.

As the plane touched down on a slightly more substantial airstrip than had greeted us at Truk, it seemed like the previous trip was a million miles away - it was a different country with new adventures ahead.

Palau is located to the west of Truk, about halfway back towards the Philippines. It's made up of a string of islands arranged vertically, and stretching around ninety miles from top to bottom. Although you may not know much about Palau, it's instantly recognisable because of an amazing group of rock islands, covered on all sides by trees stretching down to the water's edge, and that, which from the air, look like a series of round green humps lying in an azure sea.

The diving here is also very different to Truk. Whereas the previous location had been a sheltered lagoon that could often be quite silty, and all the dive sites were wrecks, here it was effectively an open ocean, with a reputation for a fantastic variety of marine life, including a large number of sharks, and some interesting wrecks on the side. There were also cave systems and large caverns to explore, as well as the world-famous Jellyfish Lake. Here, millions of jellyfish survived in a landlocked lake and migrated up and down the water column during the day/night cycle - a unique phenomenon, and one I had been eager to experience for many years.

All in all, Palau is a location with a massive variety of unique dives, and it was this appeal that made it another on the list of amazing dive locations for the series.

After a night in a hotel, it was time to board the *Palau Aggressor* liveaboard, which was to be home for the week.

The first thing that struck me about the boat was the dive tender. Most liveaboards are just where you eat and sleep and not usually where you dive from - for this there are tenders that ferry you out to the dive sites and are more manoeuvrable to be able to pick you up. These are often inflatables or RIBs, but on the *Aggressor* it was a large fibreglass-hulled boat with a full-length canopy and squared-off bow. There were spaces for the cylinders and seating for all the guests, but the really striking feature was that the whole boat was picked up by a lift at the stern of the *Aggressor* and raised up to the dive deck level. To board or leave the craft, all you had to do was step aboard - so if it was rough there was no danger of falling over in a rocking and rolling boat - fantastic system.

The aim of the dives was to shoot enough material to show off Palau's amazing diversity of locations and marine life. The sites included: three wrecks (*Teshio Maru, Iro Maru*, Jake Seaplane); three caves/caverns (Siaes Tunnel, Blue Holes, Chandelier Cave); nine reefs (German Channel, Turtle Cove, Barracks Point, Ulong Channel, Peleliu Corner, Blue Corner, Sandy Paradise, New Drop off), and Jellyfish Lake.

From a filming point of view, the same techniques used in Truk would be fine on the wrecks and would also be similar in the confined area of the cavern/caves, only here, one of the tasks was to show off the scale of the tunnels and caves relative to the rest of the dive site. Making a reef look different, however, can be somewhat more challenging, as they often all look alike, so the trick is to find something distinctive about each particular site.

For example, Ulong Channel and German Channel are, as the names suggest, long channels within the reef, so you can highlight the walls and the sandy seabed as well as showing the marine life present. Some sites might have a particular species of marine life that frequents that location - German Channel had a group of manta rays that weren't seen on any of the other sites.

There are a few sites, though, that have a reputation that precedes them. Blue Corner is one of the most famous dive sites in the world. It's made up of a reef in about twenty-five feet of water that extends to a wide corner that is swept by onshore currents. Here, you just have to take a reef hook - a strong metal hook on the end of six to ten feet of line, which you carefully secure to the coral and attach to your BC - then just let the current push against you, allowing you to 'fly' in the water and hang there effortlessly, watching the show in front of your eyes. At Blue Corner, that consists of huge numbers of sharks, as well as large humphead wrasse, which circulate past. If you should tire of this, there are numerous shoals of fish on the reef itself, as well as visiting turtles to keep you occupied.

Blue Corner is so iconic that it is usually repeated several times during a trip. The plan had originally been to dive the site on the second day and then later in the week. However, nature was to intervene, meaning the planned second visit was moved up the schedule.

From the first day of the trip the captain had received reports that a large storm system was moving into the Palau region, and he was aware that this might mean a change to the itinerary. Given that the water conditions on the first couple of days couldn't have been better, resulting in a millpond-flat, calm sea, we weren't too worried.

However, on the second day you could tell there was a nervousness amongst the crew, and by the third day we were told the storm would hit that night and we would therefore move the second Blue Corner dive to that morning, as the captain wasn't sure when we would be able to dive again. That put a whole new perspective on things and on the storm that was fast approaching - and with good reason.

The date was the 6th of November 2013 - the storm was called Typhoon Haiyan - and after sweeping over Palau it would go on to devastate parts of South East Asia, killing over 6,500 people in the Philippines.

At the time of our early morning dive at Blue Corner, all that was in the future, but the predictions were so severe that it was deemed necessary to offload all the guests and crew from the boat to a local, solidly built hotel, even though the *Aggressor* would be moored up in the harbour.

The approaching force of nature resulted in an air of apprehension, but also a certain expectancy. I had never experienced a hurricane/typhoon before, and while there was clearly an element of danger - no one knew how bad things would get - I have to say it was an incredibly thrilling feeling.

We were back in the harbour by lunchtime, having completed three dives. The rest of the day was spent preparing the boat for the coming storm and moving everyone to the hotel.

The storm hit in the middle of the night. And as we would learn later, we only caught the edge of the swirl of cloud and rain that made up the typhoon, but even so the noise was indescribable. Looking out of the hotel window at two o'clock in the morning revealed a sight straight out of a disaster movie. Palm trees were bent sideways, and much of the water in the swimming pool had been sucked out onto the pool surround.

We awoke to a scene of devastation. Trees and power lines were down and buildings with corrugated roofs no longer had them. But the wind was calming. It was remarkable how quickly the weather had passed through.

An hour or so after breakfast and we were again back on the boat. There would be no diving that day, but time was spent preparing the boat for the following days. During this time, a helicopter that operated from a facility next to the harbour took off to check out the most northerly islands of the archipelago, which had received the full force of the typhoon.

When they returned their report was grim.

On one of the islands not a single tree or building had been left standing. Fortunately, as far as we heard, there had been no loss of life - something that wouldn't be the case when Haiyan swept across the Philippines over the coming days.

As we were unaware of the tragedy that was to unfold many miles to the west, we turned our attention to the remaining days' diving. Our main concern was that the water conditions would be so disturbed that the visibility would be reduced to close to zero. Nothing could have been further from the truth. The following day, when we dived beneath the surface, the water was calm and the visibility was as though the storm had never been - quite incredible.

The final day of the trip saw a visit to one of my long-held dream dive sites - Jellyfish Lake.

I had seen this amazing location on many a natural history programme, and initially the thought of swimming with millions of small jellyfish, so tightly packed that much of the time they are only inches apart, was quite an alarming prospect. But over the years the animals had lost the ability to sting, and to brush against them was like brushing up against a small velvet cushion.

To access the landlocked lake you have a short climb up over a steep hill and then down to a wooden pontoon from which you enter the water. No suncream lotion is allowed as the chemicals can be dangerous for the jellyfish. You are also not allowed to use scuba equipment - only snorkels. It's probably a wise move, as the lower levels of the lake are highly toxic and hazardous to descend into.

But there was no need to go deep.

As you swim across the lake, at first you see just one or two individuals, but gradually the numbers increase until there are hundreds in your vision. It's a remarkable experience and one in which you only have to turn the camera on to shoot some wonderful footage.

The visit to this unique location capped off what had been an amazing trip, and together with Truk Lagoon, it provided enough material to make up two editions of *SCUBA DIVING - Underwater...*

Two other books were also added to the series.

The Red Sea, which probably represents some of the best bang for buck diving anywhere in the world, with its multitude of wrecks and world-class variety of reefs and marine life.

And the Philippines, where, in the area around Anilao,

you can find a vast array of amazing critters, which help to make the region a fascinating and memorable experience.

But there was another location I had been keen to visit for many years, and that would undoubtedly top all the others.

The Galápagos.

I'm sure we have all read about and watched television programmes of places we would like to visit, but there is nothing you can watch or read about the Galápagos Islands that can quite prepare you for the experience of being there.

Everything you have seen and heard is true and then some.

You probably know about the friendliness of the animals, and that they have no fear of Man. You probably know there is an incredible diversity of species, even between the many islands that make up the archipelago. But what you may not be prepared for is the sheer raw topography and violent volcanic nature of most of the islands. It's like stepping into *The Land That Time Forgot.*

Everywhere you look there are the brutal rugged cones of volcanos, some small, some large, and it brings to mind the description of those that first travelled the waters when they came across the islands and described them as 'hell on earth.' A far cry from the unique and treasured natural environment we associate them with today.

The islands are a province of Ecuador and lie in the Eastern Pacific, around seven hundred miles from the Ecuadorian coast. They are made up of a hundred and twenty-five islands and islets, most of which are located in a roughly oval-shaped group, with two we shall talk about later ninety miles to the north.

To reach the Galápagos you have to fly through either Quito or Guayaquil in Ecuador, and at the airport your luggage is inspected for any items that might in some way contaminate the islands. Once this check has been completed, your bags are then sealed for the flight.

When I travelled, however, before I even reached this stage, American Airlines had managed to lose my luggage - they had left it in Miami. It was the first time in many years of international flight that my bag had gone missing, and it was at the worst possible moment.

On any normal trip, losing your luggage is an inconvenience, and you may even be reunited with it before your return. But when you are flying out to a group of islands, and then staying aboard a boat that will be travelling far from shore, the chances of seeing your belongings again in time are pretty remote.

While I had taken my own advice and carried all the camera gear as hand luggage, all the dive gear was in the hold. It wasn't the end of the world, as more kit could be hired on the boat, but as any diver will tell you, when you have built up your equipment over the years to fit perfectly and be adapted to the diving you do, not having it with you is a major blow - particularly as when you're filming you need to be able to instinctively control your gear without a second thought, something that isn't so easy when using hired equipment.

So it was with a sense of frustration that I boarded the flight from Guayaquil to the small island of Baltra in the Galápagos, with little hope of seeing any of my gear again for the rest of the trip. The only slightly encouraging sign had been that while talking to the tour operator in Ecuador they seemed to act as though this was a regular occurrence and were fairly confident I would be reunited with my bag. I wasn't going to hold my breath.

On the approach to landing you have a clear view of many of the islands, and the sense of anticipation amongst those on board was palpable. You could clearly see the barren, volcanic landscape and you knew you were arriving somewhere very special - and very different.

The islands lie in one of the most volcanically active areas of the planet, and eruptions are regularly throwing up new land masses in the north-west of the group. Over time, these move steadily south-east and change in shape and form as they become ever more weather-beaten. Eventually they disappear back into the ocean from whence they came - like a giant island conveyor belt.

There are also interesting climactic conditions, which change radically, even across the small area of the group. This is broadly split between a tropical climate in the north-east and sub-tropical in the south-west. It is these conditions, as much as anything, that has led to the diversity of animals and plants.

The main cause of this difference are the currents that flow around the islands. From the east is the warm South Equatorial Current, which is bolstered from the north and east by the North Equatorial and Panama Currents. From the south, you have the cold Peru Oceanic and Humboldt Currents. And most importantly, from the west you have the cold Cromwell Current. This wells up from deep in the ocean, bringing nutrients to the region, and is responsible for much of the prolific marine life that inhabits the waters around the Galápagos. It's the strength of this current and its varying force in opposition to the other currents that determines the changing climate across the islands throughout the year.

Once through the arrival process, it didn't take long to be transported from the airport to the dive boat, the *Galápagos Aggressor III*. It was then time to settle in for the usual briefings and to go over the schedule for the week.

The itinerary was suitably ambitious.

While all the islands offer exciting and unique experiences above the water, and while there are some amazing dives to be had around them, where the diving becomes world class is around the two islands around ninety miles to the north - Darwin and Wolf. It's because of these that divers travel from far and wide across the globe. In particular, one dive site, Darwin's Arch, on the island of Darwin, can lay claim to being one of the best dive sites in the world.

The first couple of days were spent acclimatising to the diving and checking out the equipment. However, even the first few dives, in relatively low visibility, brought memorable experiences. A large Galápagos shark swam past in only ten feet of water - a sea lion joined the dive, its supple body looping and twisting around us in exuberant play. It was a great opener and only made everyone more excited for what was to come.

If you are planning a diving trip to the Galápagos, one of the things you have to consider is the change in water temperature you will experience from island to island. As mentioned, there are different currents affecting different parts of the islands throughout the year. To the south and west are colder currents, and to the north and east are warmer currents. In the real world this can result in a massive temperature difference in the water, depending on where you are diving.

For example, when I was there in August, the temperature ranged from 60–80°F / 15–26°C. In an ideal world this requires a couple of different suits to be comfortable, but as this isn't always possible, a one-piece 7mm wetsuit with a thin vest, hood and gloves pretty much covered things. The coldest temperatures were only experienced on a couple of the dives, and you can suffer through those because of the extraordinary sights you are witnessing.

On the second day, my dive bag turned up. To be honest I couldn't believe it - but somehow, someone somewhere had arranged for it to be put on a plane at Miami, transferred to a flight to the islands, put on a truck to a harbour, then loaded onto a boat and brought out to the *Aggressor*.

My faith in Mankind was restored!

The trip to the northern islands took place overnight, so as not to lose too much time in the water.

The Galápagos are very heavily protected for obvious reasons, and there are a limited number of tourists allowed there every year. This strict policy also extends to permits allocated to dive boats. In fact, the rules were so strict that we only ever saw one other dive boat for the whole duration, and never at the same island at the same time.

You are only able to travel to Darwin and Wolf if you are on a dedicated diving trip. You are also not allowed to land on the islands, and even if you could there is little to see. There is no habitation, and the bare land and rock make for inhospitable environments best left to the thousands of birds that have made them their home.

Having heard horror stories of the trip up north, it was with great relief when I opened the curtains over the porthole to look out onto the wild outline of Wolf Island having had a perfectly good night's sleep. The conditions could hardly have been better. There was a slight swell - just enough to let you know you were at sea, but nothing to send you scurrying to your bunk turning a pale shade of green.

Wolf Island was named after the German geologist Theodor Wolf and is a straggly, wild island - but the diving here is extraordinary. While around the main islands there are numerous creatures of unique interest, here there are the larger pelagic animals that people travel vast distances to see.

Over several days we saw one of the wonders of the natural world - walls of hammerhead sharks, made up of hundreds of individuals, calmly making their way through the water. It was probably one of the most impressive sights I have ever witnessed. There were so many sharks, not just in the wall, but swimming above and around us over the reef, that after a while it was quite annoying having a hammerhead in shot when you were trying to focus on other species.

There were also large numbers of eagle rays gracefully gliding over the rocks, and a family of fur seals that had made their home in a small inlet on the south of the island.

Wolf was also the only location during the trip where night dives were permitted, so there was the opportunity to shoot turtles, hunting moray eels and lobsters in the dark.

With some great footage in the can, it was time to move

the twenty miles or so further north to Darwin.

If possible, Darwin is even more isolated and bleak than Wolf. Both are the peaks of the ever-present volcanos and are linked physically deep underwater. But whereas Wolf had some character, with bays and inlets, Darwin was just a large, oval-shaped mass of land, smooth on all sides, and with no real landing place, even if we'd had permission to do so.

However, half a mile off its south-eastern tip lies a rock formation that forms a large and striking arch, known as Darwin's Arch, and if we thought the diving couldn't get any better, we were about to be blown away.

The rocks surrounding the arch drop away into deep water, and as the island is effectively in open ocean, it attracts the larger animals to collect around it. So not only do you get the schools of hammerheads, but at certain times of the year you also get whale sharks. No one quite knows why they come, but the theory is that the females collect here before heading out to deeper water to give birth. We could certainly attest to the fact that certain of the four animals that swam around us for many hours over several days were heavily pregnant, so the theory could be true.

The joy of the encounters was that the animals weren't just at arm's length, as can so often be the case. The whale sharks were swimming around, above and below, all in only twenty to thirty feet of water. It resulted in some remarkable footage, and as stated before, to me, it made Darwin's Arch one of the best dive sites in the world. I certainly think it would be very hard to beat.

Our experiences at the two most northerly of the Galápagos Islands were ones that will live with me for the rest of my life, but there was one dive, while at Wolf, that reminded me of the unpredictable nature of wildlife and that it doesn't do to take anything for granted.

A group of us were drifting with the current while carrying out a safety stop for five minutes at fifteen feet. The aim of the stop was to allow any excess nitrogen to come out of the body safely and so reduce the risk of decompression illness. The stops were really a belt and braces procedure, as we were within the limits of being able to surface without a stop, but when you are this far from any assistance, it is always preferable to be as safe as possible.

We had been drifting for a couple of minutes when a small pod of dolphins shot by - always a welcome sight - but then some other shapes materialised at the edge of visibility and started to come closer: silky sharks. Silkies are not particularly large sharks, but they are long and relatively thin, are fast and have a potential for aggression.

I have no problem with sharks in the water, like I think most divers, but you do have to remember they have teeth at one end, they are a wild animal, and you are in their world. Also, animals become more emboldened when they are in groups or packs.

As the silkies moved closer, we could see there weren't just a couple of them but more like twenty to thirty. They proceeded to encircle the group as we drifted through the water. It was rather like the Indians encircling the wagons. While I wouldn't say I was particularly scared, I was fairly concerned. A couple of times they had to be discouraged from coming closer by one of the divers bashing an individual on the nose with his camera. All it would have taken would have been for one of them to have taken a nip of someone and we could have had a serious situation on our hands.

Fortunately, all ended well and the sharks moved on, but it was a timely reminder that you can never take anything for granted in the amazing world beneath the waves.

With our days at Darwin and Wolf at an end, it was time to head back to the main group of islands ninety miles to the south.

The diving that would greet us over subsequent days would lack the 'wow' factor we had experienced up north but in its own way it was incredibly unique and just as special.

There were more sea lions on a number of dives, who made their presence felt as they swam close to and around the group, showing off their skills. There were the weird-looking and massive *Mola mola*, or sunfish, which swam lazily past with their unique tall, thin shape, and fins that stretched above and below their vertically flattened bodies. There were diving, flightless cormorants, which could certainly swim and hunt as well as any other animal in the water. And on one memorable trip in a Zodiac, we were greeted by penguins swimming on and below the surface. The Galápagos is the most northerly location where these charming and energetic animals can be found.

And then there were the marine iguanas - probably the signature animal of the Galápagos in the water, only eclipsed on land by the giant tortoises that lend their name to the islands.

The iguanas arrived on floating debris, most probably from South America, and due to the harsh nature of the volcanic landscape they found they could only survive by adapting to feed on the green algae that grows on shallow rocks beneath the surface.

They are cold blooded, so they have to frequently come out of the water to warm up their bodies in order to have enough energy to return to the sea to feed. It was quite amazing to watch, as almost to the second, hundreds of them headed for the water all at the same time.

Once in the water they can move at a reasonable speed and swim with an almost serpentine movement. They use long claws, which have evolved over the years, to cling to the sharp rocks while they feed in the constantly moving water.

Filming them was a joy.

On the surface they are very skittish, and any movement close by sends them scurrying beneath the waves. But once underwater they can be approached to within a few inches without seeming to mind at all. It allowed for some great footage of what is one of the most iconic animals of the Galápagos.

My time amongst the islands came to a close with a visit to the Charles Darwin Research Station to see some of the projects that were underway to protect the wildlife and species from overdevelopment and the impact of tourism. There is clearly much good work going on here to ensure the islands remain as pristine as possible, with tourists being restricted to visiting only certain locations, leaving many others solely for scientific research and conservation.

Following this, there was just time for a final trip to a tortoise sanctuary, where there was the opportunity to see giant tortoises in the wild in their natural habitat.

By the week's end, the SD camera cards had been filled, I'd had some of the most memorable and exciting diving of my life - and I knew the Galápagos edition of the series was going to be something special.

All that remained was for the flights home, thankfully without any loss of luggage, and then it was down to the editing and production of the book, ready for publication.

One of the key components of the books are the video sections from the different dive sites.

There is a simple but fairly involved process that results in what are hopefully short but entertaining videos edited to music, and it can be applied to any short-form project of this type.

Once you have all the footage, you need to eliminate all the technically unusable material and then sit down and watch it repeatedly. By doing this you should begin to see a shape to the video beyond the initial concept. Often you won't achieve all the shots you set out to, but you will also have gained others you never expected, and there is always that bit of magic that can happen on any dive where you see things you never knew you were going to see.

The footage you have, as well as the subject matter, will determine the style and tone of the video. It's now, though, that you will have to make one of the most critical decisions in the whole process – the music.

Music can make or break any audiovisual project, including feature films. Get it right and you can elevate often ordinary material to a special experience. Get it wrong and it can be cringeworthy. There is nothing more depressing than watching beautiful underwater footage on YouTube with someone's favourite heavy metal track running over it.

When all is finished, leave the video alone for a while, then watch it a day or so later and see if anything needs changing – hopefully, with a few tweaks here and there you will have something you can be proud of and many others will receive enjoyment from.

With the Galápagos edition complete, a sixth volume was added to the series. Entitled *SCUBA DIVING - Underwater World*, this edition includes a single dive from each of the locations in the main books, along with dives from other amazing sites around the world.

You can find more information on the series and the John McCready thrillers at www.mikesearesbooks.com.

15

Whale War III

'Belugas!'

   'I beg your pardon.'

   'No, whales.'

   'Oh, right.'

That's how it started, and things only became more bizarre from there.

When I was working out which stories to include in this book, I was also trying to decide which one would be the best to end with. Initially I thought this would be quite a hard decision, but as I looked at the various options, it became clear there was only one way to go.

The story I have chosen doesn't have any great complex diving problems to solve; there's no new or cutting edge technology, and there are no superstar names to drop. Instead, there is intrigue, suspense, drama and adventure - what more could you possibly want?

In April of 1992 the general election campaign in the UK was in full swing and it was slap bang in the middle of the silly season. Everyone was just plain bored with the mindless round of politics, and the media especially were in desperate need of something tasty to get their teeth into.

Some months earlier, in the far-flung Black Sea waters close to Sevastopol on the Crimean Peninsula, a storm had raged. The wind and waves had managed to rip a hole in the netted enclosure of a sea pen at a Russian military base. This distant, seemingly innocuous act of nature was to ultimately result in a media circus descending on the northern coast of Turkey, a near diplomatic incident between East and West, and a farcical chase between TV news crews in search of one solitary animal.

The damaged nets had been housing two beluga whales, as well as sea lions and dolphins, trained in a covert Russian military programme to collect downed torpedoes and take part in other such clandestine activities. Along with the Russians, the Americans also had a marine mammal programme, and there had even been talk on both sides of dolphins and seals being trained to deliver knockout blows to enemy divers in harbours and other militarily sensitive areas.

With the nets damaged and a clear route to the open sea created, one of these highly trained marine mammals, who had been named Tishka by the Russians, had no doubt thought it was time to take itself off on a field trip of its own without supervision from its Russian masters.

And so it came to pass that a beluga whale started its trek across the Black Sea. It headed due south, ending up at the small, sleepy town of Gerze on the northern Turkish coast. This whale, for a short period of time, would become more famous than even Moby Dick – and he too was white.

This then is the story of three of the most extraordinary and bizarre weeks of my life, leaving experiences and memories it would be impossible to forget.

After its escape from Sevastopol, the beluga had become something of a local tourist attraction at Gerze. It seemed to have befriended the local fishermen, who were feeding it regularly, and it had decided to set up home in the small bay close to the town. News of this quickly spread through the local press and further afield, and it came to the attention of Ray Gravener at British Divers Marine Life Rescue (BDMLR). Ray put together a team, including a vet, to assess the condition of the whale, to see if anything could be done about its predicament and welfare. The aim, ultimately, was to airlift the animal to the Barents Sea, where it could be rehabilitated. This was necessary, as the beluga is a cold-water mammal, preferring temperatures way below that of the Black Sea and the Mediterranean over the summer months, where it could rise far beyond the whale's normal tolerance levels, putting its life seriously at risk. There was also the ever-present problem of pollution in the Black Sea and even the possibility of radiological effects through run-off from the Chernobyl incident that could potentially harm the beluga.

This was, of course, a story ITN couldn't turn down, so after a hasty preparation I joined Sebastian Rich, Lawrence McGinty and the BDMLR team as underwater cameraman en route to Turkey to assess the situation.

It was good to see Ray again after our exploits in the Orkneys trying to track down the seal virus in 1988, but this time there was more focus to the expedition, and as we were all soon to learn, the eyes of the world would be watching our every move as the story unfolded.

Initially, it was only supposed to be a three-day trip, to assess the condition of the animal and its suitability for transportation. This would involve a visit to the government offices in Ankara to discuss the situation and receive permissions from the Minister of the Interior. However, as things progressed it became clear it was not only the practical and biological logistics that would be difficult to overcome but also the political snowball that had started rolling and was heading straight for us.

We landed at Istanbul airport on the 28th of March and immediately headed east to Ankara. I had been to Turkey several times before, and Istanbul is one of those places in the world you just have to visit – full of eastern promise as the old Turkish Delight ads said, and it certainly is… that is, if you survived the cab rides. Little did I know, but equally interesting driving awaited me in the days ahead, and at the hands of an Englishman.

The aim of the visit to Ankara was to take a petition from the BDMLR team to the Minister of the Interior to implore him to allow the whale, which had now become known as Brightness, or Aydin in Turkish, to be transported to the Barents Sea where he could be rehabilitated and then released. Ray was also desperate to prevent the Russians from coming to claim him and take him back to Sevastopol. To this end, they even had strong legal representation to back up their case, which stated that, under international law, the whale, since it was in Turkish waters, belonged to the Turkish government, and so they could decide the animal's fate – not the Russians. If you take more than a moment to think about this, you realise just how daft a statement that is – it's a wild animal, no one should own it - but as far as **BDMLR** were concerned, any legal backing, however absurd, was a useful lever to use in their quest.

There was even going to be a letter from Prince Charles to add a royal seal of approval to the operation, and somehow Sebastian had managed to secure an RAF escort of Phantom jets as the transport plane flew through British airspace. It was all starting to get slightly out of control and far more unwieldy than we had imagined.

But things had only just started warming up.

The meeting in Ankara in the minister's office turned out to be one of organised chaos. As well as ourselves, local TV crews and journalists had got wind of events and the whole episode started to turn into a media scrum. This, coupled with the minister's charming but hesitant grasp of the English language, meant we had a recipe for interesting dialogue.

The tone of the meeting was affable, but with so much riding on the outcome for **BDMLR**, there was also an air of tension as the minister listened patiently as Ray laid out the case before him. Ray was one of the most tenacious of people in his desire to succeed when it came to rescuing animals, but I had the feeling he was out of his comfort zone with a suit and tie trying to play the diplomat, and you could almost feel his desire to burst out and be in the water with his beloved whale. In contrast to this, the minister's faltering English and frequent referral to 'this little whale' added a Disneyesque slant to the whole proceedings.

After a series of staged and diplomatic overtures, both sides, although cordial, seemed to be setting out their camps. Ray and the environmentalists were polite, yet determined, in no uncertain terms, to repatriate the whale – the minister, on the other hand, listened intently, and despite no definite answer one way or the other, you got the distinct impression he didn't want to rock the boat with his larger and more powerful neighbour across the Black Sea. In other words, if the Russians wanted the whale back, it was theirs after all, so who were the Turks to stop them?

This did not bode well.

After the meeting, there was an extensive analysis and debrief amongst the BDMLR camp – rather like an exam post-mortem, where you go through every possible outcome, looking at it from every possible angle, then realising you are no closer to an answer than you had been at the beginning.

With Ray and the others putting a brave face on what appeared to me to be a major setback, we headed back to Istanbul to file a report on the progress so far.

What became something of a novelty and drove home just how small the world was, even in those days, was the fact that we would film a report during the day, edit the package with Lawrence doing a voice-over on-site, send it down the wires to London, then, as ITN had an affiliation with CNN, we could watch it on that news channel in our hotel room the next day. I know this is what happens every day, and particularly nowadays with live transmissions from war zones and the use of videophones, but when you're in the thick of it, seeing the images you shot one day on an American TV news channel the next, it's pretty cool.

The next challenge was to try to get some footage of

Brightness in the water, in his natural habitat. The only way to do this was to travel to Gerze.

There was also some urgency to the whole operation now, as there had been serious talk of the Russians coming to capture the whale and take him back to Sevastopol. Since the Turkish government seemed to be sitting on the fence on this one, there wasn't much hope they would form any sort of obstacle to the Russian action.

It was deemed to take too long to drive the 450 miles or so to Gerze, so two large Cessnas were chartered to take us there. We had been joined by Ian Sands, an ITN colleague of Sebastian's, who had flown in from a crew that had been covering the recent massive earthquake in eastern Turkey. He would help out editing the reports we filmed and get them sent back to London.

We touched down at a military air base in the rather bleak town of Sinop, east of Gerze on the Black Sea coast. Although the weather was overcast and dreary, I don't think I have ever seen a more desolate and bleak coastline as the Black Sea. The houses were drab and the roads endless and boring. It was only when the route finally twisted inland and the surroundings became more green that any semblance of depression was lifted.

After a fairly lengthy drive, we swung round a bend in the coast road, and spread out before us, across the bay, lay the small town of Gerze. This made a good establishing shot, and for the first time we got a far-off view of the town that had become the centre of so much attention. From this distance there was obviously no sign of the whale, but we were assured he came in twice a day to be fed by the fishermen, and optimistically we believed everything we were told.

The local fishermen, despite being very poor, had clubbed together to share their catch to feed Brightness, and he seemed to always come into the bay at the same time in the morning and afternoon. In fact, he had done this every day for several weeks - right up until the day we arrived.

It was like the time I had flown out to the Seychelles to help film the Subios Underwater Festival. The day I flew in, twelve whale sharks had been seen together in one bay - an unprecedented sight. Of course, once I was there, they weren't seen for the two-week duration of the trip. Then, on the last day, when I was flying out, there they were again.

Sometimes you just can't win.

With the long-distance shots in the can, we drove the final few miles down into the town itself. The place was fairly small with a couple of main streets shaped in a 'V' that led down to the harbour. We found our hotel near the quayside, but as I was to learn to my cost, it was right next door to the local mosque, which despite upgrading to modern technology to broadcast the regular calls to prayer over loudspeakers, clearly hadn't gone for the upper end of the market option. I was awoken at early hours of the morning with sound booming out through crackly speakers so distorted it made the train announcements at Clapham Junction railway station sound like a Bang and Olufsen hi-fi!

After throwing our bags into our rooms, we decided to take a look at the harbour and check out if our star performer was anywhere to be seen.

No show.

As the evening was drawing in, there was no time to go off and look for him, so we just had to be content with 'Well he's been here every day for the last three weeks. I'm sure he'll be here tomorrow.'

With no hope of seeing Brightness, it was a chance to get acquainted with the area and meet some of the locals.

Since the feelings of the people were paramount to the way the story might unfold, we dragged Ray down to the harbour to shoot a conversation between him, the local townspeople and the head of the hastily formed committee dealing with the town's new-found fame.

We at least thought we'd be in friendly hands with the locals, because, as opposed to their government, they didn't want the whale to go back to the Russians. They were so wound up about it they had even arranged for all the school kids to paint banners and form a dramatically staged protest march down to the jetty to show the depth of feeling.

This all seemed great and made fantastic visuals for the report, right up to the point where we realised they didn't want Ray to take the whale either. As far as they were concerned, it was their whale and no one was going anywhere with it.

It would take some patient scientific explanation, gentle diplomatic persuasion, and several bottles of the local tipple to win the support of these fiercely protective people.

After a slightly heated interview on the harbour, with Ray surrounded by schoolkids and locals who had never seen so much excitement, it was on to the town hall to buy those local tipples and persuade the natives to side with the environmentalists, who after all had the best interests of the whale at heart.

A few rolls of tape later, we had some interesting footage for the night's report. Seb, Ian and Lawrence went off to edit it, then they had around an hour's drive to the nearest wire transfer point to send it back to London.

After a couple of drinks in the hotel bar, I headed for bed with the hope of seeing Brightness the following day.

The next day did dawn bright and also LOUD – at about six thirty to be precise. After recovering from the rendition from the top of the minaret, there was time for a quick breakfast of rather stale, bland bread and cereal, and then it was down to planning a course of action for the day. There wasn't a whole lot we could do other than wait at the end of the jetty for Brightness to appear. After all, this was the only known place he had regularly come to, and he had done so, like clockwork, for the last few weeks.

In anticipation, we headed down to the jetty and waited… and waited… and… waited. This created a slight dilemma. Film crews are not renowned for their patience and always seem to think things should be happening for them exactly on cue - if they're not, then they'll damn well make them happen. The problem here was that you were dealing with nature, which, as was being seen, was highly unpredictable and obviously hadn't received a copy of the day's shooting schedule. So it was decided that we would go in search of the whale.

Now this wasn't a good move in my view. To go looking for a whale that could have gone anywhere in any direction was interesting to say the least. The one place in the world that people reliably knew the whale appeared was Gerze harbour. Until there were sightings to the contrary, that was the place to be to have the best chance of seeing him, but the decision was made, and so off we trotted on a wild whale chase eastwards along the Turkish coast by boat. Ian had been left with a Betacam on the jetty - just in case, but I had the underwater camera, which could provide some of the key footage we needed to shoot.

Having twiddled our thumbs and become numb in the biting wind for several hours, the not altogether unsurprising call came over the radio that the whale had turned up in Gerze. We now had the hour or so slog back to the harbour in the hope that he would still be there when we got back so we could get some underwater footage before he decided to decamp for real.

When we arrived in Gerze, there seemed to be somewhat of a circus in the harbour, with three of the local boats all out feeding the whale, which could be clearly seen, its white head bobbing above the water close to one or other of the boats. The thought then occurred to us that as the interest grew and more and more people came to see Brightness, so the harassment, noise and general activity in the water would increase and could be a factor in driving him away for good. It wasn't lost on us that we, of course, would have to be included in that group, but for the moment, he seemed to be enamoured with human contact and had no problem in approaching the small boats that drifted around him, however many people were on board.

Seb, Lawrence and Ray managed to commandeer a small rowing boat and manoeuvre close to Brightness to conduct their interviews about the state of the animal and the progress in the plans to move him. Meanwhile, I managed to slip into the water for some shots of him in his natural habitat. As we had been in such a rush to get out here, there had been no time to get hold of any scuba gear - all I had was a wetsuit, mask, snorkel and fins - so my time underwater would have to be on one breath of air. Fortunately, the harbour was fairly shallow and all the activity was close to the surface, so much of the footage could be shot at or just below the water line.

At one point he swam straight past me, barely a foot away, snapping his jaws together as a possible warning, or more probably in annoyance at this intruder into his world. Belugas are amazing creatures and are known as the canaries of the seas because of their constant chirruping and chattering underwater. This was entirely true, and I was almost spellbound as I heard a cacophony of sounds, all of which were created using nasal sacs near the blowhole. The beluga is also the only whale with an extra vertebra in the spine, allowing them to move their heads from side to side, and it was quite strange to see him actually turn his head to look at me as he swam past.

The animal himself was truly magnificent, with 'Brightness' being the perfect description. His whole body was an almost brilliant, translucent white, which shone out against the murky backdrop of the water. It was almost like having an angel swim out of the gloom towards you, which made what was to happen at the end of the trip all the more painful.

With the key shots in the can we could rest more easily. Obviously it would be great to shoot as much underwater footage as possible, but the amount we had meant that whatever unfolded in the environmental/political wrangling above water, there would always be underwater footage that could be played against it, showing Brightness in his natural environment.

It was about now though that things started to get really daft.

As the interest in the plight of the whale grew back home and around the world, and as the election news in the UK became ever more dreary, news desks started to see the Brightness story as a soap that could run and run. I mean, what could be more dramatic than a cutesy animal, stuck in the middle of a political/environmental confrontation, in a race against time for its life, played out on the world stage? They intended to milk it for all it was worth. So in the best traditions of journalism, all the papers and TV channels sent teams out to cover the story in their own inimitable styles and from every conceivable angle.

And we had everyone.

From the 'Isn't he sweet' angle, courtesy of the *Daily Mail*, who sent a female reporter to swim and 'bond' with Brightness, to the more highbrow papers that looked into the serious political implications and logistical issues concerned with rehabilitating a whale to a new location, to finally the *Daily Star*, who topped the lot with their full front page headline 'Whale War III', followed by a detailed schematic showing Brightness trying to escape the Russian military with a radar dish where his blowhole should have been and multiple rocket launchers strapped to his side.

I have heard it said that newspaper hacks sit around in the pub all evening trying to think up the most outlandish slant on a story, and I guess I had always taken this with a pinch of salt; that was until I walked into the hotel bar one evening and saw about ten of these guys, huddled in deep conversation, whiskies in hand, trying desperately to come up with new angles for the morning editions.

From the newspaper side of things it probably all came to a head when one of the tabloids reported that an SAS team was on its way to Turkey to prevent the Russians from grabbing the whale. Unfortunately, someone had got their wires crossed, resulting in three bewildered environmentalists being thoroughly searched and 'detained' at the airport when they flew into Istanbul.

Things were clearly getting out of hand, and in truth, the essence of the story was being diluted – that of the genuine survival of the whale. Also, with all this frenetic interest and people jumping into the water at every opportunity, there was the strong likelihood that the animal would just take off one day to get away from it all.

Although we were obviously part of this circus, we felt that our interest was genuine and we had originally come here to highlight the plight of the whale and bring attention to help with any rehabilitation, not to turn the whole thing into a circus.

Also, as anticipated, on the political front, things were unfortunately not looking great. It was now fairly certain the Russians would come to reclaim their whale and the Turkish government were not going to stand in their way. This prompted howls of protest from all quarters, not least the fishermen and residents of Gerze, who were now quite proud of their adopted friend who had brought all this fame to their little town. There was even an echo of 'We shall fight them on the beaches…' as the locals prepared for all-out war with the Russians to save their whale. At one point they even tried to lead him away from the harbour with fish in an attempt to stop the Russians from finding him.

However, things were to take a dramatic twist a day before the Russians arrived, and it wasn't from any sly move by the Turks, or any political shenanigans from the government. It appeared Brightness had got wind of his former captors imminent arrival and had high-tailed it off his own back. This left a lot of confused and desperate media people wondering where the next episode of the soap was going to come from. It also left us with a dilemma, and this is where the story splits into two. You could say it was where the men are separated from the boys... or, more specifically - TV crews from the printed page.

The first thing that threw the cat amongst the pigeons was the arrival of the Russians. Tension had been building for some time, as to if, and when, they would come, but come they finally did. We received reports of where they were going to land and headed off in that direction.

Since the beginning, we had been the only UK TV crew covering the story, and it was our reports, broadcast internationally, that had initially created so much buzz around Brightness. The BBC had been caught seriously napping, as they had only just contacted their Turkish affiliate, Viz News, who had sent a crew down to pick up the pieces. However, since Brightness had disappeared, the stakes had just been raised, and it was now a matter of pride within the individual organisations as to who could find him first. They had their contacts, we had ours, and nobody was sharing information.

When the Russians finally arrived in the busy port of Samsun, they must have received quite a shock. The scrum on the quayside was more reminiscent of the arrival of a rock star than journalists following an environmental story. The Russians, slightly fazed by the whole affair, looked down from the ship with bewildered faces. They were clearly used to doing things in their own time and with minimum publicity.

After the vessel had docked, their lead scientist, Dr Lev Mukhametov, made his way down the gangplank and gave an eloquent and matter-of-fact argument as to why the whale should go back to Russia. It was the usual 'He's not used to the wild, he's been trained by us, he won't survive without us,' etc. All points that were valid to a degree, but in the heat of what the story had become, factors that weren't given much credibility by the eager press pack.

While everyone's attention was fixed on the speech, three men walked almost unseen off the boat. One had a 'don't mess with me' expression, and a face that would sue if it ever cracked into a smile. The other two were less intimidating but dressed in wetsuits and carrying a bucket of fish. We were to learn later that these two were the trainers who had originally caught Brightness in the Sea of Okhotsk off eastern Russia and were here to try and lure him back. Almost before anyone had realised what was going on, all three had climbed into a black Mercedes and driven away.

I think Seb was probably the first to move, realising just what was happening. We had thrown the gear in the car and screeched out of the car park before any of the other crews had really cottoned on.

As I was thrown around on the back seat, I realised, slightly bemused, that we were now in a high-speed car chase with a bunch of Russians, two of whom were wearing wetsuits, and one, by the looks of him, who was more than likely, ex-KGB.

What followed next had to be experienced to be believed – a game of cat and mouse across northern Turkey, filled with enough deception and intrigue to fill a Tom Clancy novel. The aim - to lose Viz News and the other journalists and gain an exclusive on where Brightness had gone and what his fate might be.

Following any car at high speed is a dangerous proposition. However, following three Russians across a strange country, when they didn't want to be followed, could be construed as foolhardy. The problem was, they clearly had information as to where Brightness was, so, if we weren't going to lose the story completely, we had to follow them.

We hadn't been going long when Seb, who had been continuously glancing in his rear-view mirror, said, 'We've got a tail.'

When I looked out the back window, there, several cars back, was the Viz News crew in hot pursuit of us. It seemed like they were the only ones – all the others being left stranded at the dock in Samsun.

Looking forward was no less scary. The car was keeping a fairly consistent TEN FEET from the Russian's bumper. A quick glance at the speedo confirmed we were in interesting times - I mean, eighty miles per hour, ten feet behind a bunch of nervous Russians? Lawrence seemed fairly unfazed by the whole thing, merely reading through his notes and trying to work out something to say for his next report. At this rate I would be very surprised if there was a next report.

After about thirty miles, and with still no sighting of Brightness, the Russians pulled into a rest area to consult. Their information seemed to have lucked out. While we were watching this there was frantic activity in the Viz News car, which had skidded up barely seconds after we had pulled in behind the Russians. A minute later and their driver threw a mobile phone down and the car sped out of the car park.

Clearly they had some new intel.

We sped off after Viz News, but the Russians were a bit slow on the draw. This was starting to look like something out of a Keystone Cops' movie or the end of a Benny Hill show.

We had been going for about ten miles, with the Russians some way behind, when Seb shouted, 'Shit!' Nothing more, but he kept glancing at the dashboard. I managed a quick look myself between bouts of close encounters with alternate rear doors as I was flung from side to side on the shiny vinyl.

We were almost out of fuel.

This resulted in tension in the car that made the Cuban missile crisis look like a quiet day at the Oxford debating society, and it went on for about another ten miles.

As we were pondering what to do, realising the chase could very soon be over due to a lack of fuel, the Viz News guys careered off the road to the left a hundred yards ahead. As we swung in behind them, we spotted a petrol station across the road. The dilemma now was what to do. If the whale was here we had to film him. We might not get another chance. If he wasn't, we weren't going to get very much further without any petrol.

At this point Viz News were already out of the car, setting up a camera and tripod and running towards a small sandy beach twenty yards away. We looked out to sea, but there was no sign of Brightness.

In a split-second decision that was ultimately to change everything, Seb jumped back in the car and screeched across to the petrol station. I was still watching the Viz News guys when the Russians shot past. They had definitely seen us, but they weren't stopping.

They must have known something we didn't.

Realising the implication, Seb screamed for Lawrence, who had jumped out to grab a quick cigarette, and me, to get our butts back in the car. He was in such a hurry that the car started moving before I had even managed to open the rear door and before the petrol nozzle was barely out of the filler hole. As I dived in the back, Seb flung a handful of Turkish lira out the window, sending a pile of gravel into the air as he spun the rear tyres, and leaving a bemused garage attendant in a cloud of dust as the lira rained down around him.

The whole thing happened so quickly we were gone and dusted before the Viz News guys had even taken the camera off the tripod. It was this one quick-thinking moment that meant Viz News missed out on the whole of the rest of the story and ITN had an exclusive from here on in.

Even though we were quite a way behind the Russians when we finally made it onto the road, we had them in sight. They were catchable. By the time Viz News got going we were off the chart and they were merely racing to catch up in the hope of finding us further down the road. If we had stayed on the road they would probably have caught up at some point, but a couple of miles further on the Russians shot up a dirt track behind some trees to a lookout point on a clifftop. Here they could scan a large area of sea for Brightness. It was during this stop-off, having followed the Russians, that to our delight, we watched Viz News sail past on the main road and into the sunset, never to be seen again.

To say we had almost become friends with the guys from behind the Iron Curtain was probably stretching it a bit, but a begrudging respect certainly seemed to be growing. We hadn't managed to coax a smile out of their leader, whom I had christened 'Ivan', but we could tell he was warming to us, as the usually superior hostile sneer seemed to have disappeared. They still weren't speaking to us, so there wasn't complete détente, but we felt we were breaking through.

After about twenty minutes of sea scanning, we realised Brightness was nowhere in sight and we all piled back into our respective vehicles to continue the now familiar view of Ivan's rear bumper ten feet in front.

After another hour of formation driving, where the distance closed to about five feet on occasion, and I thought Ivan would slam on the brakes, we would pile into the back, and if the crash didn't kill us, the three perfectly aimed bullets from Ivan's undoubted sidearm most certainly would, it started to go dark.

At this point the stakes suddenly increased. Ivan, no doubt tiring of the game, decided it was time to lose us.

We now had the added problem of the Russian using the oncoming traffic as a movable chicane to try and shake us off. We're talking the car chase out of *Basic Instinct* here, where Michael Douglas is overtaking on blind corners trying not to lose Sharon Stone; something quite clearly worth dying for, but we were chasing Ivan and the fishmen - not quite the same.

Having survived the next forty miles without crashing or getting shot, we followed the Russians into a small lay-by overlooking the sea.

What was this? Surely they couldn't have seen Brightness in the dark, even though he was white. Perhaps they had night vision goggles or infrared sights.

Unfortunately, nothing so grand. They were trying to attract the attention of their ship, which had been tracking us along the coast. Perhaps the communication satellite wasn't in the right position – perhaps they needed line of sight.

Actually, it was more like line of LIGHT.

They were trying to contact the ship by flashing their headlights! As the grey hull of the vessel stood out against the black backdrop of the water, Ivan started flashing away - and I had flashbacks to Harry and Bongo in Jamaica.

It wasn't long before the Russian ship responded with its own series of flashes, and after a brief, nonsensical, illuminated conversation – we didn't understand Russian Morse code – Ivan started to walk towards us.

I was ready to run for it and Seb and Lawrence were looking slightly nervous but we needn't have worried. It seemed Ivan had decided to co-operate and suggested we find a local hotel to stay in for the night.

We eventually found an establishment that was passing itself off as a hotel on the outskirts of a small town. It was getting late, but the ice finally seemed to be thawing. Ivan even suggested we meet at six thirty in the morning, when he would take us to the boat that was going out to recapture Brightness, who had been seen in the bay. They couldn't do anything till first light, so that was why they needed the hotel. I was surprised at our new-found buddy's apparent friendship, but others were not so sure. Seb suggested we be ready to go by five thirty - just in case.

As we walked into the hotel, I thought my problems were over for the night. In fact, they were only just beginning. After mounting a wide flight of steps into the lobby, it became clear that 'seedy' wasn't quite the word for this joint. The lighting was subdued, not intentionally to create a certain ambience, though it did, but for a 'they couldn't afford the right sized light bulbs and the electricity supply wasn't reliable anyway' kind of reason. Everywhere you looked you saw rather drunken sailors tottering around arm in arm with rather scantily clad women. It soon became clear that this was the local knocking shop for Turkish sailors, a revelation backed up by Seb's comment once we hit our room. 'Keep an eye out for crabs.' I was just about to point out that we were quite a way from the sea, when I glanced at the less than clean sheets and realised that perhaps I'd better sleep with my clothes on.

After a fitful sleep, accompanied by much scratching of imaginary itches, a pillow hit me at five fifteen. When we reached the car, we were just in time to see Ivan and the fishmen climbing into the Merc.

Sons of bitches!

The lack of sleep was forgotten though, and as we threw the gear into the back of the vehicle, we managed to catch the briefest of smiles on Ivan's face as he realised he was up against worthy adversaries.

We followed them down to the quayside, where we had chartered a small fishing boat to take us out in search of Brightness.

The Russians had a boat to take them to their research vessel, which was now moored just offshore. They said we could come along, having finally accepted we weren't going to go away. This was the good news. All we had to do now was find the ever-elusive whale.

In my heart I think I hoped we wouldn't, as the discovery would inevitably lead to his recapture and being transported back to Russia, but we were here to document, not affect, and so we set out with subdued feelings but also ones of expectation.

In fairness to some of our press colleagues, Seb and Lawrence had told a few of the photographers where we were and they had come along for the final ride.

About a mile out from the shore we had our reward. There was Brightness, doggedly heading steadily east. If he kept this up for a day or so more he would cross the border into Georgian territorial waters and we couldn't have followed.

I immediately pulled on my wetsuit and jumped in with the camera. As again there was no scuba gear, I had to rely on holding my breath for any stay underwater and just hope that Brightness would come close enough for some decent shots.

What greeted me though was quite surreal. For a start the area we were in wasn't very deep - around fifteen to twenty feet - but there was some sort of halocline or thermocline a few feet off the bottom. This created a layer of silty water below and clear water above. It was in this layer that I saw Brightness, just hanging there with his tail disappearing into the silt below and his head and upper body curved over towards me, framed between the surface above and the silt layer below. It was really quite an amazing sight, but he wasn't going to stay for long, and I only managed to knock off a few shots before he disappeared into the gloom on his journey east.

Once back on board, it was time to head out towards the Russians, who, having seen what was going on, were moving in for the capture.

Their plan was to get as close as they could with the research ship, then launch a small inflatable that would take the fishmen over to the whale. They then hoped that with the lure of food and the possible recognition Brightness would show for his trainers, they might be able to lasso him and haul him on board the larger vessel on a ready-made stretcher. This of course assumed that any recognition on Brightness's part would be favourable. After all, these were the guys who had taken him into captivity in the first place and looked after him for most of his imprisonment. It was possible their mere presence would be enough to send him scurrying away.

We would have to wait and see.

Whatever happened, we were helpless to intervene and would just have to record events as they unfolded.

As things progressed, it looked as though Brightness did recognise his trainers when they approached him in the inflatable offering fish. He stayed with them as they tried to renew their relationship and regain his trust.

As was his want, Lawrence was always game for anything. The episode in Scapa Flow had proved that, along with the numerous times I had been with him when he had gone into the water with either seals, dolphins and, this time, a white whale. He had even managed to remain good humoured when the newsreader back in the studio had thought it prudent to point out that Lawrence was the one in the wetsuit!

Now he was as keen as ever to get a good piece to camera from our boat, with the Russians trying to capture the whale in the background. Since we had been asked to stay away during this stage of the capture, I had been unable to get into the water to film anything, so I was on board watching Lawrence do his thing.

All was ready for the dramatic report.

Seb had Lawrence framed nicely in the shot, the captain steered a course to keep the action in the background, Lawrence gripped the microphone, the weather was fine.

It was at this point that one of the less attentive Turkish boat crew decided to walk straight between Lawrence and the camera, stretching the microphone lead connecting the two. In his frustration, Lawrence tried to push the hapless deckhand to one side, but in the process he managed to push himself, complete with Barbour jacket full of tapes and batteries, and a fine set of green wellies, over the side. The next thing we all saw was a rather dazed and spluttering news reporter floundering around in the freezing waters of the Black Sea.

Someone yelled, 'All stop!' and I leapt in to grab Lawrence before he disappeared below the surface forever. Fortunately I had my wetsuit on in anticipation of the coming filming, but I didn't have any fins. At least I was warm and the suit provided some buoyancy to support Lawrence and his equipment-loaded jacket.

However, once I had grabbed him and started to pull him back towards the boat, the boat was either still moving or the current was taking us in the opposite direction. This was no real problem, as after all there were about ten people on the boat, one of whom at least must have had the intelligence to throw a rope to me.

As I towed Lawrence backwards I couldn't see what was going on, but there was a lot of shouting. After a couple of minutes, when no rope had appeared, I made it clear, in no uncertain terms, that I wanted one. When still no rope appeared, I turned round to see what the problem was. I was immediately confronted by ten camera lenses, everything from your average happy snap through the full pro kit of the *Daily Mail*'s photographer to Seb's Betacam.

I was so incredulous I hardly knew what to say, but after a few dire expletives, a rope finally snaked over my head and I started pulling. Of course, no one had tied off the other end, so I was acquiring a rather long length of rope in the water and going nowhere. A few even more dire expletives and the problem was sorted and we eventually made it back on board.

A rather relieved and bewildered Lawrence plonked himself down on the deck and took a few moments to get his breath back. But he didn't have long. While we'd been occupied in rescuing Lawrence, the Russians had been busy. We had barely dragged him back on board when there was a shout from the water and a Russian fist shot into the air. As we looked over, we could see Brightness had finally been snared - a lasso was clearly round his body, pulled tight behind the fins.

As we watched, the research ship closed the gap, and

all they had to do now was haul him on board. It was time to get in the water for what would prove to be some of the most distressing footage I have ever shot.

Even before I jumped in with snorkel and camera, I had a sense that I didn't really want to be filming this.

The idea was to manoeuvre Brightness towards the side of the ship and steer him into a canvas stretcher, which was suspended from a crane and had two holes for his pectoral fins. Once on the stretcher he could easily be winched aboard for the long journey back to captivity.

It was particularly poignant as, rightly or wrongly, we had all become very attached to Brightness, and we thought of him somewhat selfishly as 'our' whale. The thought of him going back into military captivity in Russia wasn't something we really wanted to dwell on.

But the job had to be done.

Once in the water I finned across to where the trainers were trying to ease him onto the stretcher.

He had been relatively calm when they had been trying to catch him earlier, so I thought this part would go fairly smoothly. But as if sensing the impending imprisonment, he had other ideas. Maybe he had remembered the harness from some distant memory, or maybe it was just the natural instinct of survival and escape from a trapped and cornered animal, but he thrashed desperately around as though his life depended on it, which as far as he was concerned, it did.

The first attempts to get him onto the stretcher failed. At the time I was only a few feet away, half-submerged, and could see everything going on above and below water. It was awful to hear the ever more frantic cries of anguish, pain and fear. Gradually, as the trainers worked to secure him in the harness, he started to tire, and eventually the thrashing began to calm, but not before the most distressing sight of all. During his valiant attempts to escape, he had scraped his delicate skin against the rusty rivets on the side of the ship and bright red blood now streamed down his glistening white body as well as the white hull of the ship. It was truly heartbreaking, and some of the small amount of seawater that had collected at the bottom of my mask was made up of tears.

But the inevitable was indeed inevitable, and as he was winched slowly out of the water, his true weight became a burden to him and all he could manage was the occasional desperate cry and slight movement of his head from side to side.

Once on board the Russian vessel, he was quickly tranquillised to try and relieve the stress of the journey ahead, and we were allowed on board for Lawrence to do a piece to camera.

Despite the sadness we all felt, I managed a small smile at the sight of Lawrence doing his report, water up to his knees, in the tank that Brightness was now quietly floating in.

With the job over, it was time to return to the UK, knowing we had covered the event with guile and cunning to keep up with the Russians and to best the BBC, but with the sadness and realisation that Brightness was returning to a life of captivity.

What lifted the spirits over the coming months, though, was that the saga was not over. Brightness managed to escape again, only to be recaptured, then escape yet again - that's one feisty little whale!

For all I know, he's still out there somewhere where the

Russians can't find him.

Once all the international pressure and hoopla had died down, they probably thought it wasn't worth the money, time and effort to catch a whale that clearly didn't want to be caught, and one that was part of a decaying and underfunded military programme, influenced more by cutbacks and budgetary considerations than the protection of a slowly disintegrating Soviet Union.

16

On Reserve

In all the years of working on underwater film and television projects, there has barely been a single job that has been boring or mundane. Every one has brought a new experience, good or bad, and has usually led to other interesting and diverse avenues for the future.

I have often been asked when I was going to get a proper job, but finding something comparable to do would be a hard task when there are so many challenges and exciting adventures to be had. It has certainly been a case of following your heart and trying to do something you love. After all, what's the point of spending most of your life doing something you don't enjoy?

I have had to be fairly ruthless with what has been included in this book, as there has been such a wealth of material to draw from, but I have tried to give an idea of some of the varied and exciting projects that are out there for people working in this field, as well as showing some of the downright daft and crazy things that can happen along the way.

Also, maybe the next time you watch an underwater sequence in a movie or on TV, you might just take a second or two to think about how much work has actually gone into producing the images you see on screen, which may last for only a few seconds.

Sadly, there hasn't been time to go into the visibility problems caused by Billy Idol's hair dye, or the prop guys who thought that dumping a tin of Marmite into a studio tank would muck up the visibility enough to make it look like murky Thames water, when a couple of teaspoons of powdered milk would quite happily have done the job.

It's also probably not appropriate to go into the problem of where to look during the filming of an adult education video involving a couple making love in a private swimming pool, and you just have to make sure everything is safe and sound!

And probably the less said the better about the producer who suggested I make the lead actress fall in love with me to get her to do the tricky underwater sequences the producer knew she didn't want to do.

Of course, not everything has been plain sailing - there has been the occasional downside, like when filming in a swimming pool where you might have thought the worst problems would be temperature or visibility, only to find the pool operator pouring concentrated sulphuric acid into the water to dilute the fifty times too much chlorine he'd already put in. The result - a trip to the hospital and a burnt airway to the lungs, reducing your breathing capacity for several months.

Then there was the time when, having been in the water for twelve hours a day, seven days in a row, with only a break to fill cylinders and have lunch, you catch an ear infection that puts you out of action for a couple of days, and the assistant producer asks if you'd mind not being paid for those days. Or the time when the bags were packed ready to fly to LA to work on a commercial with Sharon Stone in a massive underwater champagne glass, and it's cancelled almost as the taxi is arriving to take us to the airport, and all because she'd had a change of mind and didn't want to do the ad because, as we were told, she didn't like the idea of all the crew peeing in the pool.

So there have been the best of times and the worst of times, but there can hardly be many jobs where you are paid to go round the world and do what you would happily be paying to do in the first place.

For some time now my priorities have shifted towards the writing and creation of projects. There is the continued development of some of the film scripts and the *SCUBA DIVING - Underwater* series, as well as starting the series of John McCready novels. But the opportunities and experiences working underwater in the world of film and television will never be forgotten.

The rewards come not only from seeing the finished product up there on the screen but also from the often once-in-a-lifetime diving experiences you have while doing them.

And diving is a sport that virtually anyone can do.

I have taught many people to dive over the years, and there are few reasons why someone might not be able to take part. There are a small number of medical conditions that can be restrictive in certain cases, but beyond that, there really isn't any reason why you shouldn't give it a go, even if you think you could never do it.

All you need is a love of water and the will to want to try.

I was once privileged enough to take a sixty-year-old gentleman on his first ever dive in a freezing cold quarry in England. He loved every second of it.

So if he can have a go, there's no reason for anyone not to.

Diving probably represents the closest thing we will have to travelling to another planet, certainly in our lifetime. It allows you to swim weightless over coral reefs, investigate mysterious shipwrecks, and explore amazing cave systems. There are marine mammals and marine life to meet all over the world, and every encounter will leave you enthralled, enchanted, and waiting in expectation for the next one.

It also makes you realise what an incredible planet we live on, and one that should be treasured, respected and preserved for all it's worth.

So go on, why not take the plunge?

And if you do, I hope you will bring back memories and experiences you will treasure for the rest of your life.

APPENDIX

Breaking in

I have often been asked how you go about breaking into the industry and where is the best place to start. Now while there is a huge amount you can do to help yourself, as with many things, much of it is about being in the right place at the right time, coupled with a certain amount of luck and a huge amount of determination. But I'm a strong believer that to a large extent you make your own luck, so that one day you'll find yourself in the right place at the right time.

You do, of course, have to be a qualified diver and have a certain amount of diving experience. Also, a specific skill related to the film industry would be an advantage, though not entirely necessary - everyone has to start somewhere.

The job most people would probably associate with underwater film work is that of cameraman, but there are many other roles that are equally important. Remember, film-making is a team effort and never the product of a single individual.

So, what's on offer, and just how do you go about

getting into this fascinating world?

If you've ever been on a set, you will realise there are an awful lot of people that seem to be doing an awful lot of nothing. This is because experts are needed on hand at all times in all the relevant departments, in case something goes wrong, or equipment needs adjusting, or ideas change. These range from camera and sound, to props, wardrobe, make-up, lighting, special effects, stunts, and so on. In many cases these departments will also need to be utilised on underwater shoots, and you can be pretty sure that most people already working in these areas won't know how to dive.

There are also specific diving-related jobs - underwater co-ordination, diving supervision, and artist training and safety. In the latter, you may well be dealing with people who have to perform at depth, without an air supply, and who have never dived before.

Beyond these are the more senior roles of production and direction.

Once you decide on an area you would like to work in, the first thing you need is to be recognised by a professional diving or safety body in your part of the world. In the UK this is the Health & Safety Executive (HSE). From a film point of view, this means being a diver competent to undertake media diving operations. The minimum qualification for this is HSE SCUBA Diving.

The HSE recognises a number of diving qualifications, but it's always best to check with them to see if you have a qualification they accept and the requisite experience. If you have none, the best way to ensure you comply is to enrol on a specific HSE professional diver's course for SCUBA divers. This will ensure you meet any requirements that are currently in force. As regulations and specific requirements are revised from time to time you should check up on the current regulations before proceeding.

Once you have achieved a recognised qualification, you should think of it as a starting point, rather than having 'got there'. Become as experienced and proficient in your diving as possible before you even contemplate a life working underwater in film. The reason for this should be fairly obvious – when you're working your concentration needs to be on the reason you're being paid to be underwater, which is not as a diver, but for your skills in camera, safety, lighting, etc. If your diving isn't up to scratch, you'll spend more time concerned with your own safety than with the job at hand.

As well as the qualifications, you will have to undergo a full professional diver's medical every year to maintain an 'active' status with the HSE. Some positions require a current diver's first aid certificate as well. You must also dive and work regularly, particularly for those jobs involving safety work.

Once you have the qualifications, medical and experience – what next?

It all depends where you see your future lying. The following positions are just some of the key areas where divers may be needed.

Safety Diver

Unless you already have a trade in the industry that can easily be transferred underwater, safety work is probably the easiest way in. There is often the need for safety divers on shoots, particularly when there is a large underwater sequence being filmed at one of the major studios. To get in this way, it certainly helps if you are an instructor.

In the UK, the system works as follows. A diving contractor will be hired by the production company. He or she will then appoint a diving supervisor for that particular shoot. It will be down to the supervisor to organise the divers. The contractor and supervisor may be the same person, but they are the people to contact if you are interested in work, not the studios or the production company.

Having said that, a supervisor won't just want to take anyone onto a set. I have worked with many divers over the years who may have been very competent - sports or even commercial divers - but when it comes to the patience, understanding and particular demands of film work, they have been far from ideal.

You need to have a knowledge of what's required on a film shoot to be able to apply your skills safely and constructively, and this only comes from being around sets, or on location, and being prepared to listen and learn. Like in any form of diving, just because you can do it one way doesn't mean you can do it another.

Safety jobs might range from standing by for an artist, in case they fall into the water, all the way through to supervising a major drama or action sequence on a complex set with multiple artists underwater at the same time. Bear in mind, though, there's a lot of experience and learning between the two.

One interesting aspect of underwater film work is that it usually involves things you would never normally do underwater yet utilises all your normal diving skills to be able to achieve whatever's required for the particular sequence. I mean, you don't normally have a person, with no air supply of their own, tied down to the bottom of a pool or area of open water for over half an hour, but it can and has been done safely and successfully many times.

This brings us to a critical aspect of any shoot involving artists – their training. Here you will probably be dealing with people who have never dived before, and you will need to teach them just enough to be able to safely complete the shots required, which means you have to have an understanding of exactly what is needed and how to achieve it in the minimum possible time, but in complete safety. What you have to remember is that you are NOT teaching them to dive. You may, for example, not even need to mention finning action or buoyancy control. If they are twenty feet down in a gold-sequinned dress with no dive gear or fins - what's the point? You obviously need to teach enough for them to be safe, but above all, they must have absolute trust and faith in you. This needs to go far beyond a normal diving buddy situation, as their life really will be in your hands.

Stuntwork

This area of film work is probably one of the most exciting, and will involve many skills other than just diving, but if the appeal and the will is there, it can be the ultimate job. It's very well paid but also very competitive and very hard to get into. However, whereas it differs from many other areas, here there is a set formula, so to speak, for getting in.

In the UK you have to complete a number of different specified skills in a variety of different disciplines to a very high standard. While the skills required are hard to achieve, if you have enough perseverance, money and ability you can achieve them, but it's a hard slog.

For more information, contact The British Stunt Register.

www.thebritishstuntregister.com

Special Effects

Another of those exciting departments that covers a multitude of sins. These can range from explosions and mechanical effects, like the helicopter in *Leviathan*, to artistic effects, like the monster in the same film. All may require divers to work with props or rigging equipment in the water and so are good areas to look at. It can help to have some form of engineering experience, or a relative skill, to get into a special effects company, but they do occasionally take people on as assistants who can then work their way through the system. Again, if you have a recognised diving qualification and experience, this could be something a company might see as a valuable addition to the skills they can offer.

Spark/Gaffer

If you aren't interested in safety work, or have no instructional experience, then perhaps the lighting side of things is more up your street. In the strange and wonderful world of film and TV, the 'Spark' and 'Gaffer' are members of the lighting department.

Underwater, just as on dry land, there is a need for lights to be able to creatively show the action being filmed. Obviously, lights require electricity and as we all know, electricity and water don't mix. The gaffer, therefore, is a critical role on an underwater shoot, particularly from a safety point of view.

As a spark, the work will involve a lot of lugging of large, heavy lights around, but underwater will involve setting and adjusting the lights to the director's requirements. As a gaffer, or supervisor, you will be ensuring the whole location is safe from an electrical standpoint. Again, to reach this level requires years of experience in the industry to be able to anticipate any potential electrical problems and solve them before something goes seriously wrong.

To work in electrical departments, it's best to work up through the ranks to gain the relevant experience, but previous employment as an electrician will obviously give you a head start. Contact film electrical companies to see if they have any openings. All contact details for film and TV-related companies in the UK can be found in publications such as *The Knowledge* and *Kays Directory*.

www.theknowledgeonline.com
www.kays.co.uk

Camerawork

This now comes into the controversial area of 'Is it easier to teach a cameraman to dive, or a diver to operate a camera?' Overall, the eye for a shot and the ability to work a camera professionally is probably more important.

However, it doesn't of course mean that all cameramen can dive. Some will have the aptitude, some won't.

On paper, the way to work as an underwater cameraman, be it in film or on video, is to be an experienced surface cameraman first. This can be learnt through training courses or by working up through the ranks at various production companies, learning the ropes as you go. Unfortunately, this can take a long time and can also be frustrating, as there are often few places available on good camera courses, and there are only so many production companies.

There is another way, however, and one that, for some, has proven to be the best entry into their chosen field.

At the end of the day, it's a highly competitive market out there. At one end of the scale there will always be the few individuals who are well known within the industry, and for jobs with the appropriate budget, those individuals will always get the work. But there will also be countless other productions out there, with limited budgets, who don't mind who does the job so long as they get results for minimum expenditure. This is an open market.

The catch is, of course, that you will have to prove your ability and have a suitably impressive showreel in order to get the work in the first place. This, though, is down to you. You don't have to worry about getting onto any courses or working your way up through the ranks – if it's on tape or film, then obviously you can produce the work.

Probably one of the most striking examples of this is Mike Portelly, who started out in dentistry, bought his own camera and housing, taught himself how to use them, and over a number of years produced a film called *Ocean's Daughter*, which is one of the most creative underwater films ever made. He went on to become an award-winning underwater cameramen/director, responsible for such memorable commercials as the British Gas advert with babies underwater in the Red Sea, as well as countless others.

Nowadays it is possible to pick up relatively cheap digital video cameras and housings and a computer editing system for a few thousand pounds. With this kit and a bit of imagination, you can produce your own showreel to show to prospective clients. There's obviously no guarantee this will work, but at least you are doing something constructive towards your goal, and however it turns out, you are gaining experience, which can only be a good thing.

The result may be that you realise this isn't actually for you, and you could have saved yourself years of heartbreak trying to break into a highly competitive industry. But for those that do make it, the rewards can be well worth it. That said, there are probably only a handful of cameramen who earn a full-time living out of underwater work alone, so be warned.

Focus Puller

This rather strange-sounding role, is, amongst other things, the person who changes the focus of a camera during a shot. There isn't always a focus puller required underwater, but for large-scale productions they may well be used, doubling as an underwater assistant for the cameraman. As this is a specialised field in its own right, it's best to work up through the camera technician side, and the fact you can dive may be an added benefit to you securing a job in this specialised area.

Props/Wardrobe

There are a number of other departments on a film project that need to be represented underwater. These would normally be filled by people from the particular disciplines, but as HSE recognition is required, it's sometimes possible to contact companies specialising in these areas, such as props, wardrobe, art department, etc., to see if they need a hand on any underwater projects they might be involved in. If you were thinking of getting into these areas anyway and you have HSE recognition, this again might be a plus for you, as it would give a company a skill they may not currently have.

The work is relatively straightforward. If you are simply helping as an assistant because of your diving knowledge, it will involve placement of props on a set and maybe the adjustment of clothes, etc., on artists who are underwater.

If you have an artistic side that you want to develop,

there are the usual routes through art school, etc., into set design, which could then lead onto specialist niche work in underwater set design and construction. You would be amazed how often sets and props turn up made of wood or polystyrene, and when taken to the bottom of the pool or tank, to no one's surprise they float right back to the surface, as they haven't been weighted properly or designed to function in the water.

Producer/Director

For those that have grander ideas and would like to produce and direct their own projects, there are always ways in.

Again, the 'on paper' way is through recognised training courses, or the traditional route of joining a production company as a runner/assistant and working your way up. The benefit of this, of course, is that you learn the industry inside out, which is no bad thing. If you are going to produce or direct, you need to understand everyone's role and how they all work together.

An alternative route is to have such an original idea, worked out so meticulously, that nobody can say no to it. It also helps if you can bring something to the project that no one else can.

In one way, this is actually very easy. We've probably all got 101 ideas that would make great programmes or documentaries. The problem is, those ideas need to be in the right place at the right time – that's the difficult part.

The only way you can do this is by sending the ideas out to commissioning editors at the major TV companies, or large independent production companies who will have clout with the commissioning editors. There is, of course, always the danger your idea may get stolen or abused, but if it's sitting in your top drawer or on your laptop, it's not going anywhere anyway.

Once it's out there, it's just a matter of sitting back and waiting for the responses, which may take quite a while to come through. The sad thing about all this is that at the end of the day it won't necessarily be down to how good your idea is. The chances are it's a lot better than many of the programmes that actually get produced. It will be down to whether or not the concept fits into a series, or theme, that the broadcaster has space for, possibly up to a year in advance − so it really is a lottery. But, like all things, it can happen. So, if you are enthusiastic and have a thick enough skin − get writing!

Hopefully this brief round-up and the previous chapters will have whetted your appetite for using your diving skills in the film world and inspired some of you to give it a go. If you want to try - remember, it's not going to be easy, but the rewards can be truly memorable and exciting for those that make it.

Good luck!

Photographs link

To access over 300 photographs illustrating the chapters
of *LIGHTS! CAMERA! SUB ACTION!*
please go to the following link:
www.mikesearesbooks.com/lcsa-media-1.html

Please note, every effort will be made to ensure this link
remains active, but there may always be circumstances
beyond our control.

31349890R00226

Printed in Poland
by Amazon Fulfillment
Poland Sp. z o.o., Wrocław